Notes on Contributors

Ray Murphy is a senior lecturer in law at the Irish Centre for Human Rights, National University of Ireland, Galway. He is also on the faculty of the Pearson Peacekeeping Centre, the International Institute for Criminal Investigations and the International Institute of Humanitarian Law, San Remo, Italy. He is a former captain in the Irish Defence Forces, and he served as an infantry officer with the Irish contingent of UNIFIL in Lebanon in 1981/82 and again in 1989. He has field experience with the OSCE in Bosnia in 1996 and 1997, and has also worked on short assignments in west and southern Africa and the Middle East for Amnesty International, the European Union and the Irish Government.

Katarina Månsson is a doctoral fellow at the Irish Centre for Human Rights, researching for a PhD on the integration of human rights in UN peace operations. She holds a Master's degree in political science, Lund University, Sweden and a European Master's Degree in Human Rights and Democratization. She has work experience from the United Nations Office of the High Commissioner for Human Rights, the Raoul Wallenberg Institute of Human Rights and Humanitarian Law, diplomatic missions in Geneva and New York, and as a journalist.

Todd Howland is a human rights lawyer and serves as a Legal Advisor to the Humanitarian Law Project in Los Angeles, California. He directed the Robert F. Kennedy Memorial Center for Human Rights, an organization that partners with human rights advocates around the world, including a right to health advocate in Haiti (2001–2006). With the UN High Commissioner for Human Rights, he worked in the context of peacekeeping operations in Angola (1998–2001) and Rwanda (1994–96). He has also worked with NGOs including the Carter Center in Ethiopia (1992–94) and El Rescate related to El Salvador (1987–92).

Siobhan Wills has an LLM from Yale and is currently completing her doctorate, on the legal responsibilities of multi-national forces engaged in peace support, at Exeter College, Oxford University, where she is a graduate teaching assistant for the law faculty.

Clive Baldwin is head of international advocacy at Minority Rights Group International, London. He worked as Coordinator of Analysis and Reporting in the OSCE Mission in Kosovo from 2000 to 2002. He is a human rights lawyer and previously practised in London, New York and Atlanta. His most recent publication includes *Minorities in Kosovo under International Rule* (Minority Rights Group, 2006).

D. Christopher Decker is the Chief of the Security Issues Section in the Department of Human Rights and Rule of Law for the Organization for Security and

Co-operation in Europe's (OSCE) Mission in Kosovo. He is also an occasional lecturer at the International Institute of Humanitarian Law in San Remo, Italy.

Vivienne O'Connor is the rule of law project officer at the Irish Centre for Human Rights, and the Co-Director of the 'Model Codes for Post-Conflict Criminal Justice' Project. She is also an adjunct lecturer at the University of Melbourne School of Law. She holds an LLM in international human rights law and is currently completing a PhD in international human rights law focusing on the rule of law and criminal law reform in post-conflict states.

Hadewych Hazelzet works as an EU official at the General Secretariat of the Council of the European Union, Directorate General for External and Politico-Military Relations, where she was most recently desk officer for EU human rights policy. She obtained her doctoral degree from the European University Institute in San Domenico di Fiesole, Italy.

Hurst Hannum is professor of public law at the University of Hong Kong and professor of international law at the Fletcher School of Law and Diplomacy, Tufts University. He has served as a consultant to the United Nations on issues ranging from minority rights to the situations in Afghanistan, East Timor and the Western Sahara. Among his recent publications are *International Human Rights: Problems of Law, Policy, and Practice* with Richard B. Lillich and Dinah Shelton (2006) and *Negotiating Self-Determination* edited with Eileen F. Babbitt (2006).

Bertrand G. Ramcharan is Professor of International Human Rights Law at the Geneva Graduate Institute of International Studies, Chancellor of the University of Guyana, and Senior Fellow at the Ralphe Bunche Institute for International Studies at The CUNY Graduate Center. He has a doctorate from the London School of Economics and is a Barrister of Lincoln's Inn. He was a member of the UN Secretariat for 32 years and served in the position of Deputy and then UN High Commissioner for Human Rights a.i. (2003–2004) at the level of Under-Secretary-General.

Peace Operations and Human Rights

The protection and promotion of human rights has been an integral part of contemporary peace operations since the end of the Cold War. Consequently, international peacekeeping has developed into a new tool for the enhancement of human rights protection alongside existing international and regional human rights machinery.

These developments pose unprecedented challenges at the political, legal and operational levels of international peacekeeping. From a political point of view, human rights are often perceived as inimical to reconciliation and peace-building and, as a consequence, sidelined for immediate political compromises. From a legal point of view, the lack of supervisory mechanisms of the UN, the uncertainty of legal responsibility of international organizations and the difficulty of ensuring criminal responsibility of peacekeepers raise serious concerns relating to impunity and accountability. From an operational point of view, the difficulty of translating international human rights standards into practice remains a main challenge in post-conflict environments. To this aim, close and collegial working relationships are required between civilian and military peacekeepers which presupposes mutual understanding and knowledge of human rights standards.

Peace Operations and Human Rights seeks to address these and other unresolved issues concerning human rights protection in peace operations.

This book was previously published as a special issue of *International Peacekeeping*

Ray Murphy is a senior lecturer at the Irish Centre for Human Rights, Faculty of Law, National University of Ireland, Galway. He lectures in International Peace Support Operations and International Humanitarian Law.

Katarina Månsson is a doctoral fellow at the Irish Centre for Human Rights where she is pursuing a doctorate on the theme of integration of human rights in peace operations.

This publication was grant-aided by the Publications Fund of National University of Ireland, Galway.

Peace Operations and Human Rights

Edited by
RAY MURPHY and KATARINA MÅNSSON

Routledge
Taylor & Francis Group

LONDON AND NEW YORK

First published 2008 by Routledge
2 Park Square, Milton Park, Abingdon, Oxon, OX14 4RN

Simultaneously published in the USA and Canada
by Routledge
270 Madison Ave, New York NY 10016

Routledge is an imprint of the Taylor & Francis Group, an informa business

Transferred to Digital Printing 2009

Typeset in Sabon by Techset Composition, Salisbury, UK

British Library Cataloguing in Publication Data
A catalogue record for this book is available from the British Library

ISBN 10: 0-415-39489-9 (hbk)
ISBN 10: 0-415-49575-X (pbk)

ISBN 13: 978-0-415-39489-5 (hbk)
ISBN 13: 978-0-415-49575-2 (pbk)

Contents

Perspectives on Peace Operations and Human Rights

RAY MURPHY and KATARINA MÅNSSON

As the number of actors engaged in peace operations and human rights related activities has grown, there has been a corresponding increase in interest among academics in the field of human rights, peace and security. The purpose of this book has been to bring the two sides together by inviting practitioners with field experience and representatives from international organizations responsible for human rights and peacekeeping issues to share their insights and concerns with scholars and researchers working in similar fields. For the UN-espoused mantra 'from standard-setting to implementation' to come into effect it is vital to promote a continuous dialogue between practitioners, international civil servants and academics that can facilitate a mutually reinforcing synergy between the practice and theory of human rights.

Since 1985 there has been a significant increase in the number of peace operations established, with a corresponding increase in the complexity of the mandates. The traditionally passive role of peacekeepers has been replaced by a more active role of peacemaking, involving, *inter alia,* national reconstruction, facilitating transition to democracy and providing humanitarian assistance.[1] As the dynamic of conflict in the world changed, so too did the response of the UN and other international organizations and states. Contemporary peace operations are multi-dimensional in nature; according to the Pearson Peacekeeping Centre in Canada, they are:[2]

- deployed into both inter-state and intra-state conflicts;
- conducted in every phase of the conflict spectrum, from prevention through to post-war reconstruction;
- dependent on close cooperation among civilian, police, and military organizations from the international community, with parties to the conflict and war-affected populations;
- opening in new areas of international activity with conflict-affected countries, such as reforms to the security sector.

As a result, contemporary peace operations include conflict prevention, conflict mitigation, peacemaking, peacekeeping, peace enforcement, and post-conflict peacebuilding. The resolution of internal or domestic conflict is a dominant feature of recent operations and has involved the establishment of democratic governments culminating in nation building processes, as exemplified by international efforts currently underway in Kosovo. International administration of this kind, like peacekeeping itself, is not specifically provided for in the UN Charter. It is not subject to a clear UN doctrine and appears to be handled by the Department of Peacekeeping Operations (DPKO) more by default than design. Operations in Eastern Slavonia, Bosnia-Herzegovina, Kosovo and East Timor have been characterized by the UN and other international organizations assuming responsibilities that evoke the historically-sensitive concepts of trusteeship and protectorate.[3] Making such administrations accountable and preventing them from adopting neo-colonial roles is imperative. This is one context in which human rights play a central role.

Armed conflict and post-conflict situations in which peace operations deploy are often characterized by deliberate violations of human rights norms. The extraterritorial application of human rights treaties is well established in the jurisprudence of the UN Human Rights Committee and is relevant when establishing legal accountability and the responsibility of peace operations.[4] In 2004 the Committee stated:

> A State party [to the International Covenant on Civil and Political Rights (ICCPR)] must respect and ensure the rights laid down in the Covenant to anyone within the power and effective control of that State party, even if not situated within the territory of that State party...This principle also applies to those within the power or effective control of a State party acting outside its territory, regardless of the circumstances in which such power or effective control was obtained, such as forces constituting a national contingent of a State party assigned to an international peacekeeping or peace-enforcement operation.[5]

The Covenant creates a duty on a state party to ensure that members of the armed forces participating in 'peacekeeping missions or NATO military missions' are trained appropriately and familiar with the relevant human rights provisions.[6] The direct application of the ICCPR to the UN administration in Kosovo was highlighted in 2006 when the United Nations Interim Administration Mission in Kosovo (UNMIK) came before the Committee to account for the implementation of the Covenant throughout the territory of Kosovo.[7] In addition to human rights instruments adopted under the auspices of the UN, there are also a number of important regional treaties and other instruments dealing with human rights.[8] According to the European Court of Human Rights, the extraterritorial principle may also arise when control is exercised by international forces pursuant to a UN mandate.[9] A much less conservative approach has been adopted by the Inter-American Commission on Human Rights, one of two bodies in the inter-American system for the promotion and protection of human rights. The Commission has found for the extraterritorial application of human rights law in circumstances where the state merely has control over the individual complaining of a violation.[10] These regional systems have provisions governing the right to life, prohibitions on torture, cruel and inhuman treatment and also violence in general, and specifically as against women and children. As the UN is not a state, the source of its obligation to observe human rights is not without contro-versy.[11] Although not a party to the major human rights treaties, it remains a subject of international law and is as such under an obligation to protect and promote human rights.

The volume begins by addressing the question as to how peace operations can effectively operationalize human rights standards. Todd Howland suggests that one answer is to frame and evaluate peace operations according to international human rights law. Peace operations continue to be built on political and moral rather than legal grounds. As a result, peace operations lack a useful legal frame-work from which the development of post-conflict states can be assessed and the legal obligation of contributing states with respect to human rights protection can be spelled out. Taking the UN Stabilization Mission to Haiti (MINUSTAH) as a case study, Howland suggests several ways in which the International Court of Justice (ICJ) and/or the Inter-American Court for Human Rights could determine the human rights obligations of both the operation and participating member states. Closely interrelated is the issue of the extraterritorial application of human rights law to peace forces. This important aspect of human rights protec-tion by peace operations is analysed here by Siobhan Wills. Upon examination of recent case law from the ICJ and the European Court of Human Rights, Wills sup-ports the existence of a positive human rights obligation of peacekeeping forces to protect civilian populations. This stems in part from the increasing blurring of different constitutive parts of international law, especially international humani-tarian and human rights law and the law of occupation. In this regard, Wills suggests that a 'distinction between effective control for occupation and effective control for human rights law purposes' may no longer be meaningful for courts and monitoring bodies when establishing responsibility.

A more clear-cut case than Kosovo where the criteria of 'effective control' by peacekeepers is satisfied, be it under the laws of occupation or human rights law, hardly exists. Regrettably, the peace effort employed by the international commu-nity in Kosovo is a case where practice has yet to match theory. Clive Baldwin describes how both the international force (Kosovo Force, KFOR) and the human rights mission (OSCE) in Kosovo failed in meeting their human rights obli-gation to protect the minorities, due to a lack of a clear overall strategy for both actors. Reflecting upon his experience as Coordinator of Human Rights Report-ing and Analysis for the OSCE Mission in Kosovo, Baldwin shows that the diver-ging perspectives and priorities of KFOR (upholding security) and OSCE (protecting individual rights) were particularly acute with respect to the right of displaced persons to return home.

D. Christopher Decker, Head of the Security Issues Section of OSCE's Human Rights and Rule of Law Department, accounts for the human rights aspects of the transition from UN executive policing to the establishment of a democratic Kosovo Police Service. Decker identifies some key lessons for future UN police deployments and their human rights role, among others the need to approach the creation of a new local police force with a long-term perspective from the outset of a mission and the need to learn the local law. The diversity of national police cultures coupled with post-conflict legal chaos pose a real challenge for human rights protection by international peace actors. A possible remedy for dealing with deficiencies in the legal framework, especially from a human rights perspective, may lie in a set of Model Codes for Post-Conflict Criminal Justice. Vivienne O'Connor, Co-Director of the Model Codes for Post-Conflict Criminal Justice Project, outlines the human rights basis of such codes and how they could be utilized to assist in criminal law reform efforts in countries emerging from conflict.

A precondition for peace operations to succeed in fostering a human rights culture in a conflict or post-conflict country is that peacekeepers themselves act in compliance with international human rights law. There must be model actors, not only model codes. Revelations of sexual exploitation and abuse of local women and children by military and civilian peacekeepers in the Democratic Republic of the Congo shocked those unaware of such activities and tarnished the reputation of all peacekeepers. Ray Murphy, a former peacekeeper, explores the plethora of existing legal instruments outlining accountability for misconduct by UN staff. In dealing with the sexual exploitation of women and girls by UN and other personnel operating in post-conflict situations there is a limited amount the UN can do without the cooperation of troop contributing states. Despite this Murphy advocates that anyone employed by, or affiliated with, the UN must be held accountable and, when the circumstances so warrant, prosecuted. Extra-judicial factors, such as living conditions and awareness-raising on human rights standards, also play a pivotal role in preventing abuses.

Human rights integration in the field is preconditioned by effective integration at UN headquarters. Key to this equation is a strengthening in the interplay between the Office of the High Commissioner for Human Rights (OHCHR), the Security Council and the DPKO. Katarina Månsson takes the absence of specific reference to international human rights law in Security Council resolutions as one example of how lack of attention to human rights at the macro-level may effect implementation at the micro-level of peace operations. The existence of numerous institutional models of human rights integration within peace operations mirrors the constantly changing political dynamics and interests at UN headquarters. The synergy, or lack thereof, between the two levels should thus be borne in mind in any analysis on peace operations and human rights. While the UN is still learning the modus operandi of peace operations as a human rights mechanism, new actors have entered the playing field. The European Union (EU) is, alongside the African Union (AU), one of the more visible and assertive regional organization that displays significant military and civilian peacekeeping capabilities and clout. Hadewych Hazelzet of the Council of the European Union outlines the human rights aspects of the EU's past, current and future field deployments. While the EU has enhanced its record in this regard, Hazelzet identifies gaps—such as civil-military coordination and the absence of human rights at the outset of EU crisis management operations.

Humility is perhaps the starting and end point for all actors, practitioners or theoreticians concerned with human rights protection and promotion through peace operations. Professor Hurst Hannum argues that it is through humility and mutual respect that the friction between advocates for peace (mediators) and advocates for justice (human rights advocates) may best be solved. Hannum advocates a partnership approach between peace and justice actors: while human rights standards provides a 'floor of justice' below which no attempt at conflict resolution should be attempted, human rights advocates must acknowledge that positive change may more readily come about as a result of dialogue and consensus-building than through naming and shaming.

In this vein, it seems appropriate to open this volume, which has been conceived and finalized in Galway with an Irish saying, quoted by Hannum: 'May I be given the serenity to accept the things that I cannot change, the courage to change the things that I can, and the wisdom to know the difference between them'.

ACKNOWLEDGEMENT

This publication was grant-aided by the Publications Fund of National University of Ireland, Galway.

NOTES

1. John Roper, Masashi Nishihara, Olara A.Otunnu and Enid Schoettle, *Keeping the Peace in the Post-Cold War Era: Strengthening Multilateral Peacekeeping*, New York: Trilateral Commission, 1993, p.4.
2. Pearson Peacekeeping Centre Canada (available at www.peaceoperations.org/en/peace_operations.asp).
3. Mats Berdal and Richard Caplan, 'The Politics of International Administration', *Global Governance*, 2004, Vol.10, No.1, p.2.
4. Human Rights Committee, 'Comments on United States of America', para.19, UN doc. CCPR/C/79/Add 50 (1995); John Cerone, 'Reasonable measures in unreasonable circumstances: a legal responsibility framework for human rights violations in post-conflict territories under UN administration', in Nigel D. White and Dirk Klaasen (eds), *The UN, Human Rights and Post-conflict Situations*, Manchester: Manchester University Press, 2005, pp.42–80, at 46.
5. General Comment No.31, UN doc. CCPR/C/2/1/Rev.1/Add. 13 (2004) [10].
6. 'Concluding observations of the Human Rights Committee': Belgium 19 Nov. 1998, UN doc. CCPR/C/79/Add.99[14] and 12 Aug. 2004, UN doc. CCPR/C/81/BEL[10].
7. See Common Core Document, UN doc. CCPR/C/UNK/1, 13 Mar. 2006; 'Concluding Observations of the Human Rights Committee', UN doc. CCPR/C/UNK/CO/1, 25 July 2006.
8. These include the European Convention for the Protection of Human Rights and Fundamental Freedoms (1953): the African Charter on Human and Peoples' Rights (1986); the European Convention for the Prevention of Torture and Inhuman or Degrading Treatment or Punishment (1989); the Inter-American Convention on the Prevention, Punishment and Eradication of Violence Against Women (1995); the Inter-American Convention to Prevent and Punish Torture (1987); and the American Convention on Human Rights (Pact of San José, 1979).
9. *Bankovic a.o. v. Belgium a.o*, Appl. no. 52207/99, ECtHR, 12 Dec. 2001. The European Court of Human Rights held that the claims against NATO states for violation of human rights were inadmissible on the basis that the bombing occurred in territory outside the legal space of the European Convention.
10. *Coard et al. v. the United States*, Case 10.951, Report No. 109/99, 29 Sept. 1999.
11. Nigel D. White and Dirk Klaasen, 'An Emerging Legal Regime', in White and Klaasen (n.4 above), p.7; Boris Kondoch, 'Human Rights Law and UN Peace Operations in Post-conflict Situations' in White and Klaasen, p.36.

Peacekeeping and Conformity with Human Rights Law: How MINUSTAH Falls Short in Haiti

TODD HOWLAND

This article contributes to an understanding of human rights' marginalization in peacekeeping operations, and argues that international human rights law is key to enhancing operational effectiveness and accountability. Human rights have been sidelined due to their supposed irrelevance to the operational side of the UN and its component parts. Given that each member state holds binding human rights obligations based on treaty commitments, UN operations approved and funded by these member states are also bound by these obligations.[1] Further, there is a growing consensus that the UN and other multilateral institutions themselves are bound by international law, including human rights law.[2]

While the law appears to favour an interpretation that peacekeeping operations directly or in a derivative fashion have human rights obligations, there is basically no real operationalization of these obligations. Operations are conceptualized, staffed, financed, implemented and measure success without reference to international human rights law.

Human rights field operations, especially as components of peacekeeping operations, will continue to be marginalized until the UN – particularly the Security Council members and the Department of Peacekeeping Operations (DPKO) – recognizes and integrates obligations derived from human rights law. Without explicitly recognizing the human rights legal framework, the movement to mainstream human rights within peacekeeping operations seems unlikely. More broadly, the idea of integrated missions where all aspects of the UN evaluate the root causes of the conflict and work as part of the peace operation to contribute to addressing will remain fanciful.

There is a growing division between the UN's academic understanding and practice. There is an understanding in the UN of the need to address root causes of conflict (including violations of economic, social and cultural rights), the reality that all rights are interdependent, and how their respect leads to combating poverty and good governance and thereby builds the foundation for sustainable peace.[3] This recognition is trumped in practice by the way in which money flows in the UN system and to a lesser degree by a tendency of the UN bureaucracy to prioritize the protection of 'turf'.[4] This practice and how human rights law can be used as a vehicle to overcome these obstacles is discussed in this article. Accepting and applying human rights law to peacekeeping operations will trump these operational dysfunctionalities and allow the UN to cohere its academic understanding of achieving sustainable peace with the operations supposedly designed to achieve it.

The article focuses on the UN Stabilization Mission to Haiti (MINUSTAH)[5] as an example of the gulf between academic understanding of how to achieve a sustainable peace and the UN's operation for achieving it. Finally, the article will briefly discuss possible legal challenges that advocacy groups and 'progressive' member states can use to push the UN to accept and operationalize its human rights obligations in peacekeeping operations. Acceptance in this case goes well beyond the 'feel good' statements that each UN entity has a responsibility to ensure that human rights are promoted and respected through their operations in the field.[6] Human rights commitments mean that the UN operation has an obligation to facilitate measurable improvement of the human rights situation on ground. Success should therefore be measured according to human rights law, and UN organs should be held accountable to achieving these results. Such a formulation is in keeping with the common desire for accountability in the UN, but is firmly grounded in legal obligations, not the amorphous standard of some powerful member state, which appears to be the current measuring stick for accountability in the UN.[7]

Brief History of Human Rights in the Field

Human rights field operations are still a relatively new tool for the UN and the international community, with an accumulated experience of less than two decades. There are number of interesting studies, including in-depth treatments in this collection of articles, so there is no reason to repeat this material here.[8]

For the most part, the human rights dimensions of peacekeeping operations have been small. Their role has mostly been to report on compliance with human rights aspects of a peace accord or human rights obligations of the host state in general. Often these programmes have included some advocacy.[9] On a few occasions, human rights personnel in the peacekeeping operation have facilitated compliance with human rights obligations with project-based interventions with either government or civil society.[10] In addition to these primary roles, human rights field personnel have trained other elements of the peacekeeping operation to not violate human rights and hopefully to somehow contribute to achieving them.[11]

While there has been increasing discussion of 'human rights mainstreaming'[12] and how all elements of the UN can actively promote human rights, so far 'success' at mainstreaming has depended on the personality of the Special

Representative of the Secretary General (SRSG) and other mission leaders, rather than on a clear policy and understanding that the operation must comply with its human rights obligations.[13]

The movement towards creating human rights goals for the mission and helping monitor their achievement is still mostly aspirational, as most UN bureaucrats and member states do not even see this as the task of the human rights field operation. The way in which a peacekeeping mission responds to violations committed by its own forces often includes the human rights component of the operation, but the process is usually incredibly informal. Nonetheless, the recognition that UN peacekeepers can and do violate human rights is a positive development that needs to be vastly generalized for it to make a useful impact on the host society.[14]

Human Rights Law as Legal Framework for Peacekeeping Operations

Although traditional approaches to international law hold no obligation of UN member states to intervene in another country because of human rights violations, the 'responsibility to protect' is gaining more and more acceptance. Specifically, the responsibility to protect has gained significant ground through the UN reform package 'In Larger Freedom: Towards Security, Development and Human Rights for All'.[15]

But almost all past UN peacekeeping interventions have been built on political and moral grounds, and most will continue to be based on this as opposed to the legal responsibility to protect. Thus, member states have too easily moved from the idea that since they were not legally obligated to intervene, they conveniently believe that human rights law does not apply to the intervention. Pretentiously and wrongly, the interveners, acting through the UN, believed their intentions to be good and that was enough. This thinking in the humanitarian field has been difficult to overcome.[16] Recognizing that good intentions are not enough and that member states have existing human rights obligations to meet as part of the intervention are fairly novel ideas.

Perhaps a useful analogy can be borrowed from tort law. Just as in the case of the Good Samaritan, there may be no legal obligation to intervene, once the Good Samaritan does intervene, they are held liable to a standard of conduct established by law – regardless of the level of purity of motive. So it is in peacekeeping. Security Council resolutions are only sometimes guided by principle, but human rights law applies to the mission once the decision to intervene has been made.[17] There is also growing understanding of the direct application of international law to peacekeeping.[18] Statements that peacekeepers are bound by international humanitarian law and human rights law were intended to restrain malfeasance by blue helmets,[19] but this same logic should apply to the mission as a whole, and not be limited to individual acts of violence by the blue helmets.

At the same time the understanding that human rights law provides a useful framework for development practice has developed further. The human rights based approach to development has become more known and is used not simply because of the legal requirement but because of the empirical results when applied.[20] In essence, the human rights based approach to development shifts goals to the measurable improvement of the full-spectrum of human rights and requires the respect for human rights in the development process, most notably the respect for the right to participation of the beneficiaries in decisions impacting upon them.[21]

The human rights legal framework applicable to peacekeeping operations does include those treaties signed by the member states.[22] While not every state has signed and ratified each human rights treaty, almost all are party to the Convention on the Rights of the Child and the vast majority to the Covenant on Civil and Political Rights as well as the Covenant on Economic, Social and Cultural Rights. The fact that a host state (to a peacekeeping operation) is not a state party to the relevant human rights treaties does not mean that states contributing peacekeepers that have ratified these treaties are somehow not bound by them. That would be akin to having one party to a binding contract claim that because they have partnered with a third party who is not a party to the contract they no longer are bound to act in accordance with the terms of the contact. In fact, the obligation runs differently. If a party who is not a party to a contact partners with an entity that is a party to the contract, the partnership will be obliged to follow the contract. This is also the case in human rights law. Those that are bound by human rights law should insure that the partnerships they enter into act in ways that conform to their legal obligations.

While not limiting this argument to the three conventions mentioned above, the fact that they have been ratified by between 75 and 99 per cent of member states means that the obligations contained in those documents are binding on any collective enterprise created by those states, in this case, UN peacekeeping operations. While some rights contained in these conventions can be read as prohibitions on actions of blue helmets and other UN personnel,[23] of interest for this analysis is the collective obligations of states to assist other states to achieve the full respect of the rights found in the conventions.[24]

Perhaps even more important for this analysis is the progressive nature of many human rights; member states are required to improve the level of respect for rights in the conventions if they have more resources available. The idea of progressive realization has not become as concrete as it needs to be in practice. Many states do not report on compliance with their obligations in a rigorous way.[25] Many do not even present statistics that can demonstrate that over time and with greater resources the state is actually measurably improving its level of respect for the rights found in human rights law. On the other hand, many member states, for example Brazil, have taken their obligations seriously and have developed interesting indicators and are rigorously tracking their progress.[26] Such expertise could become part of a peacekeeping team sent to a country in crisis.

Here is where further attention needs to be given by UN peacekeeping operations. Often peacekeeping operations are sent to countries with a history of poor and possibly non-reporting on their human rights obligations. In fact, many of the host states for UN peacekeeping operations are dysfunctional and/or have no interest in collecting statistics on their compliance with their human rights obligations, let alone in creating benchmarks to measure their progressive realization of these rights.

Again, while member states through the UN often do not have the legal obligation to intervene, they do so anyway. When a peacekeeping mission is operationalized, the amount of money flowing toward the host country greatly increases. In the case of MINUSTAH, the annual peacekeeping budget is larger than the annual budget of the government of Haiti.[27] Not only should this give one pause in general, but it also questions whether the increase in the resources for Haiti is measurably improving the human rights situation.

Some may say that in fact this money is not for Haiti but for the peacekeeping operation. But no one will deny that the purpose of the peacekeeping operation is to benefit Haiti and its people. Thus, it is not appropriate to somehow exclude money flowing for peacekeeping as somehow 'not for Haiti'. The choice of how this money is used is not under the Haitian government's control, but that does not free the member states and the UN from meeting their obligations to progressively realize rights.

Peacekeeping operations have to a large degree been spared a human rights analysis because it is assumed that stopping the fighting in and of itself provides the largest human rights boost that the collective investment could make. But as peacekeeping moves away from observing a ceasefire in a war between two countries and toward facilitating a peace accord and internal stability (as is the case in Haiti), a much more sophisticated analysis is required to create accountability – an analysis based on human rights law.

The goal of each peacekeeping operation should be to measurably increase respect for human rights law. There should be analysis of the root causes of the conflict and of which human rights are implicated. A baseline study of the level of respect for human rights should be done at the beginning of the operation. Programmes should be put in place to measurably increase the level of respect for the target rights (those linked to the root cause of the conflict). Stopping the fighting and being present may or may not meet the peacekeeping operation's obligations, and would depend on how much money is being spent and how it is spent and whether the human rights indicators are positive because of the intervention.

While at present peacekeeping operations publish regular reports on progress, they are not grounded in human rights law. At the same time, there is a trend in development-related reports to at least discuss the human rights situation. The entire intervention by the international community should use rigorous human rights-based measures to show progress. In cases like Haiti, where there was no hot war and where political violence has continued during the UN's mission, it is far from evident that the situation has improved because of the intervention and that the root causes of the conflict are being addressed.[28]

Structural Problems Inhibiting Integrated Missions

Although in study after study the UN has clearly articulated the need to address the root causes of the conflict to achieve sustainable peace, the reality is very different.[29] A huge part of the problem is operationalizing this understanding. The principle obstacle is how money flows to a peacekeeping operation. At present, UN peacekeeping operations are paid through assessed contributions from member states. If the Security Council approves a peacekeeping operation, states are sent the bill in accord with a pre-agreed formula, and they have no option but to pay or fall into arrears.

Some countries making major contributions to peacekeeping operations have no say about their approval or how they are organized. The top two financial contributors to peacekeeping operations are the United States and Japan. Both have an interest in keeping costs down. Unfortunately, they tend to do this by limiting the scope (of the operation) and the UN entities which can access the assessed contributions and thereby limit missions basically to being blue helmets. Historically, the DPKO and, to a lesser degree, the Department of Political Affairs (DPA) were the only entities allowed into the exclusive club with access to these assessed funds. More recently, the Office of the High Commissioner for Human Rights (OHCHR) has gained some access as well as the Secretary General's Special Representative for Children and Armed Conflict, in that these entities recruit and oversee personnel integrated into peacekeeping operations. These staffers are considered to be part of the OHCHR or the Special Representative's staff, but are paid for by accessed contributions.[30] This means that most of the UN system does not have access to the assessed contributions for peacekeeping. Thus, given the way money flows in peacekeeping, very few UN entities are truly integrated into the analysis of what type of mission is needed, and even fewer are put on the ground to operationalize an integrated approach to peacekeeping.

Peacekeeping operations and UN agencies are poorly coordinated because, in part, they are financed through different pots of money, representing different donor bureaucracies with very different objectives. Peacekeeping has access to assessed contributions, a method where money flows relatively quickly. There is an urgency to move quickly, similar to how the international community should respond to human rights violations. Peacekeepers often do not partner with the host government and even keep some distance, given that they need to deal with both or all fighting factions.

Development actors are dependent on voluntary contributions, which are operationalized very slowly. While human rights violations may be ongoing, this does not usually implicate any urgency or change in the application of this method. Development actors are, for the most part, considered partners of the host government.

Both peacekeeper and development actors are in many ways so beholden to their traditional operational methods that the overarching purpose is lost in 'turf divisions' created by the way the money flows. Human rights law can change this dysfunction given that it provides a unity of purpose. Human rights law obliges the system to change not only how resources are allocated but how these monies are operationalized in countries in conflict. Bureaucratic and historic differences should not and cannot stand in the way of the UN meeting its legal obligations.

Various attempts to shore up the problem have been made, for example, making the SRSG the coordinator for the entire UN system where a peacekeeping operation exists.[31] These attempts have at least created a forum for the UN agencies or UN Country Team to speak with the people from the UN peacekeeping mission, but the reality is that they are still very different. Typically, the UN agencies have small budgets because they are working in countries where creating partnerships with the government to implement projects is difficult or impossible. Nonetheless, they have accumulated a great deal of understanding of their area of expertise and the country where they are working. The UN peacekeepers and their leadership typically have limited understanding of the country they are operating in, given that their training has been mainly military related. The vast majority of blue helmets are waiting for orders from their commanders; they typically have limited interaction with the population of the host country and may not even be able to communicate with the local population, although they have tremendous resources in comparison to the UN agencies. Most often UN agencies feel alienated and marginalized, and the leadership of the peacekeeping operation sees them as ineffective. Often tensions are significant, and animosity is common.

The problem can be quite fairly reduced to money. The agencies have no access to the assessed contributions so they will not be able to fully analyse the root causes of the problem and to operationalize programmes to address them. The blue helmets, who do have access to assessed contributions, cannot solve every problem. They simply lack the expertise. The UN Security Council has resorted to sending peacekeepers for every problem, but often sends oranges when apples are needed. The system is truly broken. It needs the unity of purpose that human rights law provides, not only to remove the dysfunctionality created by the assessed contribution problem, but also to create benchmarks for success in peacekeeping operations. Through these benchmarks accountability for all aspects of the UN participating in the mission will be ensured.

Some of the UN reforms were designed to address the gap between peacekeeping operations and the typical work of the development agencies.[32] The Peacebuilding Commission and the Standing Fund for Peacebuilding were proposed to address a serious problem but, in true UN fashion, without addressing the structural issues that created the problem.[33] The UN is unable to address the structural problem, because a number of powerful member states do not regard it as important and see change as detrimental to their interests. The Commission and Fund might help to address the gap at the margins given the desires of some states to deal with the problem, but the likelihood of that happening is being diminished by the influence of the United States and other like-minded states, which treat these new bodies as sequential to peacekeeping, rather than being integrated from the beginning.[34]

Haiti

The UN sent another peacekeeping operation to Haiti following a US-authored Security Council Resolution, a US-led military intervention following a US-brokered exit of President Aristide.[35] Untypical of peacekeeping operations, there was no hot war, and this peacekeeping operation is not supported by, or grounded in, a peace accord or even a peace process. It also has a vague mandate that leads to the lack of clarity as to how to measure the success or failure of the operation.

MINUSTAH exemplifies the need for a human rights framework for UN peacekeeping operations, given that it is far from clear what in fact its purpose is. Critics of the mission see it as a US-created entity occupying Haiti in order to facilitate a political change acceptable to the US government that could not have occurred democratically.[36] Supporters view it as a mission that has prevented Haiti from becoming torn by civil strife, and that has been restoring order so that democracy can take root.[37]

The human rights approach reminds everyone that the purpose of the mission is to measurably improve the full-spectrum of human rights as tied to the root causes of the conflict in Haiti. This approach provides a framework that is not value neutral, but reflects the values of the vast majority of UN member states. It also provides a means for measuring the progress of UN peacekeeping operations in non-traditional settings, where there is neither hot war nor a peace accord between factions. Given the recent rapid destabilization in Haiti, the importance of such a framework is accentuated. Under such conditions it is doubly important that intervention be conducted not according to the wishes of a few influential states but for the amelioration of the worsening conflict. All of this can be achieved without having to enter speculative polemic regarding why the UN is in Haiti again, which focuses attention more on intentions than on impact.

The UN should and still needs to collect the baseline data necessary to measure the present level of respect for human rights in Haiti. Within this baseline, specific rights should be targeted as linked to the root causes of the conflict. It then needs to measure whether it is facilitating or concretely contributing to improvement. The UN peacekeeping efforts should be part of the entire enterprise for change. The present separation of the International Cooperation Framework for Haiti and MINUSTAH and the lack of an integrated evaluation of the entire enterprise using the human rights-based approach should be addressed.

In fact it is just this type of problem that should be of importance to the OHCHR. At present, the OHCHR fields a few Human Rights Officers to the mission in Haiti, who are engaged in the traditional fieldwork of monitoring and a bit of capacity building. In addition, however, the OHCHR HQ should be concerned with the bigger picture and be pushing practical structural reforms. The OHCHR should radically rethink its approach to its participation in this type of mission. It needs to push much harder for the human rights framework to inform how the mission is structured and staffed and how it meets its obligations.

While numbers are hard to come by, discussions with those in Haiti indicate that government services, especially in the rural areas, have gone from bad to close to non-existent following the arrival of the UN peacekeepers.[38] Similarly, barely functioning local governments have become close to extinct.[39] Political violence has ebbed and flowed during the UN peacekeeping presence, but it has not ended, and there is no reason for it to end without some kind of political accord or solution to the underlying conflict. Most importantly, the Haitian people, who are supposedly the beneficiaries of the international intervention writ large, are to a large degree not participants in any shape or form related to the decisions impacting on their lives. Again, they have not seen any peace dividend, and the international community would be hard pressed to demonstrate one.

The fact that the UN peacekeeping budget is larger than the annual budget of the Haitian government begs the question: 'what impact could be achieved if the peacekeeping money was used differently?' First, one should ask whether the mission has concretely contributed to an increase in the level of respect of human rights. This is difficult, if not impossible, to answer in the affirmative, given the lack of baseline data. But interviews with people in Haiti do not indicate that it is the case.[40] Second, has the mission defined certain rights that need attention and visible improvement in order to address the root causes of the conflict? It is unclear if any such analysis exists, and it does not appear that there are any robust integrated UN programmes to address them.

In fact, the UN agencies such as the UN Development Programme and World Health Organization are marginalized. Normally they have limited funds and no access to assessed contributions in the context of huge needs.[41] Many observers and donor states regard the Transitional Government as corrupt or illegitimate,[42] and the Caribbean Community and Common Market (CARICOM) was unwilling to recognize it.[43] Although the government is the partner of the UN agencies, they have provided little funding. In addition, less than one per cent of the current peacekeeping budget goes to projects or programmes.[44] Amazingly, it appears that MINUSTAH does not even have the staff to effectively utilize such funds, given that blue helmets are not recruited for their project management skills. This means there is a significant funding gap for actions that could help to create an immediate transformation in Haiti, despite the significant UN presence. The peacekeepers who have little or no project money and in reality very little to do, relative to, say, in Lebanon, where monitoring a ceasefire can be a daily task. The UN agencies see promises of money on the horizon but no immediate funds or ability to implement projects.

MINUSTAH is symbolic of much needed UN reforms. Has this operation produced results commensurate with member state investment and values? Unless we define the desired results, it is impossible to say whether money and hope have been wasted. Without a human rights framework to determine success or failure, it is hard not to conclude MINUSTAH has been a waste of hope. So many Haitians have been disappointed or disillusioned with the UN peacekeeping mission that advocates are looking at ways to make it more effective.[45]

Possible Legal Challenges

There are several hurdles for advocates to clear in order to be able to use human rights law as a benchmark to measure the success of peacekeeping operations. The fact that the UN peacekeeping operation to Haiti (and other places) is not in conformity with its human rights obligations, does not mean change will happen easily or quickly. For the most part, arguments regarding peacekeeping mandates and their implementation remain on a political rather than legal level. The most influence is exercised by members of the UN Security Council, and then by the UN Secretariat, specifically the DPKO.

While advocacy groups have attempted to tweak mandates and their implementation for human rights reasons,[46] these efforts have normally addressed a specific right or small set of rights and do not challenge the operation's conceptualization, staffing and implementation as being bound by human rights law. To some degree, the reason is that some of the most influential human rights groups are still overly focused on political and civil rights.[47] Another reason is that the host state is usually a human rights violator, and so much attention flows to it as opposed to the intervention.

Using legal challenges can help to ensure that interventions should actually facilitate change in the host state. Holding UN peacekeeping operations accountable for conforming to international human rights law and thereby maximizing its contribution to positive human rights change in the host country is long overdue.

While the OHCHR has pushed 'mainstreaming' of human rights into all aspects of the UN,[48] it has not advocated aggressively that peacekeeping operations are bound, and should be guided in their conceptualization and organization, by human rights law and that the UN and member states should be held accountable for meeting their human rights obligations in the context of international interventions.[49] Even if the OHCHR began to advocate this position, it is not certain that it would achieve the needed change. In part this derives from the small and to some degree marginalized position of the OHCHR within the UN. It is also because of the difficulty that ideas have – no matter how valid – in overcoming bureaucratic protectionism and methods growing out of the way money flows through the UN system. Finally, as the OHCHR has gained some credibility it has often pushed positions that other entities in the UN see as impractical, which makes internal progress slow.[50]

It is theoretically possible for the OHCHR as part of the UN Secretariat to call upon a UN agency, the Economic and Social Council or the General Assembly as a whole, to request an advisory opinion from the International Court of Justice (ICJ) to clarify UN peacekeeping operations human rights legal obligations.[51] It is not clear that the OHCHR is willing or politically positioned to successfully make this argument in the UN system. Without the weight of an ICJ opinion, it is difficult to imagine how the OHCHR could muster sufficient power within the UN system to actually change the way money flows to peacekeeping operations – something essential to the ability of peacekeeping operations to measurably facilitate improvement in the human rights situation in situ.

More likely, a member state or advocacy group could find a specific UN peacekeeping operation in violation of its human rights obligations. A good example would be MINUSTAH. MINUSTAH and the member states that support it could be challenged as not being in conformity with its human rights obligations. In this case there are at least three possible avenues.

First, a member state could bring an action against the UN itself for violating its human rights obligations by the way it conceptualized, staffed and implemented an operation. This would be a legally interesting challenge, given that the UN does have an international legal personality and has litigated against a member state in the ICJ.[52] It is not clear whether at this juncture the ICJ would entertain a case from a state against the UN. This question has been discussed by others, but until it is litigated it is unclear if this avenue of holding UN peacekeeping operations accountable for their human rights obligations is feasible.[53] Another issue is whether a state would be willing to bring such an action. In some ways litigating against the UN seems politically more palatable than litigating against other member states, but filing a contentious claim against other states is a more legally secure route.

Second, a UN member state could litigate against other states before the ICJ, arguing that they are not meeting their human rights obligations through their financial, technical and other support they are giving to MINUSTAH. While on relatively sound legal footing,[54] the problem with this avenue is the politics of bringing other states to the ICJ. While, for example, the CARICOM states have been very critical of MINUSTAH, they would risk a great deal of political capital if they were to bring their major donors before the ICJ. The legal question involved is valid and overdue for serious consideration, but many states could react negatively to being brought to court. One option would be for the CARICOM countries to put together a larger group of countries including some donors, like Norway, in order to minimize possible negative ramifications. Another route would be for a member state that typically curries limited favour with donor countries to bring the action, such as Cuba or Venezuela.

The third possibility is to use the regional human rights systems to interpret and establish the human rights legal obligations applicable to UN peacekeeping operations. This is already happening. Zanmi Lasante, a Haitian human rights organization focusing on the right to health, with the support of the Robert F. Kennedy Memorial Center for Human Rights and the International Human Rights Clinic of the New York University Law School, approached the Inter-American Commission on Human Rights (IACHR) for a general interest hearing regarding the human rights obligations of member states of the Organization of American States operating bilaterally or multilaterally in Haiti. The hearing was held on 3 March 2006.

During the hearing, the IACHR was requested to: (1) send an onsite visit to Haiti; (2) request an advisory opinion from the Inter-American Court of Human Rights regarding the human rights obligations of OAS members working in Haiti; (3) appoint a special rapporteur on economic and social rights to monitor whether measurable progress is being made in Haiti.

All three actions would help to establish that human rights obligations apply extraterritorially and that member states do not leave their human rights obligations at home when they cross a border and operate bilaterally or multilaterally in another country. The actions would also help to establish that more than one state, in this case the host, Haiti, can hold human rights obligations to the same people – in this case to the supposed beneficiaries of the intervention, the Haitian people.

While an ICJ decision may force more rapid change, at this juncture it is not certain that the resolution would be favourable or even whether such an action will be brought. On the other hand, an action to the IACHR has been brought. Once the regional body establishes the principle, it will be politically more palatable for the OHCHR to assert legal duties, not just amorphous 'responsibilities', on UN entities and states and demand that they facilitate measurable improvement in the human rights situation in the countries where they intervene.

Conclusion

It is long overdue that the human rights obligations of UN peacekeeping operations are recognized, leading to modification of how such missions are financed, conceptualized, staffed and implemented. This change will work to fill the gap between conceptual understanding of the need to address the root causes of the conflict and the real operational capacity of the UN to do so. Additionally, the recognition of the human rights legal framework will create benchmarks that are internationally acceptable and empirically linked to peace-keeping effectiveness. Finally, and very importantly, the articulation of specific human rights goals linked to the root causes of the conflict will create a means to measure and hold accountable UN peacekeeping operations.

Ensuring that UN peacekeeping operations conform to human rights law should be a welcome development, given the link between addressing the root causes of the conflict and sustainable peace. Unfortunately, because this change (already legally mandated) would challenge bureaucratic interests and undermine a number of coveted financial and operational modalities, there will continue to be a great deal of resistance.

But change is overdue. MINUSTAH is just one example of a waste of hope and money. The UN can do much better, and member states must allow it to do so. Unless legally mandated to change, the UN will only make minor and marginal changes without achieving great strides in operationalizing its understanding of the need for integrated peace missions that facilitate the transition from conflict to sustainable peace.

Thus, 'progressive' member states and advocacy groups have a role in imposing the pre-existing, but yet unrecognized, obligations deriving from a human rights legal framework on UN peacekeeping missions. Without it, medioc-rity and the protection of short-term interests and turf will continue to prevail in UN peacekeeping missions over maximizing contributions to improving the human rights situation. With this change, the UN will increase the possibility that its peacekeeping interventions will actually lead to sustainable peace.

ACKNOWLEDGEMENT

The author would like to thank his research assistant Chris Saeger as well as Monika Kalra Varma, Sushetha Gopallawa and Dino Kritsiotis for their input and feedback during the development of this article. The opinions and errors herein are solely those of the author.

NOTES

1. Kenneth Watkin, 'Controlling the Use of Force: A Role for Human Rights Norms in Contemporary Armed Conflict', *American Journal of International Law* [hereafter *AJIL*], Vol.98, No.1, 2005, pp.1–34; Theodore Meron, 'The Humanization of Humanitarian Law', *AJIL*, Vol.94, No.2, 2000, pp.23–78.
2. Ken Roberts, 'Second Guessing the Security Council: The International Court of Justice and Its Powers of Judicial Review', *Pace International Law Review*, Vol.7, No.282, 1995, pp.281–328; Thomas Franck, 'The "Powers of Appreciation": Who is the Ultimate Guardian of UN Legality', *AJIL*, Vol.86, No.3, 1992, pp.519–23; The International Law Associations 2004 Berlin Conference Report *Accountability of International Organizations* (www.ila-hq.org/pdf/Accountability/Final%20Report%202004.pdf); Bernd Martenczuk, 'The Security Council, the International Court and Judicial Review: Lessons from Lockerbie', *European Journal of International Law*, Vol.10, No.3, pp.517–47 and Jose E. Alvarez, 'Judging the Security Council', *AJIL*, Vol.90, No.1, 1996, pp.1–39; Brian D. Tittemore, 'Belligerents in Blue Helmets: Applying International Humanitarian Law to United Nations Peace Operations', *Stanford Journal of International Law*, Vol.33, 1997, pp.61–118.
3. Proponents of the 'broad' concept of human security articulated in the UN Development Programme's 1994, *Human Development Report*, and the Commission on Human Security's 2003 report, *Human Security Now*, argue that the threat agenda should be broadened to include hunger, disease and natural disasters because these kill far more people than war, genocide and terrorism combined (see, www.humansecurityreport.info).
4. See, e.g., 'In Haiti, rhetoric trumps human rights,' *Boston Globe*, 16 Aug. 2005.
5. Security Council Resolution 1529, UN doc. 1529, 29 Feb. 2004, and 'Statement by the Secretary General', UN doc. S/PRST/2006/1, 6 Jan. 2006.
6. *Memorandum of Understanding Between the Office of the High Commissioner for Human Rights and the Department of Peace-Keeping Operations*, 5 Nov. 1999 (www.unhchr.ch/html/menu2/4/mou_dpko.htm). See also Office of the High Commissioner for Human Rights, *Annual Appeal 2005* (www.ohchr.org/english/about/docs/appeal2005.pdf), pp.31–93.
7. 'Bolton Says UN Corruption Unacceptable, Needs Fixing', *Human Events*, Vol.61, No.36, 2005, p.793.
8. See in particular Vivienne O'Connor in this volume.
9. Todd Howland, 'Mirage, Magic, or Mixed Bag? The United Nations High Commissioner for Human Rights' Field Operation in Rwanda,' *Human Rights Quarterly*, Vol.21, No.1, pp.1–54.
10. Todd Howland, 'UN Human Rights Field Presence as Proactive Instrument of Peace and Social Change: Lessons from Angola', *Human Rights Quarterly*, Vol.26, No.1, pp.1–28.
11. For example the Pearson Peacekeeping Centre has developed several courses, some in cooperation with the OHCHR and other UN agencies, on human rights training for peacekeepers (www.peaceoperations.org/en/os/os_courses.asp).
12. 'Mainstreaming human rights refers to the concept of enhancing the human rights programme and integrating it into the broad range of United Nations activities, also in the areas of development and humanitarian action.' OHCHR website (http://193.194.138.190/development/mainstreaming.html).
13. See, e.g., Hurst Hannum, 'Human Rights in Conflict Resolution: The Role of the Office of the High Commissioner for Human Rights in UN Peacemaking and Peacebuilding', *Human Rights Quarterly*, Vol.28, No.1, pp.1–84.
14. See Ray Murphy in this volume: 'An Assessment of UN efforts to Address Sexual Misconduct by Peacekeeping Personnel'; Secretary-General's Bulletin on *Observance by United Nations forces of international humanitarian law*, UN Doc. ST/SGB/1999/13, 6 August 1999 (www.un.org/peace/st_sgb_1999_13.pdf).
15. UN doc., A/59/2005, 21 March 2005.
16. Mary Anderson, *Do No Harm*, Boulder, CO: Lynne Rienner, 1999; Hugo Slim, 'Positioning Humanitarianism in War: Principles of Neutrality, Impartiality and Solidarity', *Development in Practice*, Vol.7, No.4, 1997, pp.342–57.
17. Articles describing the legal obligations of the UN include: Ved P. Nanda, 'Accountability of International Organizations: Some Observations', *Denver Journal of International Law and Policy*, Vol.33, No.379, 2005, pp.379–90 and Terry D. Gill, 'Legal and Some Political Limitations on the Power of the UN Security Council to Exercise Its Enforcement Powers under Chapter VII of the Charter', *Netherlands Yearbook of International Law*, Vol.26, 1995, pp.33–138.

18. Joseph P. Bialke, 'United Nations Peacekeeping Operations: Applicable Norms and the Application of the Law of Armed Conflict', *The Air Force Law Review*, Vol.50, 2001, pp.1–63; Daphna Shraga, 'UN Peacekeeping Operations: Applicability of International Humanitarian Law and Responsibility for Operations-Related Damage', *AJIL*, Vol.94, No.2, 2000, pp.406–12; UN Secretary-General's Bulletin, *Observance by United Nations Forces of International Humanitarian Law*, UN doc. ST/SGB/1999/13 (1999), reprinted in 38 *International Legal Materials* 1656 (1999); 2004 Report of the International Law Association Committee on the Accountability of International Organizations (www.ila-hq.org/htlm/layout_committee.htm).

19. Jennifer Murray, 'Note: Who will Police Peace-Builders? The failure to Establish Accountability for the Participation of U.N. Civilian Police in the Trafficking of Women in Post-Conflict Bosnia and Herzegovina', *Columbia Human Rights Law Review*, Vol.34, No.2, 2003; 'Report of the Special Committee on Peacekeeping Operations and its Working Group at the 2005 substantive session', UN doc., A/59/19, 1 Mar. 2005 (www.un.org/Depts/dpko/dpko/ctte/5919.pdf?Open Element); 'Sexual Abuse in Peacekeeping Report "Hard and Unvarnished Look" at Serious Problem, Reforms Must Be Quickly Implemented, Says Secretary-General', UN Press Release SG/SM/9778, 3 Mar. 2005 (www.un.org/News/Press/docs/2005/sgsm9778.doc.htm).

20. Anita C. Edwin and Sriprapha Petcharamesree, *A Human Rights Approach to Development: A Source Book*, Books for Change, 2003.

21. See e.g., Office of the High Commissioner for Human Rights, *Frequently Asked Questions on a Human Rights-Based Approach to Development Cooperation*, New York: United Nations, 2006.

22. Ralph Wilde, 'Legal "Black Hole"? Extraterritorial State Action and International Treaty Law on Civil and Political Rights,' *Michigan Journal of International Law*, Vol.26, 2004–05, pp.739–806.

23. See in particular Commission on Human Rights resolution 2002/14 on the situation of human rights in the Democratic Republic of the Congo, 19 April 2002, which condemns 'The widespread use of sexual violence against women and children, including as a means of warfare'.

24. See article 2 paragraph 1 of the International Covenant on Economic Social and Cultural Rights, 16 Dec. 1966 (www.unhchr.ch/html/menu3/b/a_cescr.htm) and its General Comment by the Office of the High Commissioner for Human Rights, 'The nature of States parties obligations (Art. 2, par.1)', 14 Dec. 1990 (www.unhchr.ch/tbs/doc.nsf/(symbol)/CESCR + General + comment + 3.En? OpenDocumen)

25. See Anne F. Bayefsky, *The UN Human Rights Treaty System: Universality at a Crossroads*, Ardsley, NY: Transnational Publishers, 2001, esp. pp.201–14.

26. United Nations Development Programme, *Human Rights Development Report 2000*, p.96.

27. The Haitian government had annual revenues of about US$400 million in 2004 (www.cia.gov/cia/publications/factbook/geos/ha.html), whereas the approved 2005 MINUSTAH budget was US$518.30 million, UN doc. A/60/176, 1 Aug. 2005.

28. The performance report of MINUSTAH, while not rigorously based on human rights, indicates that many benchmarks were not reached. Note that these measures do not include the money and actions of the International Cooperation Framework for Haiti, which should be integrated into such an analysis. United Nations, 'Performance report of the budget of the United Nations Stabilization Mission in Haiti for the period from 1 July 2004 to 30 June 2005', UN doc. A/60/646, 6 Jan. 2006.

29. 'The causes of conflict and the promotion of durable peace and sustainable development in Africa', UN doc. A/52/871–S/1998/318, 13 April 1998 (www.un.org/ecosocdev/geninfo/afrec/sgreport/index.html). See also 'Implementation of the recommendations contained in the report of the Secretary-General on the causes of conflict and the promotion of durable peace and sustainable development in Africa', UN doc. A/59/285, 20 Aug. 2004 (www.un.org/documents/ga/docs/56/a56371.pdf).

30. 'The Impact of Armed Conflict on Children', UN doc. A/51/306.Add.1, 6 Sept. 1996 (www.un.org/special-rep/children-armed-conflict/KeyDocuments/Report/A-51-306-Add-1English.html#Top).

31. For example this was the case in Angola, where I served, and it did create a good deal of tension.

32. 'Strengthening the United Nations: an Agenda for Further Change', UN Doc. A/RES/57/300, 7 Feb. 2003 (http://daccessdds.un.org/doc/UNDOC/GEN/N02/561/30/PDF/N0256130.pdf).

33. Following the creation of the Peacebuilding Commission by the General Assembly on 20 December 2006, the Secretary-General was instructed by the General Assembly to create the Standing Fund for Peacebuilding (www.un.org/ga/president/60/summitfollowup/pbcpr051220.pdf).

34. Broadly, see the debate in Nassrine Azimi and Chang Li Lin (eds), *The Nexus Between Peacekeeping and Peacebuilding: Debreifing and Lessons*, Den Haag: Kluwer Law International, 2000. For specific information on the Peacebuilding Commission, see its website (www.un.org/peace/peacebuilding) and the Secretary-General's 2nd addendum to the *In Larger Freedom* report: 'Peacebuilding Commission: Explanatory Note by the Secretary General', 19 April 2005 (www.un.org/largerfreedom/add2.htm).

35. Christopher Marquis, 'Aristide Flees After a Shove From the U.S.', *New York Times*, 1 Mar. 2004, pp.A1-A10. See also Security Council Resolution 1529 (n.5 above). There were two previous major missions to Haiti: UNMIH, Sept. 1993–June 1996 and MICIVIH, 1993–97. The launch of another mission less than ten years later highlights the need to more clearly define the success of such missions in terms of measurably improving the human rights situation.
36. Amy Goodman (ed.), *Getting Haiti Right This Time: The US and The Coup (Read and Resist)*, Monroe, ME: Common Courage, 2004.
37. See e.g., International Crisis Group, 'Haiti's Transition Hanging in the Balance', Latin America/Caribbean Briefing No.7, Port-au-Prince/Brussels, 8 Feb. 2005.
38. Interview with Loune Viaud of the Haitian NGO, Zanmi Lasante, Cange, 22 March 2006.
39. See also Walt Bogdanich and Jenny Nordberg, 'Mixed U.S. Signals Helped Tilt Haiti Toward Chaos', *New York Times*, 29 Jan. 2006, Sect.1, pp.1–10.
40. Ibid.
41. Interview with Nancy Dorsinville, Harvard School of Public Health, Cambridge, MA, 15 February 2006.
42. See e.g., 'Caribbean Countries Fail Corruption Test', *The Jamaica Observer*, 28 Oct. 2005 (www.jamaicaobserver.com/magazines/Business/html/20051027T210000-0500_91229_OBS_CARIBBEAN_COUNTRIES_FAIL_CORRUPTION_TEST.asp).
43. 'Haiti's interim prime minister asks for OAS election support', *Caribbean Net News*, 7 May 2004.
44. See MINUSTAH budget, UN Doc. S/2005/313/add.1, 23 June 2005.
45. Interview with Viaud (see n.38 above).
46. See e.g., Human Rights Watch, 'UN: Darfur Needs Strong Protection Force' (http://hrw.org/english/docs/2006/04/20/sudan13237.htm).
47. Joe Oloka-Onyango, 'Reinforcing Marginalized Rights in an Age of Globalization: International Mechanisms, Non-State Actors, and the Struggle for Peoples' Rights in Africa', *American University International Law Review*, Vol.18, pp.851–911.
48. 'All UN entities have the responsibility to ensure that human rights are promoted and protected through and within their operations in the field.' Internal OHCHR document distributed to field presences in December 2006.
49. Some scholars have asserted that the UN needs an ombudsperson to help move the organization in that direction. Florian Hoffman and Frédéric Mégret, 'Fostering Human Rights Accountability: An Ombudsperson for the United Nations,' *Global Governance*, Vol.11, 2005, pp.43–63.
50. Discussion with DPA and DPKO staffers, New York, 22 February 2006. One example cited was the sheer number of human rights indicators being pushed by the OHCHR that made the project unrealistic.
51. While the WHO has brought an action to ICJ on the illegality of nuclear weapons, it was rejected by the Court. The WHO would be in a better position, juridically speaking, to bring an action on whether MINUSTAH and peacekeeping mission in general are meeting their obligations to facilitate measurable increases in the right to health. But to get to this stage the General Assembly of the WHO would have to approve the request for an advisory opinion to the ICJ, which some WHO members are likely to oppose. See 'Legality of the Threat or Use of Nuclear Weapons: Advisory Opinion of 8 July 1996', (ww.icj-cij.org/icjwww/idecisions/isummaries/iunanaummary960708.htm).
52. International Court of Justice, *Reparation for Injuries Suffered in the Service of the United Nations*, advisory opinion of 11 April 1949 (www.icj-cij.org/icjwww/idecisions/isummaries/iisunsummary490411.htm)
53. Martenczuk (n.2 above).
54. See in particular the ICJ ruling 'Armed Activities on the Territory of the Congo (Democratic Republic of the Congo v. Uganda)' 19 December 2005 (www.icj-cij.org/icjwww/ipresscom/ipress2005/ipresscom2005-26_co_20051219.htm) and compare with the ICJ's ruling in Bosnia Herzegovina vs. Yugoslavia (Serbia and Montenegro), 'Case Concerning the Convention on the Prevention and Punishment of the Crime of Genocide', *AJIL*, Vol.87, No.3, 1999, pp.505–20.

The 'Responsibility to Protect' by Peace Support Forces under International Human Rights Law

SIOBHAN WILLS

The applicability of international human rights law extra-territorially has major implications for peace support forces, since troops, even when they are engaged in UN operations, remain bound by the rules of international law to which they would be bound if they were acting independently of the UN.[1] The case law of international and regional courts and treaty bodies largely supports the view that a state's obligation to respect and ensure international human rights laws outside its territorial boundaries can arise in three circumstances: (1) where a state is in control of territory outside its borders; (2) where the actions of a state agent bring persons or property under their direct control, for example by kidnap or detention; (3) in recognized exceptions to the territorial principle of jurisdiction generally characterized by localized state control or authority, for example embassies and vessels flying the state's flag.

Control of Territory

Two decisions in 2004 and 2005 of the International Court of Justice (ICJ) affirm that human rights treaties apply to territory under the de facto 'control' or 'authority' of a state party. In 2004, in its Advisory Opinion on *The Legal Consequences of the Construction of a Wall in the Occupied Palestinian Territory* (hereinafter *Israeli Wall*) the ICJ stated that all the human rights treaties to which Israel is party are applicable in the Occupied Palestinian Territories (except to the extent that it has formally derogated from them), as well as the human rights obligations that constitute customary law.[2] In December 2005 the ICJ held that Ugandan forces in occupation of the Ituri district in the Democratic Republic of the Congo were required to uphold all the human rights treaties to which Uganda is party.[3] Regional human rights courts have adopted similar positions[4] with the exception that in *Bancović* (which concerned claims by relatives of those killed in the bombing of the Serbian television station by NATO forces during the 1999 Kosovo campaign), the European Court of Human Rights (ECtHR) held the case inadmissible for lack of jurisdiction on the grounds that the Convention operates 'in an essentially regional context and notably in the legal space (*espace juridique*) of the Contracting States.'[5] Nevertheless in the subsequent *Issa* case (which concerned claims that Iraqi shepherds had been murdered by the Turkish army during the course of operations in northern Iraq in 1995), the Court implied that the Convention is applicable beyond the regional limits of Europe if the contracting state is exercising de facto control over the territory.[6]

The Actions of a State Agent Bringing Persons or Property under its Control

Human rights treaties may also apply extra-territorially even where the state does not have control over territory, in cases where individuals or property are brought within the jurisdiction of parties to a human rights treaty by the actions of state agents bringing them under the state's control, for example by detaining them. The principal justification for this category of jurisdiction is that articulated in the *Lopez* case in which the UN Human Rights Committee held that it would be unconscionable to interpret the International Covenant on Civil and Political Rights (ICCPR) in such a way as to permit a state party to perpetrate violations of the Covenant on the territory of another state that it could not perpetrate on its own territory.[7] The European and Inter-American Courts of Human Rights (ACtHR) have taken a similar approach.[8]

Recognized Exceptions to the Territorial Principle

The ECtHR has also recognized that certain activities or places that are accepted as being within a state's authority fall within a well-established exception to the territorial principle of jurisdiction such as 'cases involving the activities of its diplomatic or consular agents abroad and on board craft and vessels registered in, or flying the flag of that State.'[9] In the view of the UK High Court in the *Al-Skeini* case, a military prison falls within this group. The Court stated that:

> it is not at all straining the examples of extra-territorial jurisdiction ... to hold that a British military prison, operating in Iraq with the consent of the Iraqi sovereign authorities, and containing arrested suspects, falls within even a narrowly limited exception exemplified by embassies, consulates, vessels and aircraft, and in the case of *Hess v. United Kingdom*, a prison.[10]

Implications for Peace Support Forces

In its General Comment No. 31, of 29 March 2004 the Human Rights Committee made it clear that the applicability of human rights treaties extends to peacekeeping forces:

> A State party must respect and ensure the rights laid down in the Covenant [ICCPR] to anyone within the power and effective control of that State

party, even if not situated within the territory of that State party...This principle also applies to those within the power or effective control of the forces of a State party acting outside its territory, regardless of the circumstances in which such power or effective control was obtained, such as forces constituting a national contingent of a State party assigned to a national peacekeeping or peace-enforcement operation.[11]

Peace support forces are frequently likely to find themselves in situations where human rights abuses are being committed by one or more of the belligerent parties, and the question arises as to what extent the force has an obligation to intervene to prevent them. Most human rights treaties encompass both negative and positive obligations, either explicitly or implicitly. However, even in the case of non-derogable rights, the positive obligation to secure is not an absolute one. In *Osman v United Kingdom* the ECtHR stressed that where there is an allegation that the authorities have violated their positive obligation to protect the right to life it must be established:

that the authorities knew or ought to have known at the time of the existence of a real and immediate risk to the life of an identified individual or individuals from the criminal acts of a third party and that they failed to take measures within the scope of their powers which, judged reasonably, might have been expected to avoid that risk.[12]

In the case of *Mahmout Kaya v Turkey*, the ECtHR reiterated that the duty to protect did not extend to the population as a whole:

the positive obligation must be interpreted in a way which does not impose an impossible or disproportionate burden on the authorities. Accordingly, not every claimed risk to life can entail for the authorities a Convention requirement to take operational measures to prevent that risk from materialising. For a positive obligation to arise, it must be established that the authorities knew or ought to have known at the time of the existence of a real and immediate risk to the life of an identified individual or individuals from the criminal acts of a third party and that they failed to take measures within the scope of their powers which, judged reasonably, might have been expected to avoid that risk.[13]

Nevertheless despite these qualifications, the potential for positive obligations under human rights law has far-reaching implications for troops. For example, it seems at least plausible that military camps belonging to a state's forces would fall within the 'narrowly limited exception' to the territorial limits of jurisdiction exemplified by embassies, consulates, vessels, aircraft and prisons.[14] If that is the case, the compliance of the DUTCHBAT contingent of the UN Protection Force (UNPROFOR) in the 'evacuation' of the refugees sheltering in its military camp at Potocari, Bosnia, prior to their massacre by Serb forces, should be assessed in the light of human rights treaties to which the Netherlands was party. There is ample, though not unchallenged, evidence that troops 'knew or ought to have known at the time of the existence of a real and immediate risk' to the lives of the men in the camp,[15] and there are credible allegations that the force 'failed to take measures within the scope of their powers which, judged reasonably, might have been expected to avoid that risk.'[16] One Dutch soldier claims that he took photographs of Dutch troops assisting in the separation of the men from the women.[17] No derogations are permitted in respect of the right to life under any human rights treaty, with the exception of the European Convention (ECHR) which, under Article 15, allows for derogation, to the extent strictly necessary in the exigencies of the situation, in respect of deaths arising from lawful acts of war. The massacre at Srebrenica was not a lawful act of war.

Similarly it could be argued that the conduct of Belgian troops immediately prior to the massacre in 1994 of 2,000 Rwandans that had sought refuge at their camp at Kicukiro, should be assessed in the light of the human rights treaties to which Belgium is party. The Rules of Engagement under which the force was operating stated that certain 'ethnically or politically motivated criminal acts' would 'morally and legally require UNAMIR [the UN Mission to Rwanda] to use all available means to halt them.'[18] Despite this, when the Belgian forces requested permission to withdraw from the camp they failed to inform their commanding officer of the presence of 2,000 refugees in the camp and the fact that the Interhamwe Hutu militia had been stationed outside with their machetes for days.[19] Amongst those killed at the camp was a prominent politician, Boniface Ngulinzira, whom UNAMIR had undertaken to protect. He had been brought from his house to the camp by his UNAMIR guards.[20]

However the situation that is likely to raise the most difficulty in future operations is the extent of the positive obligations of peace support forces in situations comparable to occupation. The applicability of human rights law in situations where a state is in effective control of territory is not limited to formally recognized cases of occupation. In 1998, the Human Rights Committee stated that it was 'concerned about the behaviour of Belgian soldiers in Somalia under the aegis of the United Nations Operation in Somalia (UNOSOM II).'[21] The Committee reiterated its concerns in 2004:

> The Covenant automatically applies when it [the State party] exercises power or effective control over a person outside its territory, regardless of the circumstances such power or effective control was obtained, such as forces constituting a national contingent assigned to an international peacekeeping force or peace support operation.[22]

However the jurisprudence on the human rights law obligations of occupants is relevant to peace support forces, for two reasons. First, troops engaged in post-conflict operations, or deployed into 'failed states', may find themselves the only effective authority in the area and hence may be subject to the laws of occupation. Second, decisions of the ICJ reflect a growing acceptance of 'convergence' principles (at least in certain circumstances) with regard to the relationship between international humanitarian law (IHL) and Human Rights Law. Walter Kälin, the UN Special Rapporteur on human rights in Kuwait following the Iraqi invasion in 1991, describes the convergence approach as: 'The application of both sets of norms (cumulatively whenever possible) as they reinforce each other; thus one should speak of a unified complex of HUMAN RIGHTS norms under different institutional umbrellas'.[23]

Theodore Meron has argued that 'the convergence between humanitarian and human rights law is progressing rapidly' and that 'although these systems of protection continue to have different institutional 'umbrellas'...a strict separation between the two is artificial and hinders efforts to maximize the effective protection of human rights'.[24] While this view of the relationship between IHL and international human rights law is controversial it is, to some extent, borne out by the fact that the International Committee of the Red Cross (ICRC) itself, in its 2005 study on Customary International Humanitarian Law, seems to view the two regimes holistically, particularly as regards the force's relationship with the local population.[25]

The ICJ in both the *Israeli Wall* opinion and the *Case Concerning Armed Activities on the Territory of the Congo* (hereinafter *Congo*) seemed to regard the applicability of occupation law as virtually synonymous with the applicability of human rights law, based on the fact that effective control is a key criterion under both regimes.[26] Article 42 of the Hague Regulations provides that: 'Territory is considered occupied when it is actually placed under the authority of the hostile army. The occupation extends only to the territory where such authority has been established and can be exercised'. Article 43 states that: 'The authority of the legitimate power having in fact passed into the hands of the occupant, the latter shall take all measures in his power to restore and ensure as far as possible, public order and safety, while respecting unless absolutely prevented, the laws in force in the country'.

Brookes L.J. of the UK Court of Appeal, in considering the applicability of The Human Rights Act 1998 to UK occupying forces in Iraq, argued that:

> it is quite impossible to hold that the UK, although an occupying power for the purposes of the Hague Regulations and Geneva IV, was in effective control of Basrah City for the purposes of ECHR jurisprudence at the material time. If it had been it would have been obliged, pursuant to the *Bankovic* judgement, to secure to everyone in Basrah City the rights and freedoms guaranteed by the ECHR. One has only to state the proposition to see how utterly unreal it is. The UK possessed no executive, legislative or judicial authority in Basrah City, other than the limited authority given its military forces...For the purposes of completeness, I should make it clear that I reject the arguments by the claimants to the effect that occupation for the purposes of the Hague Regulations must necessarily be equated with effective control of the occupied area for ECHR purposes.[27]

However Lord Justice Sedley disagreed:

> In respectful disagreement with what Brookes L.J. says in paragraph 124, I do not see why the presence or absence of civil power for effective control in international law should be tested by asking whether there is sufficient control to enforce the full range of [ECHR] Convention rights.... What

seems to me more material is the fact that ... the United Kingdom was an occupying power within the meaning of Article 42 of the Hague Regulations because the Basrah region was under the authority of its armed forces. Article 43 then makes it incumbent upon the UK, 'to take all the measures in [its] power to restore and ensure, *as far as possible*, public order and safety, while respecting, *unless absolutely prevented*, the laws in force in the country'.

No doubt it is absurd to expect occupying forces in the near chaos of Iraq to enforce the right to marry vouchsafed by Article 12 or the equality guarantees vouchsafed by Article 14 [of the ECHR]. But I do not think effective control involves this.... It does not make the occupying power the guarantor of all rights; nor therefore does it demand sufficient control for such purposes. What it does place upon the occupier is an obligation to do all it can.[28]

Lord Justice Brookes' argument can be criticized on the grounds that there is a very strong emphasis in IHL on the protection of civilians, and to suggest that the occupant has no obligation to comply with the international human rights standards set out in treaties to which it is party *in so far as it has the power to do so*, would seem to undermine the spirit of the Conventions. On the other hand Sedley L.J. seems to be arguing that occupation law itself requires an occupant to apply international human rights standards. A more conservative approach would be to hold that the applicability of human rights law derives from the human rights regime and not from occupation law. It is not immediately clear how the Article 43 obligation to ensure 'public order and safety' encompasses an obligation to secure rights protected under international human rights treaties unless those rights were already part of the existing local law.

Some commentators have interpreted *'l'ordre et la vie publics'*, the French text equivalent of 'public order and safety', as encompassing all *'qu'il s'agit des fonctions socials, des transactions ordinaires, qui constituent la vie des jours'* [matters relating to social functions and common transactions that make up everyday life].[29] The ICRC states that it is a principle of customary law that human rights law 'applies at all times'.[30] It could be argued that an obligation to restore all those ordinary functions that constitute daily life, read in the light of human rights law development since the drafting of the Geneva Conventions (in particular the customary law rule that human rights law applies at all times, including in armed conflict) encompasses a requirement that the occupant respect and ensure 'as far as possible' the international human rights standards protected by customary international law and those treaties to which it is a party. However such an approach would require a significant reappraisal of the relevant provisions of the Hague Regulations and of Geneva Convention IV. None of the delegates to the *Diplomatic Conference of Geneva 1949* considered a proposal by the Mexican delegate to include a reference to human rights standards in Article 64 of Geneva Convention IV important enough to make any comment on it worth recording, let alone adopt it.[31] However case law of the

ICJ, and to an extent the ICRC's study on Customary International Law, provide some support for a re-interpretation of Article 43.

In assessing the scope and meaning of customary rules of IHL, the ICRC study refers frequently to international human rights law. Chapter 32 of the ICRC's study is on 'Fundamental Guarantees', which are described as 'overarching rules' that 'apply to all civilians in the power of a party to the conflict and who do not take direct part in hostilities'.[32] The study lists nine 'fundamental guarantees' of customary IHL: each rule is supported by state practice from human rights law as well as IHL.[33] The introduction to the chapter states that this was done 'not for the purpose of providing an assessment of customary human rights law, but in order to support, strengthen and clarify analogous principles of humanitarian law.'[34] The introduction concludes by saying that: 'It is beyond the scope of this study to determine whether these guarantees apply equally outside armed conflict although collected practice appears to indicate that they do'.[35]

On a semantic level it is quite difficult to appreciate how rules of customary IHL intended for the protection of civilians that do not participate in hostilities, could be applicable where there is no armed conflict. However on a practical level it is possible to see how such an approach could be relevant given that forces (especially those engaged in peace operations) are frequently deployed into situations where force is used but does not reach the level of armed conflict, or where there is an armed conflict but the force is not party to it.

The ICRC approach to the determination of customary rules of IHL implies that certain customary rules of international law that are similar in both IHL and human rights law have now developed to such an extent that for many purposes distinctions in their originating source are no longer significant (at least in the context of 'fundamental guarantees'). This does not resolve the problem of jurisdiction under human rights law but it does suggest that courts and monitoring institutions, when determining whether an occupant has effective control for the purposes of human rights law, may be likely to 'shortcut' the analysis of effective control criteria to the point where there is no distinction between effective control for occupation and effective control for human rights law purposes. If this approach is consistently adopted then for all practical purposes the Article 43 requirement that occupants observe and ensure all applicable human rights law (an obligation that can only be derived from the customary law status of the principle that human rights law remains applicable in armed conflict) will generally be taken to imply that the occupant must observe and ensure, so far as is possible, all the human rights treaties to which the occupying state is party, all the human rights treaties to which the occupied state is party, and customary human rights law – except to the extent of any measures taken pursuant to a declared derogation that are strictly necessary in the exigencies of the situation. This would seem to be the approach taken by the ICJ.

In its two most recent decisions on occupation, the *Israeli Wall* opinion and the *Case Concerning Armed Activities on the Territory of the Congo* the ICJ has treated the status of occupation as in itself triggering jurisdiction under human rights laws to which the occupant is party. In the latter case, the court, having concluded on the basis of the evidence that Uganda was the occupying power in Ituri at the relevant time, stated that:

> As such it was under an obligation, according to Article 43 of the Hague Regulations of 1907, to take all the measures in its power to restore, and ensure, as far as possible, public order and safety in the occupied area, while respecting, unless absolutely prevented, the laws in force in the DRC. This obligation comprised the duty to secure respect for the applicable rules of international human rights law and international humanitarian law, to protect the inhabitants of the occupied territory against acts of violence, and not to tolerate such violence by any third party.
>
> The Court having concluded that Uganda was an occupying Power in Ituri at the relevant time, finds that Uganda's responsibility is engaged both for any acts of its military that violated international obligations and for any lack of vigilance in preventing violations of human rights and international humanitarian law by other actors present in the occupied territory, including rebel groups acting on their own account.[36]

The Court then listed all the human rights and humanitarian law treaties that it considered applicable to Uganda as occupier. The Hague Regulations were held to be applicable on the basis that they are customary law. The following treaties were then listed along with the dates of accession by both parties: the Geneva Conventions and Additional Protocol I, the ICCPR, the African Charter on Human and People's Rights, the Convention on the Rights of the Child and its Additional Protocol on the Involvement of Children in Armed Conflict. However the significance of the fact that the occupied state, the DRC, was also party to these Conventions was not discussed at all. The mere listing of these treaties as applicable, without analysis, suggests that, in the Court's view, occupation constitutes jurisdiction for the purposes of human rights law. In addition to violations committed by Ugandan troops the Court accepted evidence that Ugandan forces had failed to take action to put an end to violence that had resulted in some 100,000 deaths and the displacement of some 500,000 people, in particular that 'UPDF [Uganda Peoples Defence Force] forces stood by during the killings and failed to protect the civilians.'[37] The Court found by 16 votes to 1 that Uganda had violated its obligations under international human rights law and international humanitarian law both by direct acts 'as well as by its failure, as an occupying Power, to take measures to respect and ensure respect for human rights and international humanitarian law, in the Ituri district.'[38]

The tenor of the ICJ's decisions in the *Congo* case and the *Israeli Wall* opinion implies that the obligation on forces to protect the human rights of the local population may arise not only under human rights law but also directly under IHL through Article 43 of the Hague Regulations. Whilst in any individual case the applicability of occupation law and/or human rights law may be disputed on the facts, the developing 'convergence' between the two regimes is likely to enhance the expectation of both the local population and the international media that troops should provide protection from human rights abuses.

Conclusion

The International Commission on Kosovo in its follow up to the Kosovo Report, examined the post-conflict administration established by SC Resolution 1244 (10 June 1999) and argued that 'greater efforts should have been taken from the inception of the occupation to protect civilians in Kosovo, and to establish the Rule of Law,'[39] comments that imply that the Commission views the administration as an occupation. Referring to the framework of contextual principles that should govern humanitarian intervention that it had proposed in the Kosovo Report,[40] the Commission recommended that, taking into account lessons learned from the transitional administration in Kosovo, a new provision emphasizing the importance of providing protection to minorities should be added, so that it should now read:

> There must be even stricter adherence to the laws of war and international humanitarian law than in standard military operations. This applies to all aspects of military occupation, including post-cease-fire occupation, *and imposes a particular duty on occupying forces and their administrative counterparts to give the highest protection of threatened segments of the civilian population, including the prevention of acts of revenge and retribution* [original emphasis].[41]

The Commission's references to the Kosovo administration as an occupation are perhaps surprising given that Resolution 1244 said nothing at all about the laws of occupation or the larger body of general IHL. Nevertheless it is an indication that there is increasing recognition that UN forces, and their administrative counterparts, may be involved in operations that are closely akin to occupation and that the principles of occupation may be considered relevant, even if only by analogy.

The UN Secretary-General stated in 2005 that the UN must be prepared to commit to longer involvement in post-conflict situations since all too often, 'a fragile peace has been allowed to crumble into renewed conflict.'[42] It is envisaged that the newly created Peacebuilding Commission will be heavily involved in this process.[43] It is inevitable that peace support forces will be involved in such operations. The strong emphasis on human rights protection in decisions of the ICJ and human rights treaty bodies will require all peace support forces deployed into these situations to be aware of their potential obligations under human rights law, in particular the fact that they may have positive obligations to provide protection. Such responsibilities are in line with the increasingly accepted proposition that the international community (via its institutions) has an 'international responsibility to protect' people from serious violations of human rights. It is a proposition endorsed by the Secretary-General's High level Panel on Threats, Challenges and Change,[44] by the General Assembly at the World Summit in 2005 and by the Security Council in its third resolution on the Protection of Civilians in Armed Conflict, Resolution 1674 adopted on 28 April 2006.[45] Training and planning for peace operations should reflect the fact that troops will be expected and may be legally obligated to provide that protection. Failure to do so is to put troops into an untenable situation where they cannot carry out the tasks they are expected to do, leading to loss of morale[46] and loss of the respect of the local community.[47]

In the light of these developments it is inexcusable to deploy troops into situations where they may find themselves responsible for extensive administrative and security tasks, for example in 'failed' states such as Somalia or in post-conflict administrations such as Kosovo and East Timor, without sufficient recognition (and appropriate mandate, resources and training) of their potential responsibilities under human rights law, in particular recognition that the obligations of the force are not limited to ensuring that their own conduct is of a high standard but also that they may be required to secure, in so far as it is in their power to do so, the human rights of the local population.

ACKNOWLEDGEMENT

This article is based on a small section of the author's 'Occupation Law and Multi-National Forces: Problems and Perspectives', *British Yearbook of International Law*, 2006, and is published here with permission.

NOTES

1. Adam Roberts and Robert Guelff, *Documents on the Laws of War*, Oxford: University Press Oxford (3rd edn), 2000, p.723.
2. International Court of Justice, *The Legal Consequences of the Construction of a Wall in Occupied Palestinian Territory*, Advisory Opinion, 9 July 2004, *International Legal Materials (ILM)* 1009, 2004.
3. International Court of Justice, *Case Concerning Armed Activities on the Territory of the Congo: Democratic Republic of the Congo v Uganda*, 19 Dec. 2005, para.217.
4. European Court of Human Rights: *Loizidou v. Turkey* (40/1993/435/514) Judgement (Merits) (1996); *Cyprus v Turkey* Judgement of 10 May 2001, App. No.27581/94; *Djavit An v Turkey*, Judgement of 20 February 2003, App. No.20652/192 2004; Inter-American Commission on Human Rights, Case 11.589, *Alejandre and Others v Cuba*, Report No 86/89, 29 Sept. 1999.
5. European Court of Human Rights, *Bancović v Belgium and 16 Other Contracting States* (52207/99) 2001, para.80.
6. *Issa and others v Turkey* App. No.31821/96 Judgement, 16 November 2004, para.74.
7. United Nations Human Rights Committee, *Delia Saldias de Lopez v. Uruguay*, Communication No.52/1979 (29 July 1981), para.12.3, UN doc. CCPR/C/OP/1 (1984), para.88; Communication No.R.13/56, para.10.3, UN doc. Supp. No.40, A/36/40 (1981), para.185.
8. *Bancović v Belgium* (see n.5 above), para.68; *Drozd and Janousek v France and Spain* Judgement 26 June 1992 Series A No.240, 29 and *Ilascu and others v Moldova and the Russian Federation*, Application No.48787/99, Admissibility Decision, 4 July 2001, 21 website text; Inter-American Commission on Human Rights, Case 11.589, *Alejandre and Others v Cuba* (see n.4 above), para.25. However under *Bancović* jurisdiction does not extend outside the *espace juridique* of the Convention: *Bancović v Belgium* (n.5 above), para.47.
9. *Bancović v Belgium* (n.5 above), para.73.
10. *The Queen on the application of Mazin Jumaa Gatteh Al-Skeini and others v Secretary of State for Defence* [2004] EWHC 2911 (Admin), paras.286–7.
11. General Comment No.31, UN Doc.CCPR/C/2/1/Rev.1/Add.13, 2004, para.10.
12. European Court of Human Rights, *Osman v United Kingdom*, Judgement of 28 October 1998, Application No.87/1997/871/1083, Reports 1998-VIII, para.116.
13. *Mahmout Kaya v Turkey*, European Court of Human Rights, App. 22535/93, Judgement 28 March 2000, para.86.
14. *The Queen on the application of Mazin Jumaa Gatteh Al-Skeinii* (see n.10 above), paras.286–7.

15. Philip Corwin, *Dubious Mandate: A Memoir of the UN in Bosnia, Summer* 1995, Durham: Duke University Press, 1999, p.212; General Assembly report A/54/549,15 November 1999, Report of the Secretary-General pursuant to General Assembly resolution 53/55, 'The fall of Srebrenica', paras.341–3; The testimony of Major Franken in the Krstić trial confirms that the force knew that a massacre was about to take place: Major Franken's testimony, T. 2008-2009: *Krstić* ICTY IT-98-33-T, Judgement (2 Aug. 2001). However the 'Summary for the Press' of the report 'Srebrenica – a 'Safe' Area: Reconstruction, Background and Consequences of the Fall of a Safe Area', 10 April 2002, undertaken by Netherlands Institute for War Documentation, states that 'Deputy Dutchbat commander Franken ... *could not* have suspected that this would lead to the mass slaughter of these and many other men who fell into the hands of the Bosnian Serbs during their flight to Tuzla', para.11 [original emphasis] (www.srebrenica.nl/en/a_index.htm)
16. A case concerning the family of one survivor is currently being brought against the Netherlands: *H. Nuhanović v de Staat der Nederlanden* 28 October 2004, Hof 's-Gravenhage (Court of Appeal, The Hague).
17. Major De Ruijter of the Dutch Military Intelligence Service took the film in for development but through some 'very bad luck' it was destroyed. However, the Dutch press noted that the leaked Ministry of Intelligence report stating that the film was 'destroyed' had been signed on 25 July 1995: one day before the film was developed. 7 Dec. 2002, 'Just Bad Luck Film Roll Was Destroyed', (www.nisnews.nl/dossiers/srebrenica/srebrenica.htm).
18. 'Report of the Independent Inquiry into the Actions of the United Nations during the 1994 Genocide in Rwanda', United Nations: New York, 15 Dec. 1999, p.5.
19. Romeo Dallaire, *Shake Hands with the Devil*, London: Arrow, 2004, p.290.
20. Report of the Independent Inquiry ... Rwanda (see n.18 above), p.13.
21. Concluding Observations of the Human Rights Committee: Belgium 19 Nov. 1998, UN doc. CCPR/C/79/Add.99, para.14.
22. Concluding Observations of the Human Rights Committee: Belgium 12 Aug. 2004 UN doc. CCPR/C/81/BEL, para.10.
23. Walter Kälin, *Human Rights in Times of Occupation: The Case of Kuwait*, Berne: Law Books of Europe, 1994, pp.26–7 (original emphasis).
24. Theodore Meron, *Human Rights in Internal Strife: Their International Protection*, Cambridge: Grotius Publications, 1987, p.28.
25. Jean-Marie Henckaerts and Louise Doswald-Beck, *Customary International Humanitarian Law*, Cambridge: Cambridge University Press, 2005, pp.300–305.
26. Several judges, while agreeing with the Court's conclusions, expressed concern at the poor quality of the analysis of relevant IHL: *The Legal Consequences of the Construction of a Wall in Occupied Palestinian Territory* (see n.2 above), Separate Opinion Judge Higgins, para.40; Separate Opinion Judge Kooijmans, para.10; Separate Opinion Judge Owada, para.24.
27. *The Queen on the application of Mazin Jumaa Gatteh Al-Skeini* (see n.10 above), paras.124–7.
28. Ibid., paras.195–6.
29. Ministere des Affaires Étrangères, Actes de la Conférence de Bruxelles de 1874 (Paris 1874), p.23 quoted in Edmund H. Schwenk, *Yale Law Journal* Vol.54, No.2, pp.393, 398; Marco Sassòli, 'Legislation and Maintenance of Public Order and Civil Life by Occupying Powers', *European Journal of International Law*, Vol.4, No.16, pp.661, 663.
30. Henckaerts and Doswald-Beck (see n.25 above), pp.300–305.
31. *Final Record of the Diplomatic Conference of Geneva 1949*, Vol. II a, pp.670–72.
32. Ibid.
33. Ibid., pp.306–83.
34. Ibid, p.299.
35. Ibid.
36. *Case Concerning Armed Activities on the Territory of the Congo* (see n.3 above), paras.178–9.
37. Ibid., para.209.
38. Ibid., paras.209, 345. The case may have implications for the UN Mission in the Democratic Republic of the Congo (MONUC). In mid-2006, the UN was investigating allegations that, during joint operations with DRC forces, MONUC repeatedly stood aside and watched as DRC forces killed civilians and torched their huts in a series of attacks against villages in the Ituri district. *The Guardian* (London) 'UN accused over Congo village massacre', 18 June 2006; Channel 4 (UK TV) 'Unreported World – The UN's Dirty War', broadcast 23 June 2006. The legal position is more complicated than that of Ugandan forces since MONUC is not in occupation. However, MONUC is authorized to use all necessary means to ensure the

protection of civilians: S/RES 1565 (1 Oct 2004); S/RES 1592 (30 March 2005); S/RES 1635 (28 October 2005); S/RES 1649 (21 December 2005).

39. Independent International Commission on Kosovo, *Follow up to the Kosovo Report: Why Conditional Independence?*, 2001, p.37 (available at www.kosovocommission.org).

40. Independent International Commission on Kosovo, *Kosovo Report*, Oxford: Oxford University Press, 2000, pp.193–5.

41. The Commission emphasized that 'even in the context of a humanitarian intervention backed by UN authority, there exists an international duty to comply with these guidelines'. Independent International Commission on Kosovo, *Follow up to the Kosovo Report: Why Conditional Independence?* (n.39 above), p.36.

42. 'Secretary-General Calls Endorsement of Peace Building Commission a Turning Point in Remarks Following Historic Event', SG/SM/10277 GA/10440, (www.un.org/News/Press/docs/2005/sgsm10277.doc.htm).

43. Ibid.

44. Report by the Secretary-General's High Level Panel on Threats, Challenges and Change, *A More Secure World: Our Shared Responsibility*, paras.201–3.

45. A/RES/60/1, 24 October 2005, paras.97–105; S/RES/1674, 28 April 2006, [4].

46. Netherlands Institute for War Documentation, *Srebrenica 'A Safe Area': Reconstruction, Background, Consequences and Analyzes of the Fall of a Safe Area*, Pt II, Ch.8, Sect.13, 'Peacekeeper Stress', 2002; John Sloboda, James Kemp and Chris Abbot, *Putting People First: The Way Forward for the UK Armed Forces*, Oxford Research Group, 5 July 2004 (www.oxfordresearchgroup.org.uk/publications/briefings/puttingpeoplefirst.htm).

47. UK Ministry of Defence, Joint Warfare Publication 3.50 *The Military Contribution to Peace Support Operation*, 2nd edn, Joint Doctrine and Concepts Centre, Shrivenham, 2004, p.306.

Implementation through Cooperation? Human Rights Officers and the Military in Kosovo, 1999–2002

CLIVE BALDWIN

At the end of NATO's war with the Federal Republic of Yugoslavia (FRY), carried out in the name of the human rights of the inhabitants of Kosovo, the UN Security Council passed Resolution 1244. This authorized both the creation of a NATO-led peacekeeping force, and a United Nations Mission in Kosovo (UNMIK), which would run an interim administration until the final status of Kosovo was resolved.[1] Human rights were supposed to be at the heart of this. The Organization for Security and Cooperation in Europe (OSCE) was made responsible for 'institution-building', and one of its largest departments was Human Rights and the Rule of Law.

Despite this, nearly seven years later the human rights situation in Kosovo remains one of the worst in Europe, particularly for Kosovo's minorities. Ethnic cleansing took place in 1999 despite the presence of the international administration and peacekeeping forces, and happened again in 2004.[2] Today thousands of Kosovo's Serbs, Roma and even Albanians (those who lived in areas of Serb dominance) remain displaced, too afraid to return home.[3] The international community, including the military and the human rights officers, can therefore be said largely to have failed in what they set out to achieve in 1999.

This article analyses the way in which human rights officers and the military component of the international presence in Kosovo tried, but largely failed, to work together in the critical early years of their deployment (the time of the author's experience there). It will explain how the lack of an overall strategy for both the military and human rights presence contributed to this. It will focus on two key issues, the rights of minorities (particularly the displaced), and the justice system, where human rights officers and the military should have worked together towards a common goal, but usually failed to do so.

To understand these problems it is necessary to understand the structure of the human rights and the military components of the mission operating in the province.

A Very Large Human Rights Mission: the OSCE

The OSCE is an international organization that emerged in the early 1990s as a development of the Cold War Conference on Security and Cooperation in Europe (CSCE). Its membership consists of every European state, every state of the former Soviet Union, the United States and Canada. It is in essence a conflict-prevention organization. Originally it focused on monitoring military agreements, but since 1990 its main area of work has been democratization and the protection and promotion of human rights. The OSCE has developed particular areas of specialization: elections, minority rights and the media. It has also established long-term missions in various countries, the largest of which have been in Croatia, Bosnia and Herzegovina and Kosovo. The OSCE has a very small secretariat in comparison with the size of its field missions, so the largest of these missions have been, essentially, fully autonomous. Staff in most of the field missions have been persons seconded by OSCE member states, nearly always on short-term (six month or less) contracts.

The Prequel: the Kosovo Verification Mission (KVM)

Although there was a small OSCE mission in Kosovo in the early 1990s, international involvement began in earnest with the deployment of the OSCE's Kosovo Verification Mission (KVM) in autumn 1998.[4] This mission was a requirement of the deal negotiated by Richard Holbrook with President Slobodan Milošević of Serbia–Montenegro that year to avert the threat of NATO bombing. The OSCE mission was set up to monitor the ceasefire between the FRY forces and the Kosovo Liberation Army (KLA), and therefore was largely military-orientated. However, a human rights component was also established, which monitored alleged human rights violations by both the FRY forces and the KLA and reported on these. Human rights officers of the KVM included human rights professionals but also, due to the nature of this mission, former military and police officers. As a result, the KVM mission focused on reporting of criminal activities that amounted to human rights abuses. This became most apparent in the killings at Račak in January 1999, which were reported on by the OSCE. The process that followed led to the withdrawal of the KVM and the NATO bombing of Yugoslavia. Subsequently, the OSCE published its account of human rights violations during the KVM,[5] which have been used in trials of persons involved in human rights abuses at that time, notably Milošević.

Compared with what came later, the OSCE's KVM can be regarded as an example of good cooperation between the military and human rights officers.

Both were part of the same mission, with the same basic aim, to monitor and report, a task which both were able to do within their respective areas of expertise.

During the NATO bombing campaign, the OSCE maintained a mission working with the Kosovan refugees. The OSCE, along with the military, was therefore the first organization to arrive in Kosovo following the end of the bombing. After much initial confusion about the organizational structure of the interim administration in Kosovo, a 'four pillar' structure emerged. UNMIK, headed by a Special Representative of the Secretary General (SRSG), was responsible for the administration of Kosovo. This was to be done through four pillars, one of which was the responsibility of UNMIK itself, and involved administering what became, essentially, ministries and local government. The other three were run by the UN High Commision for Refugees (UNHCR), OSCE and EU missions in Kosovo (although the UNHCR later pulled out of the pillar structure and was replaced by a second UNMIK pillar responsible for 'security and justice'). Other UN institutions (for example, the World Health Organization and the Food and Agriculture Organization) had missions in Kosovo but these were separate from UNMIK.

There were two other human rights bodies in Kosovo at this early stage apart from the OSCE. The SRSG appointed a human rights adviser, a senior human rights expert, at the start of the mission. The human rights adviser to the SRSG worked closely with the OSCE, but resigned after six months and was not replaced.[6] The Office of the High Commissioner for Human Rights (OHCHR) also had a separate office in Pristina, outside of UNMIK structures.

The OSCE, however, had the 'mandate' for human rights,[7] and developed a large Department of Human Rights and Rule of Law, with, at the start of this period, officers in each of Kosovo's municipalities. However, the human rights work of the OSCE suffered from a lack of overall strategy and confusion over responsibilities. Its role within UNMIK was unclear. In effect the OSCE, with a separate structure, had a role that was partly monitoring UNMIK from the outside. It was rarely consulted by UNMIK and therefore ended up similar to an NGO in reporting and publishing on human rights violations as the only way to influence change. At the same time UNMIK, when faced with criticism of its human rights record by the OSCE, claimed that one branch of the UNMIK mission should not be criticizing another. On occasions, UNMIK tried, sometimes with success, to prevent or water down such criticisms.[8]

Within the OSCE itself, much confusion remained about how it should operate. This is not surprising given that Kosovo represented a unique situation. The OSCE Mission had four major thematic departments (Human Rights/Rule of Law, Elections, Democratization, and Media) each with officers in the municipalities, and each with very different tasks. However, the OSCE mission had many former military officers on its staff and in effect ended up trying to run a military structure parallel to one based on thematic issues. This military ideal aimed at a centralized, hierarchical structure where OSCE staff would report to the heads of OSCE's regional offices who would instruct them on the OSCE needs of the day. Another aspect of the military mindset in parts of the OSCE was the running of a Situation Centre, requiring daily reports on the 'situation' in OSCE officers' Area of

Responsibility. This was obviously in conflict with the needs of a human rights/rule of law department for specialist officers working only on human rights issues. This tension was never adequately resolved. In practice, while the appearance of a military structure was set up, in reality the Human Rights Division was able to operate autonomously, with a large number of specialist human rights officers.

Although the OSCE in Kosovo had one of the largest human rights missions in the world per head of population, the Human Rights/Rule of Law Department itself also suffered at times from a lack of a clear overall strategy. Again, it should be emphasized that this is far from surprising in such a unique mission. The author was quite surprised on his arrival in January 2000 to find that only a minority of the human rights officers had experience or qualifications in the field of human rights (at that time a majority had non-human rights backgrounds, including former police, journalists, humanitarian aid workers – and a few were ex-military). This changed, but only gradually. To begin with the human rights work did have a relatively clear strategy, that of monitoring. Most of the staff were ex-KVM officers, and it was very much a development of that work. In December 1999, the OSCE Mission published a summary of its work and findings in monitoring human rights from June to October that year, under the same title ('As Seen, As Told') as that of the KVM report.[9] This monitoring approach also fitted in with the desire of the ex-military in the OSCE for a 'situation report' as human rights officers often reported daily on crimes taking place against minorities.

As time went on the OSCE had to find a clear role in not only monitoring but also improving the human rights situation. This was made very difficult at all times by the confusion over who held ultimate authority in Kosovo, as well as what the final status of Kosovo would be. In mid-2001 the author conducted a review of the OSCE's human rights work in Kosovo up to then. The review found significant frustration among human rights officers owing to the perception that the human rights division itself was run on military lines, with a 'command and control' mentality that was considered inappropriate for human rights work. The (military) idea of situation reporting and a command structure based on regional offices was also rejected as inappropriate, as all it seemed to result in were human rights reports which had no impact on the overall human rights situation. Instead, the Human Rights Division was restructured to focus on five key thematic issues (property, anti-discrimination, gender, training, security). With the security area it was decided to focus on the police rather than on the military, partly as the experience until then was that it was very difficult for human rights officers to have any impact on KFOR. This restructuring was not without its opponents, particularly those in OSCE who wanted the hierarchical, situation reporting approach – but the change was pushed through as no alternative was offered.

KFOR

Like everything else in Kosovo, KFOR was itself an exceptional mission. Ostensibly led by NATO, and reporting to Brussels, it included forces from outside NATO, such as troops from Russia and the United Arab Emirates. A KFOR command structure was set up with a COMKFOR (Commander KFOR) based in Pristina, and five regional brigades, led by respectively: the French (in the north); Italians (northwest); British (centre, including Pristina); Germans (southwest) and Americans (southeast). Within each brigade were units from other countries. However, the source of instructions for each particular unit was often unclear. National authorities retained a large degree of control over their units in Kosovo; and each brigade developed its own identity. COMKFOR's role was often uncertain. The famed military strength of simple command and control did not happen.

Also notable about Kosovo was the lack of civilian control of the military. Unlike the situation in East Timor, where the military reported to and were controlled by the civilian UN SRSG, in Kosovo, KFOR was an entirely separate unit. The SRSG had no authority over KFOR, which created its own policies (and indeed individual units and brigades in turn often created their own).

This also led to a distinct lack of clear strategy in KFOR, in line with a track record remarked on by General Rupert Smith: 'The starting point to understanding all operations in the Balkans in the 1990s, including the NATO bombings of 1995 and 1999, was that they were without strategies'.[10] This was made much worse in Kosovo by the confused and divided command structure of KFOR, and the lack of civilian control. At least in discussions with OSCE, KFOR would describe its understanding of the mandate as being simply: 'Ensuring public safety and order until the international civil presence can take responsibility for this task'.[11] In practice, however, this could mean putting their own 'force protection' as their top priority and therefore doing very little. For some KFOR brigades, though, it could go to the other extreme, of involvement with non-military activities such as criminal justice.

Minorities

The priority for human rights officers and nominally the military during this period was the situation of minorities, particularly Serbs, Albanians (in Serb-majority areas) and the Roma (including Ashkaelia and 'Egyptians'). KFOR and the OSCE were the first international organizations to arrive in Kosovo after the departure of the FRY authorities. Unfortunately, the vacuum in authority had already been filled by extremists who targeted minorities, resulting in a major flight of minorities. Albanians targeted Serbs, Serbs in turn targeted Albanians, and both Albanians and Serbs targeted the Roma. This first wave of ethnic cleansing under the international administration went on for several months, to the great surprise of most observers.[12] The response of the OSCE Human Rights Division was to document the problems. Besides publishing *As Seen As Told*, the OSCE issued, jointly with UNHCR, a series of ten reports over four years setting out the problems of the minorities. Minorities that remained faced ongoing harassment and threats to their lives and wellbeing, and their situation became the priority for the OSCE Human Rights Division for most of this period. As a result human rights officers generally ended up developing a deep understanding of the situation of minorities in their area, particularly their security concerns.

This could have led to a close working relationship with KFOR, which was responsible for the 'safe and secure environment', but which rarely had detailed intelligence on the situation of minorities in their area, and whose lack of knowledge of local circumstances was compounded by the rotation of KFOR soldiers every six months. However, such a close relationship rarely developed. It occurred at times in particular locations, but not at a Kosovo-wide level. As the human rights mission became more human rights-orientated and less geared towards military/situation reporting, the lack of common ground between the two groups became even more apparent.

This was not helped by the lack of an overall strategy by KFOR, due to the diverse command structure described above. Decisions about how to deal with minorities on the ground were made by local commanders, with responses varying widely. KFOR, with over 50,000 troops at the start, seemed curiously reluctant to assert its authority against those carrying out and supporting the ethnic cleansing and harassment of minorities. In fact, human rights officers were told on many occasions that the priority for KFOR was 'force protection' (protecting itself before others).

KFOR's policy towards the remaining minorities differed greatly between the different national contingents. In some parts of Kosovo KFOR troops permanently guarded and escorted minorities at all times, but the overall security and confidence of minorities to live a normal life rarely increased. In the north (the French-led brigade's area of operations), the city of Mitrovica was allowed to be divided by its river (it previously had not been) with the northern part becoming Serb dominated and the Albanians dominating the south. The Roma were expelled from their quarter, which was burned down, and they did not return. Any attempt to extend UNMIK authority in the north or to return Albanians resulted in Serb riots. KFOR rarely took any preventive action. In the centre of Kosovo, British KFOR troops referred repeatedly to the need to apply the lessons learned from Northern Ireland. Foot patrols were carried out regularly, which initially reassured the local minorities. However, very few displaced persons returned, and in 2004 many of the remaining minorities fled. In the German southwest a 'tough' policy was introduced, including strict curfews and restrictions on freedom of movement. This appeared more successful in reassuring minorities, but, as will be described below, it did nothing to assist return. In 2004, ethnic cleansing took place on a large scale in this region, as it did in central Kosovo.

As a result, the international community failed on the critical issue of minority security. Human rights experts, although documenting the situation and attacks at length, were rarely able to go beyond this to offer solutions. Recommendations coming from OSCE were usually those requested by minorities, namely increased KFOR protection, which was not viable in the long term. KFOR was rarely willing to listen to the OSCE, which it regarded as unqualified to comment on military matters.

At the same time, KFOR was unable to offer any solution beyond the temporary posting of armed guards. This was because as an army they were not qualified to do what was essentially policing work, but with the lack of UNMIK police they were required to become involved. The international community as a whole can be said to have accepted ethnic cleansing as a *fait accompli*, most dramatically in Mitrovica but in effect across Kosovo. Instead of arresting the perpetrators and their supporters, KFOR adopted a strategy of negotiation. Force protection was a priority rather than minority protection.

It is uncertain whether a different approach could have worked in the circumstances in bringing at least a common approach between human rights and military experts. Clearly human rights workers are not security experts, and it would be very frustrating for military officers to be lectured on how to conduct military operations. On the other hand, army officers are not experts on security in the wider sense (including policing and reassuring vulnerable groups). Assuring the security of the vulnerable is a key human rights issue, and human rights experts need to be involved in finding policies that will do this.

Return

The biggest attempt to organize cooperation during this period was the creation in spring 2000 of a Joint Committee for the Return of Kosovo Serbs (hereinafter the Joint Committee). This began as an attempt to deal with the chronic lack of coordination of return policy across Kosovo. Before its creation, separate parts of KFOR, UNMIK and even Western countries' offices/embassies conducted their own plans for the return of Serbs in different parts of Kosovo. The Joint Committee was set up by the heads of UNMIK, UNHCR, OSCE and KFOR to try to coordinate policy, both at a Kosovo-wide and local level.[13] The fact that it was restricted to Kosovo Serbs for the first year (not Albanians or Roma) indicates that it was a largely political organization. Yet it managed to produce a basic set of guiding principles and policy recommendations, based on the basic right of everyone to return, as set out in Security Council resolution 1244. Putting this into practice in particular locations, however, proved difficult.

The lack of unified command within KFOR again proved to be an obstacle to close cooperation. The OSCE and UNHCR, already used to working together on minority reports, found it relatively easy to pass on information and instructions from the Joint Committee to their municipal offices and to receive the necessary information about the situation on the ground (this became more difficult as staffing was reduced and the OSCE changed its *modus operandi*). UNMIK found such coordination more difficult due to the lack of organized structures as local government was set up. But, generally KFOR proved the most difficult. The author, as a member of the Joint Committee working group, had a productive relationship with KFOR staff there. However, KFOR brigades and commanders in the field often proved reluctant to accept decisions made by the Joint Committee in Pristina. For example, the British brigade at one point adopted its own plan for the return of Serbs to its region, without consultation. In some parts of Kosovo close working relationships were established, but these were often due to the individuals concerned.

One fundamental problem caused tension between the OSCE and KFOR on the issue of return. The OSCE, approaching matters from a human rights viewpoint, stressed the right of all displaced people to return, as set out in resolution 1244. This, the OSCE said, meant that KFOR, by exercising powers similar to that of a state authority, was first under a duty not to hinder the return of any displaced person to their homes, and second was under a positive duty to assist displaced people to return. KFOR, on the other hand, referred to its mandate under resolution 1244 to 'establish a secure environment in which refugees and displaced persons can return home in safety'.[14] KFOR interpreted this to mean that it had the right, and indeed the duty, to strictly control possible return until a safe environment had been secured. Some KFOR commanders went so far as to actually regard returning Serbs as a threat to safety and good order and would therefore discourage return. The OSCE also pressed for the full protection of the right to property, as one of the most important rights of the displaced and, indeed, central to security. However, KFOR rarely shared this opinion, and human rights officers often complained that KFOR preferred not to evict Albanians who were illegally occupying Serbian property (or vice versa) in their area because of the risk of disorder.

There was persistent tension between the OSCE and KFOR in the German area, as Serbs often complained to the OSCE that KFOR had set up checkpoints that prevented Serbs from visiting their homes. The attitude of the local KFOR commanders at times appeared to regard return as a threat to public order. Indeed, it probably was in the short term, but the fact remained that the Serbs had a fundamental right to return, which was one of the most important rights the whole international community was supposed to protect. It was only when the Serbs threatened to boycott the 2001 election due in part to this issue that action was taken. COMKFOR requested a full background briefing from the OSCE, which led to an investigation and a major change in local KFOR policy.

Security and Justice

The issue of the rights of minorities was one where the OSCE and KFOR appeared to share the same aims, but found it difficult to work together. On the issue of the justice system, the OSCE and KFOR increasingly found themselves opposed to each other, with the classic division of human rights monitors accusing the military of violating basic human rights, especially with regard to detention, whilst the military accused the human rights monitors of requiring measures that would negatively impact upon security.

The roots of this dilemma lie in the confusion over who was responsible for security. Under resolution 1244, KFOR had responsibility for 'ensuring public safety and order until the international civil presence can take responsibility for this task'.[15] As stated above, KFOR and the OSCE were the first international bodies to set up in Kosovo. It took UNMIK much longer in 1999 to become fully operational, particularly the UNMIK police force, which did not reach full strength until 2000. The first trials did not begin until 2000. UNMIK established a Department of Judicial Affairs, and declared that justice and policing were too 'sensitive' to hand over to Kosovans during this period.

The OSCE had a range of responsibilities beyond monitoring the human rights situation, such as supporting the development of institutions to protect human rights, including an Ombudsperson's office. It created a legal system monitoring section which produced public reports on the criminal justice system, including issues of detention. During the critical period of 1999, then, KFOR was responsible for security whilst the OSCE had responsibility for trying to ensure human rights compliance. In fact, relations were often productive during this period as it was clearly an emergency situation. KFOR found itself responsible for detaining persons, but at the OSCE's request accepted the need for these detentions to be reviewed by an emergency team of judges.

By the end of 1999, the future of the justice system in Kosovo seemed clear. Each of the five KFOR brigade areas had a firm plan to hand over policing and detention functions to UNMIK. Such handover of responsibilities did take place. During discussions with KFOR commanders at the time, the OSCE was told that KFOR welcomed this as they felt they should not have a role in this type of work. The OSCE did not begin fully monitoring the legal and detention system until the end of 1999.

During 2000, the security situation deteriorated in Kosovo, particularly in Mitrovica. One response was, belatedly, to introduce international judges into the judicial system. However, another response was for KFOR to once again get involved in justice and detention issues. By then, however, a justice, police and detention system was already in place under UNMIK's authority, and the OSCE was monitoring it. KFOR's role was very unclear, and, as in other areas, whatever action was taken depended very much on local commanders. What did happen, in late 2000, was extra-judicial detention of suspects by US KFOR which reopened its detention facility in its Camp Bondsteel base. To begin with it seemed to comply with the rule of law: the first time an international judge ordered two persons detained by KFOR released, KFOR complied. However it did not do so again, claiming the power under its mandate to detain people at will.

The OSCE, now monitoring the justice system, began criticizing this extra-legal (and therefore arbitrary) detention, at first privately, but when this had no effect, publicly. Instead of ending its detentions, KFOR involved UNMIK in the process. US KFOR began to detain people whose release had been ordered by international judges, on the basis that they had 'other evidence' which they refused to share. After pressure from KFOR, the political adviser to the SRSG issued 'detention orders' in the name of the SRSG that he claimed could override court orders.

Although the use of extra-judicial detention was started by US KFOR, it involved the rest of KFOR. Other KFOR brigades began handing over detainees to US KFOR who detained them in Camp Bondsteel. KFOR began interfering in ongoing police investigations, notably following the bombing of the 'Niš Express' bus full of Serbs in early 2002. The main suspect, in detention under police investigation, was taken from Pristina Detention Centre by US KFOR and subsequently escaped from their custody. KFOR produced three other suspects whom they claimed to have evidence against, but refused to produce this evidence in court. A judge therefore ordered their release, but they were then detained by KFOR claiming to act on a SRSG order. In the run-up to the 2001 elections Serbs pressed for a full investigation of the bombing, whilst OSCE and the

Ombudsperson publicly criticized the use of arbitrary detention by the SRSG and KFOR. Instead of a full investigation leading to judicial proceedings, the SRSG promulgated a special law, creating a 'tribunal' of persons to review the detention of these three persons.[16] This tribunal was appointed by the SRSG, and its members were flown into Kosovo for one hearing lasting one day. To the surprise of nobody, it ruled that the persons should be detained. They were subsequently released, without charge, after the elections. With the brief conflict in Macedonia in 2001, US KFOR detained hundreds of Albanian men it suspected of being involved in that conflict. Again, no evidence was ever produced in court.

Arbitrary detention and violation of court orders became the biggest issue for the OSCE, and indeed for almost everyone involved in human rights and the rule of law in Kosovo. Preventing arbitrary detention is one of the most important human rights and is central to the rule of law. KFOR's actions led to a major and public undermining of this right, which was made much worse by the fact that judicial rulings were ignored. Given the involvement of the SRSG, the UN's commitment to the rule of law was also severely brought into question. Given that private discussion led nowhere, the OSCE was forced to publicly condemn the practice in its reports. Both UNMIK and KFOR officials expressed their displeasure at being criticized in public, but no change in practice took place. The Criminal Defence Resource Centre, a body set up by the OSCE, began filing cases for submission to the European Court of Human Rights against Germany, France and Norway for the involvement of their soldiers in handing over persons to US KFOR for illegal detention.[17]

KFOR, and US KFOR in particular, ended up claiming that human rights monitors, including the OSCE, had no right to monitor their activities or visit the people held in detention. KFOR also refused to allow the Ombudsperson to visit the detainees. In 2000, UNMIK passed Regulation 2000/47 which granted both UNMIK and KFOR complete immunity in Kosovo from any legal proceedings, a quite extraordinary claim for bodies that were acting as Kosovo's government. As a result, many claims from Kosovans about seizure of property by KFOR were therefore unable to be taken to court. Shortly after the period covered by this article, KFOR refused to allow the Council of Europe's Committee for the Prevention of Torture the right to visit the detention centres in Camp Bondsteel. The Committee pointed out that it had the right to access every other detention centre in Council of Europe countries.

One of the main reasons KFOR ended up in such a situation was, again, the lack of clarity over who was responsible for what. The lack of civilian control meant that KFOR could set its own policies and areas of operation and in many ways force UNMIK to follow rather than the other way around. In particular, the military was seen as responsible for 'security' and indeed, deferred to on any aspect of security, including the justice system, despite the obvious lack of military expertise in dealing with justice. The military collect evidence in secret, whereas a court requires evidence to be presented in public. Rather than adapt to this, KFOR still insisted on the right to detain people without presenting evidence, and UNMIK greatly compromised the justice system in an attempt to reconcile this.

One other problem highlighted by the detention crisis that made cooperation between the military and human rights officers very difficult was the question of hierarchy. Despite the confusion in the KFOR command structure, policy issues would be referred to the highest authority. When dealing with other international organizations, the military expected a similar hierarchy to apply (they would go through the head of the department or mission). However, the approach of a human rights field mission, especially after the restructuring referred to above, was to delegate as much decision-making power to those in the field, who often knew much more about what was going on. It was very frustrating for them not to be able to speak to KFOR officers in their area of responsibility.

Conclusion

An international peacekeeping force and human rights mission started working in Kosovo at the same time. Both appeared to have the same overall aim – the implementation of human rights in Kosovo. After three years, however, the record was largely one of failure, particularly on the two critical issues of the protection of minorities and the rule of law, as illustrated by the problem of illegal detentions. As to the issue of minorities, ethnic cleansing took place and was not reversed, and the various international bodies were not able to work together to produce a solution that would greatly improve their security and ensure return. As to the issue of rule of law, the original plan for a clear handover to a civilian justice system was stopped and seriously undermined by the widespread use of arbitrary, extra-judicial detention by KFOR.

Whilst on many individual occasions human rights officers and military personnel could work together, this would largely consist of human rights officers providing information to the military. Cooperation on a common return policy proved to be very difficult, even within organized frameworks like the Joint Committee on Return. On detention issues the military and human rights components of the mission found themselves on opposite sides.

Kosovo is a special case, particularly in the size of both the military and the human rights mission, the absolute autonomy given to KFOR and the confusion over responsibilities. But the following key lessons can be learned:

Military security and human rights are not the same. There has been much discussion in the past decade about the military and human rights work 'coming together'. In fact the two are, and always will be, very different. Trying to imply they are similar will only lead to confusion and mutual misunderstanding. What is needed is a clear understanding of each other's role and professional skills in a particular context. The only area where the military and human rights will have very similar roles is in monitoring the behaviour of another government, as happened during the KVM. Even then, the distinction must be clear – human rights experts monitor human rights, and the military monitor military issues – both requiring particular expertise.

Do not have the military doing non-military work. 'Mission creep' can spread, sometimes against the will of the military, but sometimes with their support.

Often at the root of this is a belief that the military can do all security work better than civilians, and when there are any security problems, the solution is to increase the military's power and responsibilities. In fact the military have a specific, but limited competence and should not act outside of this.

Do not have human rights officers doing non-human rights work. Like the military, human rights officers can end up working outside their areas of expertise. In Kosovo, this was because of the lack of a clear understanding as to what human rights work actually is, and the lack of qualified staff. In particular, the temptation to have human rights officers doing pseudo-military intelligence work of situation reporting should be avoided. The independence of human rights work – and the need to assess and report on the basis of objective criteria – should be the top priority of anyone setting up a human rights mission.

The military need to overcome the hierarchy issue when working with other organizations. It will be almost impossible for the military to work with non-hierarchical organizations if they expect them to have the same structure as they do. The military must find a way of working in these circumstances.

Human rights officers have to have confidence in themselves. Some human rights officers working in Kosovo at times seemed to be overawed and overimpressed by the military and were reluctant to raise issues with them. It was notable that these human rights officers were usually those without a human rights background. Therefore it is vital that human rights officers in a mission are properly trained and qualified.

The military need to have clear civilian control. The lack of civilian control over KFOR made it very difficult to deal with KFOR, and led to the disaster of the detention issue. Peace operations must have clear civilian control on the ground.

Security is too important to be left to the generals. The military deals with one type of security – that requiring weapons and bombs – and intimidating those who may be intimidated by this. This is very important, but it does not mean they are the best to deal with all the other types of security, especially policing and the rule of law. Human rights and security are inextricably linked but too often find themselves set against each other. In fact human rights protection is a fundamental part of long-term security, which both human rights officers and the military need to understand.

Strategy, strategy, strategy. This is where human rights professionals can learn most from the military. For centuries, the best soldiers have understood that above everything else they need a clear goal and strategy before determining day-to-day tactics. Yet this is exactly what was missing on all sides in Kosovo. Whilst human rights tactics will be very different from those used by the military, the key elements of military strategy should be required study for any human rights activist.

The military and human rights are very different worlds and should remain so. Attempts to bring them too closely together will weaken both. When both are genuinely working towards the same aims, they can work well together – but only if the overall strategy, goals and professional expertise on both sides are fully understood and respected.

ACKNOWLEDGEMENT

The author was the Coordinator of Human Rights Reporting and Analysis for the OSCE Mission in Kosovo from January 2000 to July 2002. The article is based on his experience during that period. It is a personal opinion and does not reflect the opinion of the OSCE.

NOTES

1. See the relevant UN documentation (at http://daccessdds.un.org/doc/UNDOC/GEN/N99/172/89/PDF/N9917289.pdf?OpenElement).
2. See the BBC report (http://news.bbc.co.uk/2/hi/europe/3551571.stm).
3. In its last report in March 2005, UNHCR's position was that Kosovo Serbs, Roma and Albanians in a minority position still required international protection due to a well-founded fear of persecution (www.unhcr.ch/cgi-bin/texis/vtx/home/opendoc.pdf?tbl=SUBSITES&id=425545362).
4. See J.-R. Michel Maisonneuve, 'The OSCE Kosovo Verification Mission', *Canadian Military Journal*, Spring 2000, pp.49–54 (available at www.journal.dnd.ca/engraph/Vol1/no1/pdf/49-54_e.pdf).
5. OSCE, *Kosovo/Kosova: As Seen as Told, The Human Rights Findings of the Kosovo Verification Mission*, Warsaw: Office for Democratic Institutions and Human Rights, 1999.
6. A long dispute ensued between the SRSG's office, DPKO and the OHCHR over who had the right to appoint a human rights adviser. After 18 months a person was appointed to be responsible for 'communities and returns' rather than human rights.
7. Decision No. 305 of OSCE Permanent Council, 1 July 1999.
8. See BBC, 'OSCE: Kosovo Courts biased against Serbs', 18 Oct. 2000 (http://news.bbc.co.uk/2/hi/europe/978633.stm).
9. OSCE (see n.5 above).
10. Rupert Smith, *The Utility of Force: The Art of War in the Modern World*, London: Allen Lane, 2005, p.333.
11. S/RES/1244, para. 9(d).
12. See in particular OSCE (n.5 above).
13. The author was the OSCE's representative on the Kosovo-wide working group.
14. Para.9(c).
15. Para.9(d).
16. UNMIK Regulation 2001/18.
17. Two cases (*Saramati v. France, Germany and Norway* and *Behrami & Behrami v. France*) are pending before the Court's Grand Chamber and were due for public hearings on 15 November 2006. In accordance with the rules of the Court, the Chamber decides on both admissibility and merits of the cases.

Enforcing Human Rights: The Role of the UN Civilian Police in Kosovo

D. CHRISTOPHER DECKER

The synergy between human rights and policing is not always a comfortable one, especially in the post 9/11 era when, it might be argued, human rights have been eroded in favour of security issues. Yet police, as a main actor in upholding internal security, play an important role in safeguarding the human rights of the individual: through overt actions to protect, and by refraining from committing acts that might violate human rights. When UN human rights bodies or NGOs examine a state's human rights record, the police often receive detailed scrutiny. This was certainly true in Kosovo in 1999 when attention focused on the treatment of ethnic Albanians by the Serb police forces. After the NATO bombing, and the establishment of the United Nations Interim Administration Mission in Kosovo (UNMIK), the most pressing need in Kosovo was to establish some degree of law and order. Human rights might have been highlighted in the world media during and after the bombing, but it was not the single most important goal of the mission. Instead the goal was to stabilize the situation and create order.

With the pull-out of Serb forces in 1999, no domestic police force existed. Consequently, there was an urgent need for a police force in Kosovo. The UN Secretary-General proposed a three-stage process for UNMIK in the field of police and security. The first stage was to establish KFOR supremacy in maintaining law and order, with advice from UN Civilian Police (CIVPOL) officers. The second stage was the handover of policing to UNMIK CIVPOL officers, assuming executive policing powers, and the establishment of an indigenous police force, the Kosovo Police Service (KPS). The third and final stage was the transition of executive policing to the KPS, with an advisory and monitoring role for CIVPOL.[1]

While CIVPOL initially may not have focused on human rights, international human rights standards soon became an integral part of all of its work. This article focuses on both the human rights problems facing CIVPOL in the various phases of its development and the human rights achievements of CIVPOL. After outlining the background to CIVPOL and its establishment in Kosovo, the article will describe the three stages laid out by the Secretary-General. However, due to the significant emphasis on training and capacity building of the KPS, *four* distinct phases in the development of effective policing and security in Kosovo can be identified: (1) executive policing; (2) capacity building of KPS; (3) the transition of executive policing from CIVPOL to KPS; and (4) monitoring the KPS. It should be emphasized that while the initiation of each phase had a definite starting point, none of the phases has yet reached a conclusion. This is largely due to the fact that CIVPOL officers may still intervene in police work even though their primary task is monitoring. Similarly, there are some 'sensitive' units where transition has not taken place and where CIVPOL maintains executive policing powers.[2]

For purposes of clarity, in this article the term 'CIVPOL' or 'CIVPOL officers' refers to the Civilian Police Division of the UN Department of Peacekeeping Operations (DPKO) or any international police officers serving in the division. The term 'UNMIK Police' refers specifically to the CIVPOL mission in Kosovo and/or the international officer serving in the mission. 'KPS' refers only to local Kosovan police officers,[3] and the term 'police' generally refers to both KPS and UNMIK Police.

CIVPOL and the Kosovo Mission

Prior to 1989, only three UN peace operations contained CIVPOL components: the Congo (1960–64), West New Guinea (1962–63)[4] and Cyprus (1964–).[5] The 1990s saw an enormous increase in the number and scope of UN peacekeeping missions, for which reform of national police according to principles of democratic policing has became a key function. Of the 16 ongoing peacekeeping missions throughout the world, 11 have CIVPOL components.[6] Regardless of the mandate, whether vested with executive or monitoring responsibilities, CIVPOL should always operate in accordance with human rights standards.

UN Security Council Resolution 1244, establishing UNMIK, contained several provisions concerning the security of Kosovo. Paragraph 5 established an international civil and security presence. Paragraph 10 laid out the tasks of the international civil presence, including, *inter alia*, 'maintaining civil law and order, including establishing local police forces and meanwhile through the deployment of international police personnel to serve in Kosovo; [and] protecting and promoting human rights'.[7] Just two days after the adoption of Resolution 1244, the Secretary-General submitted a report to the Security Council where he outlined the initial roles and responsibilities of the interim civil administration. At the top of the list was the creation of the Office of Police Commissioner, an international police force, riot police and border police.[8] A month later, the

Secretary-General described the massive civil security problem in Kosovo in the following terms:

> The security problem in Kosovo is largely a result of the absence of law and order institutions and agencies. Many crimes and injustices cannot be properly pursued. Criminal gangs competing for control of scarce resources are already exploiting this void. While KFOR is currently responsible for maintaining both public safety and civil law and order, its ability to do so is limited due to the fact that it is still in the process of building up its forces. The absence of a legitimate police force, both international and local, is deeply felt, and therefore will have to be addressed as a matter of priority.[9]

The response of the UN was to pour human, material, and monetary resources into Kosovo in an attempt bring normality to the province. The introduction of Police was slow. Eventually, however, UNMIK had the largest deployment of Police officers to date.

Executive Policing

One of the major obstacles faced by the UN at the beginning was a shortage of qualified staff that could carry out state-like functions. Nowhere was this more apparent than in the police and justice sector.[10] As has been seen in Afghanistan and Iraq, international forces have difficulty establishing law and order after the overthrow or breakdown of government. Kosovo was perhaps the first stark example of this. Although NATO troops were initially tasked to uphold law and order, many contingents were reluctant to take on a policing role.[11] The complete collapse of the legal system exacerbated the situation. During the previous ten years the Serbian-dominated Yugoslav government had prevented Albanians from taking office in state institutions. As a result, few Albanian judges or police officers had exercised public functions since 1990.[12] With Serbs fleeing Kosovo and Albanians not yet returning, or sufficiently qualified,[13] it was not possible for UNMIK to simply reform the police and judiciary. An entirely new legal system, including a new police force, was needed.[14] In the interim, UNMIK needed a police force to carry out day-to-day policing so as to maintain law and order. This meant the creation of the largest international executive police force to date. Executive policing 'refers to the power and practice of law enforcement by international police within a particular territory. This power derives from the assumption by the UN of sovereign authority over the area (either all or part of a state) and its practice from the establishment of a transitional administration.'[15]

The effectiveness of UNMIK Police in exercising executive authority was initially hampered because the UN was unable to recruit sufficient numbers of officers. While the Secretary-General urged states to send CIVPOL officers, only 1,100 had arrived by September 1999 and numbers continued to be boosted until 2002.[16] The other problem that plagued UNMIK Police was the concentration of international police in Pristina city and region, leaving very few deployed in other areas.[17] The Secretary-General also noted that there was an urgent need for human rights and legal advisers for UNMIK CIVPOL.[18]

The following sections examine some of the major human rights issues confronting UNMIK Police in the period when it had sole executive policing authority.

Rights of Arrested Persons

Lack of clarity about the applicable law in Kosovo at the outset of the operation created problems for UNMIK. UNMIK Regulation 1999/24 created four possible sources of applicable law:

- the law in Kosovo as it existed on 22 March 1989;
- UNMIK Regulations;
- the law applied in Kosovo between 22 March 1989 and 12 December 1999 (the date UNMIK Regulation 1999/24 came into force) if in favour of a criminal defendant or if it fills a legal gap where no law from March 1989 exists; and
- international human rights standards and laws.

While there was confusion in the courts concerning the hierarchy of law, especially when certain articles of the FRY Criminal Procedure Code conflicted with the European Convention for the Protection of Human Rights and Fundamental Freedoms (ECHR), the FRY Criminal Procedure Code itself was not readily available to UNMIK Police officers, nor was there training on the Code.

One area where this resulted in constant human rights violations concerned the length of detention.[19] Under international human rights law, Article 9 and 14 of the International Covenant of Civil and Political Rights (ICCPR) and Article 5 and 6 of the ECHR provides a framework to protect persons subject to any form of arrest or detention. Article 9(1) of the ICCPR states: 'Everyone has the right to liberty and security of person. No one shall be subjected to arbitrary arrest and detention. No one shall be deprived of his liberty except on such grounds and in accordance with such procedures as are established by law.' Article 5(1) of the ECHR has similar wording. Articles 9(4) of the ICCPR and 5(3) of the ECHR state that persons arrested or detained shall be brought promptly before a judge. The purpose of this right is to ensure that an independent and impartial judiciary can check the power of the police to arrest and detain. Under international human rights law there is no clearly defined standard in relation to the length of time a person can be held before being brought before an independent judge. The UN Human Rights Committee has stated that it should be within a few days.[20] The European Court of Human Rights has determined that a period of four days and six hours, in a terrorism case, constituted a violation of the right to be brought promptly before a judge.[21]

In Kosovo, under the FRY Criminal Procedure Code (CPC) police were required to bring an arrested person before a magistrate within 24 hours.[22] There were exceptions to this '24-hour' rule, including a few dealing with situations where the police could demonstrate that it was impossible to bring the arrested person before a magistrate.[23] In these situations custody could last for a maximum of three days from the moment of apprehension.[24] This became known as the '72-hour' rule. While 72-hour detention was supposed to be an exception, it became the rule and in many cases even the 72-hours rule was breached. Unfortunately, UNMIK Police issued instructions which stated that 'when a suspect is placed in a detention centre, the case must be presented to the public prosecutor within 72 hours of arrest'.[25] It was noted by the Organization for Security and Co-operation in Europe (OSCE) that this mistake had been brought to the attention of UNMIK Police. Despite this, during the first half of 2000 the OSCE 'was not aware of 'any cases where the procedures of the FRY Criminal Procedure Code (CPC) have been followed'.[26]

This systematic violation of the CPC was well documented and lasted until 2001.[27] Isolated cases still occurred in 2002. In 2003, however, the OSCE undertook a monitoring programme on the rights of arrested persons and found that out of 183 cases only two exceeded the 72-hour period. In both, the arrested person was mentally disabled.[28] Currently, cases where arrested persons are in police custody for a period exceeding 72 hours are extremely rare. This is usually due to the lack of other services, such as resources for juveniles or police officers unsure of how to treat mentally ill persons. In fact, in many areas of Kosovo, officers are now reluctant to keep people in custody over 24 hours because most officers feel that the holding facilities are inadequate or not numerous enough to hold more than one person. The conditions in holding cells are another area where UNMIK Police and KPS have struggled to meet international human rights standards.

As a result of conflicting instructions issued to both UNMIK Police and the KPS and a lack of knowledge of the FRY CPC, human rights standards were persistently violated. In 2004, the Provisional Criminal Procedure Code of Kosovo (PCPCK) came into force.[29] From the time of its adoption in July 2003 until it came into force in April 2004, the Kosovo Police Service School (KPSS) trained all 7,000 KPS and Border/Boundary Police on the new PCPCK. This provides that '[a] person deprived of liberty under the suspicion of having committed a criminal offence shall be brought before a judge promptly and at the latest within 72 hours of the arrest and shall be entitled to a trial within a reasonable time or to release pending trial'.[30] Additional training and the establishment of just one time limit have greatly reduced violations of the right to liberty and security of persons in Kosovo.

Holding Cells

In 1999, there was a serious shortage of holding cells where the police could hold arrested persons. Even if it had been possible to deploy CIVPOL quickly, this problem would have seriously hampered effective law enforcement. In addition, while UNMIK Police was aware that the conditions of the existing holding cells did not meet international standards, very little was done to address the situation. In 2002, the OSCE carried out an assessment of all the holding cells in Kosovo.[31] This report found that there were problems with the size of the cells, the lack of bedding, poor sanitation and inadequate procedures for feeding detainees.[32]

In particular, many cells were not of sufficient size to house the number of detainees. Due to years of neglect by the Yugoslav government, the cells were in a general state of disrepair. Additionally, beds were not always provided for arrested persons even though they were being held overnight. Often only a mattress was left on the floor with a blanket. These conditions were made worse by the fact that many of the holding cells in police stations were situated in the basement, resulting in dampness, poor ventilation and poor lighting.

Unfortunately UNMIK, which held initial responsibility for the holding cells, decided that the responsibility should be shifted to the Kosovo Consolidated Budget (KCB). This meant that there was no money to refurbish the holding cells until it could be put into the 2004 budget. In response, the Deputy Police Commissioner for the KPS (an UNMIK Police officer), the OSCE, the UN High Commissioner for Human Rights, and UN Office for Project Services developed a project proposal to solicit money from donors to make the holding cells comply with international standards. While initially the fundraising was unsuccessful, the KPS budget provided funding to refurbish and build new cells, representing about a third to one half of all the cells in Kosovo during 2005. Subsequently, in December 2005, the Italian government pledged 1.4 million euros to the holding cell project. This amount should allow for the completion of all the required work on the holding cells in order to meet international standards.

The effort of UNMIK Police in refurbishing the holding cells in Kosovo marks a significant step in their endeavours to implement human rights standards. KPS Station Commanders, through the holding cell project and OSCE reports on the holding cells, have learned what the international standards are and have taken a keen interest in the conditions of arrested persons. The work undertaken by UNMIK Police officers on this project and the subsequent interest of the KPS in the conditions of the holding cells demonstrates the positive affect CVIPOL can have on human rights.

Lessons from Executive Policing

It is clear that the CIVPOL mission in Kosovo could have proceeded more smoothly, especially during the initial executive period. Because of problems resulting from police officers not knowing the FRY CPC,[33] there are efforts to create 'universal' criminal and criminal procedure codes so that future CIVPOL missions will not face the same problems.[34] Furthermore, it has taken the UN more than five years to begin to get the holding cells up to proper international standards, and what success has been achieved is due to the individual efforts of senior UNMIK Police officers rather than institutional support from the UN.

In 2000, UNMIK Police developed a human rights training course for incoming officers and specialized human rights training programmes for investigators dealing with arrest, detention, search and seizure.[35] A Human Rights Office was established, attached to the Police Commissioner's Office. This office acted as liaison to other human rights offices and assisted in developing the Policy and Procedure Manual.[36] The police also adopted codes of conduct for the KPS and UNMIK Police, which embodied many human rights standards.

UNMIK Police also created an Internal Investigation Section for UNMIK Police officers and a Professional Standards Unit for KPS officers. These units are responsible for investigating police officers and offering a remedy to any persons who believe that their rights were violated by UNMIK Police or KPS officers. These efforts were made principally because the Kosovo mission marked the first large-scale executive policing mission, and the UN had much to learn concerning human rights and officer discipline. Many human rights issues arose in relation to UNMIK Police, partly because the UN was not prepared for a CIVPOL intervention of this type. There have been several studies undertaken by UNDP and other institutions on CIVPOL and post-conflict security in Kosovo, as a result of which lessons have been learned, and one hopes that the same mistakes will not be repeated.[37]

Capacity Building of the KPS

Capacity building of the KPS is one of the most important tasks that UNMIK Police has undertaken in Kosovo. This is crucial; in contrast with the situation pertaining in most other countries, the official KPS training period is a matter of weeks rather than years. In this way, it is the on-the-job capacity building that will be the lasting legacy of UNMIK. If the UN fails to create an effective, accountable and human rights compliant police force, the people of Kosovo will suffer adverse effects long after the UN has gone.

Initially the training period for KPS officers was four weeks. This training was undertaken by the OSCE, which founded the KPSS. The first 200 cadets were taken into the police school on 7 September 1999 and within five weeks they were on the street, working alongside UNMIK Police officers for field training.[38] As time went on the length of the course increased and by mid-2006 it was 20 weeks.[39]

Much of the emphasis in the initial training was to teach KPS cadets basic policing methods and to instil the principle of 'do no harm'. Human rights training has been incorporated into the basic training as the course has lengthened in duration. Since 2000, there has been an in-service training course concerning human rights for KPS officers.[40] As the basic course evolved, so too has the teaching of human rights. Initially it was a stand-alone course, but this changed to facilitate human rights mainstreaming throughout the training syllabus so that it is now akin to a 'golden thread' within the entire course.[41] However, the practical application of human rights to on-the-job situations is learned by KPS through the UNMIK Police officers and senior KPS officers, who were themselves taught by UNMIK Police.

Use of Force

One of the most important aspects of being a police officer is the ability to use force, but this power comes with many restraints. It usually takes officers a great deal of classroom training and field experience to learn how to use force properly. Due to the short duration of the police school training programme, most KPS officers needed to learn how to use appropriate force while on the job. In this way it became very important for UNMIK Police officers to effectively train KPS in this highly subjective and pedagogically difficult area.[42]

A recurring problem has arisen in relation to the use of firearms. As mentioned above, CIVPOL officers bring their skills with them from their home country, and each country has differing standards on the use of force; this is particularly true of the use of lethal force. These differences arise not only between African and European states, but also amongst European/Western states. The United States is one of the largest contributors to UNMIK Police in Kosovo, but its rules governing use of force are significantly different than those in Europe. American police officers can fire more than one round at a suspect without it being deemed excessive force, whereas in Sweden, for instance, an officer may fire one round and they are then required to reassess the situation before discharging a further round.[43] As CIVPOL officers have not been trained in accordance with a uniformed standard for the use of force, there is always the possibility that, when carrying out executive policing functions, they will use excessive force contrary to local law. Not only were the use of force standards unclear for CIVPOL when exercising executive authority, but KPS officers had to learn how to use appropriate levels of force from already confused UNMIK Police officers.

These initial problems were partly alleviated by the adoption of the KPS and UNMIK Police policy and procedure manuals, which contained directives on the use of force. The KPS Policy and Procedure Manual (PPM) is under constant review so that the KPS can adapt to safety and security concerns as they arise. Furthermore, as part of the KPS policy on the use of force, a KPS officer is required to complete a report each time an incident takes place where a KPS officer uses force. These incidents are then reviewed internally by other KPS officers who sit on a Use of Force Board whose function it is to determine whether appropriate force has been used. If the Board determines that excessive force has been used, it can recommend changes in policy or training to the Police Commissioner.[44] Allegations of excessive use of force are also investigated by the Professional Standards Unit.

Rights of Arrested Persons

UNMIK Police were required to focus much attention on arrest and detention issues. To date there is no classroom training for KPS officers in relation to the custody of prisoners. Everything that KPS officers learn about the practical treatment of prisoners is taught by UNMIK Police officers on the job. In turn, the OSCE Department of Human Rights and Rule of Law has assisted UNMIK Police in assessing the treatment of arrested persons in Kosovo, so as to assist UNMIK Police and KPS officers in identifying areas where shortcomings existed. For example, in 2003 it was found that nearly all persons interviewed by the OSCE did not have defence counsel during police questioning, even though arrested persons have the right to free defence counsel under the applicable criminal procedure law. While some arrested persons responded that they did not seek a lawyer because they were innocent of the charges against them, others stated that they thought they would be required to pay for the lawyer's services even though they had been informed that the services were free. This demonstrated a clear lack of understanding of the importance of the right to defence counsel. In response, the OSCE and senior UNMIK Police officials designed new forms and implemented new procedures to ensure that arrested persons are fully informed of their right to defence counsel.

Internal Complaints Mechanism

Lastly, the issue of police accountability is an aspect of capacity building where CIVPOL plays a significant role.[45] As discussed in the section on Executive Policing, both the KPS and UNMIK Police have internal investigation units. However, internal investigations are a very sensitive issue irrespective of the police department under consideration. There are cultural legacies in Kosovo from the 1990s when the police forces were not accountable. The population is not experienced in seeking redress against government bodies, let alone the police. At the beginning of the mission Kosovans were unclear what institutions were responsible for which issue. This meant that they often went to KFOR, the OSCE or NGOs to get their problems solved. In recent years Kosovans seem more willing to file citizen complaints against the police, and the police have recognized a responsibility to investigate all complaints.

In October 2005, transition of the Professional Standards Unit from UNMIK Police authority to KPS took place. Currently there are UNMIK Police monitors that examine the cases during and after the investigation. These UNMIK Police officers work with the Professional Standards Unit to improve the quality of the investigations. Basic investigatory skills still need to be reinforced by UNMIK Police at various levels, not just within the Professional Standards Unit. For example, KPS officers are still learning the skills needed to identify pertinent witnesses, ask proper probative questions, and conduct thorough follow-up investigations. Without these skills the KPS officers in the Professional Standards Unit will not be successful and this could lead to a breakdown in confidence in the ability of the KPS to investigate and discipline itself. If this were to occur a lack of accountability would certainly follow.

Capacity building of the KPS is continuing in many different units and being accomplished mostly by the police school and UNMIK Police officers. However, other organizations such as UNDP are assisting with training officers on a wide variety of topics, including management skills and procurement. The capacity building of the KPS is a project for years to come. At the time of writing, talks on the future of Kosovo's status were underway. The international community is especially concerned about protecting the minorities that remain in Kosovo after a determination of status has occurred. The role of the KPS will be central in ensuring their long-term safety. On account of concerns surrounding how the Provisional Institutions of Self-Government (PISG), bodies run by the Kosovans, including the KPS, will treat the minority population once the UN mission leaves, there will be further involvement by international organizations in Kosovo. This will primarily involve additional capacity building and monitoring for compliance with democratic policing standards. The capacity building phase will not be completed on some levels in the foreseeable future. What will change is that CIVPOL will most likely complete its mission by the end of 2006 or by mid-2007. At that point the EU will probably have some role in Kosovo, although its resources seem to be quite stretched at present.[46] Human rights will remain a central issue in the capacity building of the KPS in the foreseeable future.

Transition to KPS Executive Policing

A critical task for UNMIK Police was preparing police stations and KPS officers for the transition to executive policing.[47] Prior to transition, the KPS is still subservient to UNMIK Police. However, once transition is completed, UNMIK Police officers are no longer supposed to intervene, except in situations where a human rights violation might occur or when a KPS officer's acts might lead to death or injury.

In order to analyse the needs of the KPS, a Transition Unit was set up by UNMIK Police administration. Some of the critical tasks of transition required CIVPOL officers to determine the proper staffing levels of stations in order to ensure their ability to function effectively. This included trying to find the proper balance of gender, ethnicity and rank. Logistical issues also played an important role. These included, among others, ensuring there was a basic level of communication equipment, vehicles, and support staff during the transition period. UNMIK Police officers were also required to ensure that officers understood policies and procedures such as how to deal with juveniles, victims of domestic violence, citizen complaints, and relations with KFOR.

In some cases KPS officers needed to be redeployed between stations in order to ensure that each station had an appropriate number of officers. During transition, the number of higher ranking officers needed for each station was determined. However, due to the lack of senior ranking KPS officers at the beginning of transition, not all the posts could be filled. In some cases this also applied to 'specialized' units such as the Domestic Violence Units and the Community Policing Units at individual stations. A lack of officers in these units could contribute to an ineffective victims' advocacy scheme. Furthermore, Community Policing Units carried out efforts to build trust between minority communities and the KPS. When understaffed, the units were unable to carry out these activities.

An issue that became evident to UNMIK Police concerning human rights amongst KPS officers related to the theoretical knowledge and the application of human rights in KPS officers' daily work. Interviews were undertaken with KPS officers in various stations. No real patterns emerged. It was clear in some stations that officers lacked both basic knowledge about human rights and how human rights impact on their daily work. In other stations KPS officers demonstrated clear knowledge of human rights, but lacked the ability to transform their knowledge into their daily policing activities. For example, KPS officers did not always make the connection that by not strictly adhering to the rights of arrested persons, they were potentially violating that person's human rights. The KPS Training Unit addressed this issue by carrying out remedial training on human rights for all 7,000 KPS officers and this was completed by April 2006.

After the transition of police stations, UNMIK Police monitors are permanently deployed in the stations as an Executive Adviser (usually the former UNMIK Police

Station Commander) and an Operational Monitor (usually the former Deputy Station Commander). The role that the CIVPOL officers play is one of continued facilitation of transition, advising and monitoring. The transition of UNMIK Police from executive and managerial positions did not go smoothly in all areas and many UNMIK Police officers were uncertain about their role after transition was complete.

Monitoring

UNMIK Police began their last phase at the end of 2002 by designating certain UNMIK Police officers as international monitors. Several reporting forms were developed to look at a range of issues that KPS officers face in their daily work. These included arrests and prisoners, managerial skills, crime scene procedures, case disposal, calls for service, traffic procedures, and non-compliance toward UNMIK Police. UNMIK Police officers have been completing these forms throughout Kosovo and the information is collected in a central database.

The work that UNMIK Police conducts in relation to monitoring is important because personnel with a police background are able to assess the professional performance standards of KPS officers. While outside monitors can assist and help in making independent assessments of the KPS, only other police officers are qualified to assess and offer advice and training on issues that will make the KPS a more effective police service. Moreover, the information collected by UNMIK Police officers can be used to extract lessons learned and pinpoint training needs that should be addressed through the KPSS or the in-service KPS Training Unit.

The large numbers of monitoring forms being completed by the UNMIK Police monitors allows senior police administration to have a large sample size at their disposal. In turn, this permits the administration to draw conclusions about the KPS as a whole, or to look at the practice of individual stations. This information can be very useful in determining training needs in specific stations or regions. Likewise, if an adverse trend were to appear throughout Kosovo, the administration can see this and either issue clarifying bulletins or design retraining for the whole of the KPS.

UNMIK Police have been joined in the work of monitoring by the OSCE's Department of Human Rights and Rule of Law, which in 2001 appointed a Legal Adviser for Police and Human Rights. In 2002, greater resources were dedicated to the issue and a section was created within the department, the Security Issues Section. In addition to the Legal Adviser, human rights officers and assistants were hired for each region. The goal of this section is to assist all stakeholders in helping create an effective, accountable and human rights compliant police service for the people of Kosovo. This is accomplished by working with the police in monitoring certain human rights issues, writing up the monitoring findings, developing recommendations and helping implement those recommendations with UNMIK Police and KPS. This monitoring has been successful because UNMIK Police and KPS have seen a need for an independent group to look at its practices and they have been open and responsive to the recommendations included in the reports. There is recognition amongst UNMIK Police that the mission must leave Kosovo with the best police force possible, and the only way to do that is to explore all the shortcomings and develop plans to deal with them. Because a human rights compliant police force is at the core of the concept of democratic policing, the partnership between UNMIK Police and the OSCE was required and has been successful.

Conclusion

In the early stages of UNMIK there were several failures by CIVPOL which hampered its effectiveness. Inadequate numbers and delays in deployment at a time when minority communities were being subjected to reprisals caused serious credibility problems for UNMIK.[48] Internal discipline within UNMIK Police also proved problematic. On several occasions there were officers that might have committed crimes and/or human rights violations, but they were not disciplined and were merely sent home. In the early years, repatriation from the mission was seen as a punishment. However, officers were sent home and faced no other repercussions, a situation which did not serve the interests of justice.

There were 6,500 CIVPOL officers and over 5,000 KPS serving at the high-point in the mission's staffing. As of late-2006, there were roughly 8,000 KPS officers and 1,800 CIVPOL officers. KPS officers have executive authority in nearly every unit and station in Kosovo. Transition at the senior management level has yet to take place, but it is envisaged that KPS officers will begin shadowing senior CIVPOL officers in 2006 and take some degree of operational control.[49]

Some very important lessons have been learned during the various stages of the CIVPOL mission in Kosovo. Clearly there is a need to have more CIVPOL officers at the ready to be deployed shortly after the cessation of a conflict. Unfortunately, this mistake seems to have been repeated in both Afghanistan and Iraq. Once security forces lose control of a territory it can take years to re-establish law and order. This lack of rule of law clearly has an adverse impact on human rights. Another lesson from Kosovo is the need for CIVPOL officers to know the local law. Because it will not always be practical for potentially thousands of CIVPOL officers around the world to be trained on one state's criminal and criminal procedure laws, the development of model criminal and criminal procedure codes, if adopted by the UN, should greatly benefit future missions in overcoming legal uncertainty and ensuring human rights compliance. Lastly, when states, either in coalition or through the UN, decide to intervene within a state, they must do so with the plan of making a long-term commitment. It is simply not possible to bomb a territory for three months (in Kosovo's case) and then plan to reconstruct in a matter of a few years. This lack of long-term vision and commitment can be seen in the training of the KPS. Had there been a 10–15 year plan for the KPS, officers could have received a proper 2–4 year police academy training. A longer training period would have provided the KPS officers with a better background and a far better understanding of policing and hopefully human rights.[50]

CIVPOL has played an important role in Kosovo. It had complete responsibility for civilian law and order in Kosovo for four years. It would not have been possible for NATO forces to have acted as the police force for Kosovo because most military forces are not prepared or trained to carry out police activities. Although CIVPOL were late in arriving, they were able to establish a degree of normality for the population. CIVPOL was also integral in providing the necessary field training for the new KPS officers. The short duration of KPS cadet training meant it was absolutely necessary for the new KPS officers to receive field training from experienced police officers, even if the field training did not always reinforce the KPS training. CIVPOL officers also prepared the KPS to take over executive police functions and were the only body with the expertise to create the conditions necessary for handover of stations and units to KPS officers. Lastly, monitoring has become an important part of CIVPOL duties in Kosovo. Unfortunately it does not appear that much has been done with valuable lessons learned that could be fed back into training, both cadet and in-service, to enhance the professionalism of the KPS as a whole.

Overall, CIVPOL has made an invaluable contribution to the safety and security of the people in Kosovo. Despite all the criticism of CIVPOL, it has done much to promote and protect human rights. However, more could have been accomplished earlier in the mission and it is hoped that future missions may learn lessons from the obstacles that CIVPOL has confronted in Kosovo.

ACKNOWLEDGEMENT

The views expressed in this article are solely the author's and do not represent the views of the OSCE or the UN Mission in Kosovo.

NOTES

1. 'Report of the Secretary-General on the Interim Administration in Kosovo', UN Doc. S/1999/779, paras.61–5, 12 July 1999.
2. For instance there has been no transition in the Regional Mitrovica/Mitrovicë police, or in the Serious Crimes Squad within police headquarters.
3. The term 'Kosovan' is the officially recognized word for people from Kosovo according to UNMIK reporting guidelines.
4. Duncan Chappell and John Evans, *The Role, Preparation and Performance of Civilian Police in United Nations Peacekeeping Operations*, International Centre for Criminal Law Reform and Criminal Justice Policy, 1997, p.19 (www.icclr.law.ubc.ca/Publications/Reports/Peacekeeping.pdf).
5. See www.un.org/Depts/dpko/dpko/civpol/2.htm.
6. See United Nations Peacekeeping Operations, Background Note, www.un.org/Depts/dpko/dpko/bnote.htm.
7. UN Security Council resolution 1244, para.11, (i),(j), 10 June 1999.
8. 'Report of the Secretary-General Pursuant to Paragraph 10 of Security Council Resolution 1244 (1999)', UN Doc. S/1999/672, 12 June 1999.
9. 'Report of the Secretary-General on the Interim Administration in Kosovo' (see n.1 above), para.6.
10. David Marshall and Shelley Inglis, 'The Disempowerment of Human Rights-Based Justice in the United Nations Mission in Kosovo', *Harvard Human Rights Journal*, Vol.16, 2003, pp.100–101.
11. Ibid., p.109.
12. Ibid., p.97.

13. 'Report of the Secretary-General on the Interim Administration in Kosovo' (see n.1 above), para.13.
14. The Secretary-General made this point in his report to Security Council, ibid., para.18.
15. Renata Dwan, 'Introduction', in Dwan (ed.) *Executive Policing: Enforcing the Law in Peace Operations*, SIPRI Research Report No.16, Oxford: Oxford University Press 2003, p.1.
16. 'Report of the Secretary-General on the Interim Administration in Kosovo', UN Doc. S/1999/987, 16 Sept. 1999, paras.6, 120.
17. Ibid., para.26.
18. Ibid., para.29.
19. Colette Rausch, 'The Assumption of Authority in Kosovo and East Timor: Legal and Practical Implications', in Dwan (n.15 above), p.18.
20. UN Human Rights Committee, *General Comment No.8*, para.2, UN doc. HRI\GEN\1\Rev.1 at 8 (1994).
21. *Brogan v U.K.* A/145-B (1988) 11 European Human Rights Reports (EHRR), 117.
22. Federal Republic of Yugoslavia Criminal Procedure Code (FRY CPC) Art. 195.
23. Police were allowed to extend custody: in order to establish identity, verify an alibi; if the arrested person's identity could not be established or if other circumstances exist which suggest the arrested person may attempt escape; if there was a founded fear that the arrested person would destroy the traces of the criminal act or if particular circumstances indicate that he would hinder the investigation by intimidating witnesses or accomplices; or if particular circumstances justified a fear that the criminal act would be repeated or an attempted criminal act would be completed or a threatened criminal act committed.
24. FRY CPC Arts.195 and 196.
25. UNMIK Police, *Operational Bulletin No.15*, 17 May 2000.
26. OSCE Legal System Monitoring Section, 'Six Month Review of the Criminal Justice System February–July 2000', 2000, p.27.
27. Ibid.; OSCE Legal System Monitoring Section, 'A Review Of The Criminal Justice System 1 September 2000–28 February 2001', 2001, pp.19–20; OSCE Legal System Monitoring Section, 'Review Of The Criminal Justice System October 2001', 2001 pp.20, 42–4.
28. There are many problems in Kosovo with regard to the treatment and housing of mentally ill persons. There are only two rooms in Pristina Hospital to accommodate mentally ill persons that might harm themselves. Furthermore, there is only one mental health facility in Kosovo and it has been the subject of human rights concerns. See Eric Rosenthal and Éva Szeli, *Not on the Agenda: Human Rights of People with Mental Disabilities in Kosovo*, Mental Disability Rights International, 2002 (www.mdri.org/pdf/KosovoReport.pdf).
29. UNMIK Regulation No. 2003/26, 6 July 2003.
30. Provisional Criminal Procedure Code of Kosovo, Art. 14(2).
31. The standards that the holding cells were being measured against were primarily those set forth in the Council of Europe's European Convention on the Prevention of Torture, Inhuman or Degrading Treatment (ECPT) and the interpretations of the Convention by its enforcement body the Committee for the Prevention of Torture. Additionally, the UN Standard Minimum Rules for the Treatment of Prisoners was also used. In 2004, the ECPT became applicable in Kosovo through an agreement between the SRSG and the Secretary-General of the Council of Europe.
32. OSCE Security Issues Section, 'The Holding Cell Report', 2002 (on file with the author). The OSCE points out that it did not find any mistreatment of detainees, but did find that police officers were often expected to buy arrested persons food because there was no budget set aside for feeding detainees.
33. It was common knowledge within the mission that it had been suggested to UNMIK Police officers to 'use the law from your own country as a guide', since so few officers knew what the criminal procedure was. Kosovo does not seem to be the exception, but part of the common practice. See David H. Bayley, *Changing the Guard: Developing Democratic Police Abroad*, New York: Oxford University Press, 2006, p.101.
34. See www.nuigalway.ie/human_rights/Projects/model_codes.html.
35. UNMIK Police, *Annual Report 2000*, p.9 (available at www.unmikonline.org/civpol/reports/report2000.pdf).
36. Ibid.
37. *Inter alia*, UNDP, *Light Blue: Perceptions of Security and Police Performance in Kosovo*, 2004; Anna Khakee and Nicolas Florquin, *Kosovo and the Gun: A Baseline Assessment of Small Arms and Light Weapons in Kosovo*, UNDP/Small Arms Survey, 2003; Erin Mobekk, *A Brief History of Policing Peace Operations in the 1990s*, 2004 (www.undp.org/bcpr/jssr/4_resources/documents/CICS_Mobekk_2004_Brief%20History%20Policing%20Peace%20Operations.pdf).

38. 'Report of the Secretary-General on the Interim Administration in Kosovo' (n.16 above), para.30.
39. OSCE Mission in Kosovo, Police Education (available at www.osce.org/kosovo/13216.html).
40. UNMIK Police (n.35 above), p.9.
41. Rather than the cadets receiving just a three-hour course on basic human rights, the idea behind the 'golden thread' is that every class that cadets take has human rights content.
42. The success of this training method has been questioned, and it has been suggested that a core group of field training officers should be created by CIVPOL. Robert M. Perito, 'National Police Training within an Executive Police Operation', *Executive Policing: Enforcing the Law in Peace Operations*, SIPRI Research Report No.16, in Dwan (n.15 above), pp.92–3, 100.
43. Discussion with a firearms instructor at the Kosovo Police Service School, Pristina 2002. See also Rausch (n.19 above), p.25.
44. KPS, 'Policy and Procedure Manual, Use of Force Review Board P-4.45', 16 Jan. 2003.
45. For a discussion about the importance of accountability in police reform see Chuck Call, 'Challenges in Police Reform: Promoting Effectiveness and Accountability', IPA Policy Report, New York: International Peace Academy, 2003, pp.8–10.
46. The EU currently has police missions in Bosnia-Herzegovina, the former Yugoslav Republic of Macedonia, Palestine and the Democratic Republic of Congo.
47. For an in-depth examination of various models of transition see Eric Scheye, 'Transitions to Local Authority', in Dwan (n.15 above), pp.109–19.
48. There is a belief that the lack of UNMIK Police was a contributing factor in the March 2004 riots in Kosovo, which led to further attacks against minority communities in Kosovo. See also Clive Baldwin's article in this issue.
49. The case as of February 2006. International Crisis Group, 'Kosovo: The Challenge of Transition', Europe Report No.170, 17 Feb. 2006, p.6.
50. Call (see n.45 above), p.5.

Rule of Law and Human Rights Protections through Criminal Law Reform: Model Codes for Post-conflict Criminal Justice

VIVIENNE O'CONNOR

> It is essential, if man is not to be compelled to have recourse, as a last resort, to rebellion against tyranny and oppression, that human rights should be protected by the Rule of Law.
>
> Preamble, *Declaration of Human Rights*

In the last few years, the centrality of the rule of law to UN peace operations has increasingly been acknowledged.[1] In the words of the Secretary-General: 'it is by reintroducing the rule of law and confidence in its impartial application that we can hope to resuscitate societies shattered by conflict'.[2] The rule of law is recognized as an inherent element in ensuring long-term sustainable peace, economic and political development in post-conflict states.[3] As expressed in the Universal Declaration of Human Rights, quoted above, the rule of law is also intrinsically linked to the protection of human rights. The UN has been engaged in rule of law related tasks since its earliest peace operations in Angola, Namibia, West Papua and the Congo. Since that time, it has been involved in a whole range of activities such as training of criminal justice actors, monitoring of criminal justice institutions, law reform and institution building, to name but a few. In the executive missions established in East Timor and Kosovo, the mandate of each peace operation went further in devolving full responsibility for upholding and enforcing the domestic criminal law in both territories to the UN.

This article concentrates on one specific rule of law task, namely criminal law reform. It examines the inter-relationship between the rule of law, criminal law reform and the protection of human rights in post-conflict societies. In this context, it also discusses the potential relevance and value of model criminal codes, developed as part of the Model Codes for Post-conflict Criminal Justice Project, to the criminal law reform process and to the enhancement of human rights protection in post-conflict states. This article first examines and deconstructs the definition of the rule of law as set out in the report of the Secretary-General on The Rule of Law and Transitional Justice in Conflict and Post-Conflict Societies[4] (hereinafter 'Secretary-General's Rule of Law Report') with a view to demonstrating the theoretical links between the rule of law and human rights. Second, it looks at a variety of rule of law tasks that have been undertaken in efforts to operationalize the rule of law principle in UN peace operations, in particular criminal law reform. Thirdly, the article focuses on the practical relationship between criminal law reform and the protection of human rights in light of the UN's field experience in reforming criminal laws in Kosovo, East Timor and Cambodia. This section also critically examines law reform efforts in these peace operations and details international calls for the creation of tools to assist those involved in the law reform process. Finally, it looks at how law reform tools, in the form of model codes, may be employed to enhance human rights protections in post-conflict states.

Defining the Un-definable: What is the Rule of Law?

An obvious starting point for discussing the rule of law in peace operations is the question: what is meant by the 'rule of law'? Criticisms abound that the concept of the rule of law is so often used, or misused, that it has been rendered meaningless.[5] There is a huge body of legal and political theory that discusses the meaning of the rule of law. The aim of this section is simply to provide a short conceptual backdrop from which to understand the definition of the rule of law as contained the Secretary-General's Rule of Law Report and its relationship with international human rights norms and standards.[6] This definition is relied on as the working definition of the rule of law in the context of peace operations.

Scholars of legal theory have debated the meaning of the 'rule of law' since the time of the early Greek and Roman civilizations.[7] Early legal theory focused more on the meaning of 'law' as opposed to 'rule of law' with two predominant schools of thought: legal positivism and natural law. The proponents of legal positivism hold that law should be understood and analysed without reference to morality or notions of 'higher laws'.[8] In contrast, proponents of the natural law maintain that 'true' law is not value-free.[9] The natural law position can be summed up by the Latin maxim, *lex iniusta non est lex*, meaning that an unjust law is not a law. If the rule of law is taken in its simplest and most uncontested form, meaning that the state rules by law and is ruled by law, it is clear that legal theorists' differing perceptions of the meaning of the rule of law are based on competing definitions of what 'the law' is.

While some legal theorists, such as Ronald Dworkin, argue convincingly that morality and individual rights form part of the law, and by necessary implication the rule of law,[10] legal positivism has been predominant in most of the later twentieth century thinking on the definition of the rule of law. In assessing whether the rule of law exists in a particular state, the focus of legal positivists is not on the substantive quality of the law in the state, but instead on its procedural rationality.[11] In the absence of substantive quality as a criterion for determining the law's validity, according to Brian Tamanaha, 'the positive law came to a point in its own nature – to legality – for legitimation'.[12] Thus, the law is deemed valid where it possesses certain procedural qualities, as opposed to the substantive qualities that are reminiscent of natural law theory. According to Lon Fuller, rule of law exists in a state where the law is general, is publicized, does not operate retroactively, is generally understood, is non-contradictory, is capable of compliance, is constant, and finally, where there is a congruence between the declared rule and official action.[13] Other such formalistic conceptions of the rule of law have been espoused by scholars such as Max Weber[14] and Jürgen Habermas.[15] Habermas, in particular, holds that democracy, rather than the 'rule of law', is the mechanism by which the law is imbued with the preferences and values of the members of society. Thus, values are 'injected' into the law through a democratic process in which elected representatives are responsible for enacting laws.[16]

This view on the indirect conference of values on the law through the modality of democratically elected representatives also finds favour with liberal democracy political theorists.[17] Liberal democracy theory holds that the existence of the rule of law is not premised on the law *per se* but that, to be valid, the law must derive from rights-bearing, equal human subjects under a democratic system of governance.[18] This power is checked through the mechanism of separation of powers. The idea of a government bound by law, first postulated by thinkers such as Aristotle and Montesquieu,[19] came to the fore after the promulgation of the Magna Carta in England in 1610, and has since been a fundamental tenet of constitutionalism and rule of law theory.[20]

Despite their potential to provide a solid conceptual framework for rule of law actors in peace operations, legal and political theories are often absent in contemporary discussions on the definition of the rule of law. There are a multitude of actors engaged in rule of law activities in post-conflict states and consequently a multitude of differing definitions of the rule of law.[21] Some actors have used the phrase 'rule of law' colloquially and have equated it with 'law and order', a related but different concept.[22] Many of these definitions are over-technocratic and confuse the creation of legal, judicial and law enforcement institutions with the creation of the rule of law. Given that earlier rule of law efforts in post-conflict states were largely reactive, with little time to gain a conceptual grounding prior to their execution, it is no surprise that it has taken awhile for theory to catch up with practice. A universally agreed upon definition of the rule of law is thus still elusive. Indeed it may remain perpetually elusive, as is an agreed upon conception of 'the law'.

Within the context of the UN and its work in the rule of law sphere, it seems, however, that a definition has been agreed upon. In September 2003, speaking at the Security Council debates on 'Justice and the Rule of Law: The United Nations

Role', Hans Corell, then UN Legal Counsel, asked about the phrase 'rule of law': 'what do we mean by that?'[23] His question was answered nearly a year later in the Secretary-General's Rule of Law Report.[24] It states that:

> The rule of law is a concept at the very heart of the Organizations' mission. It refers to a principle of governance, in which all persons, institutions and entities, public and private, including the State itself, are accountable to laws that are publicly promulgated, equally enforced and independently adjudicated, and which are consistent with international human rights norms and standards. It requires, as well, measures to ensure adherence to the principles of supremacy of the law, equality before the law, accountability to the law, fairness in the application of the law, separation of powers, participation in decision-making, legal certainty, avoidance of arbitrariness and procedural and legal transparency.

Rather than adopting a wholly technocratic definition of the rule of law, the UN has defined the concept of the rule of law by reference to sound political and legal theory. The elements of legal and political theory that require that the law is supreme, that all persons are accountable to it and that the power of the state is checked by the separation of powers are all present in the definition. There are also elements of Lon Fuller's positivistic definition of the rule of law with the definition's reference to procedural and legal transparency, lack of arbitrariness and legal certainty. Interestingly, the UN definition requires that the law contains certain substantive elements prior to it being rightly seen as complying with the rule of law principle. The concept of 'divine law' employed by natural law scholars to define the requisite substantive element of 'true' law is not employed. Instead, the UN definition of the 'rule of law' provides that law must be embued with the values and norms of international human rights law. Thus, the UN definition of the rule of law signals a rejection of the positivistic approach of value-free law. It also makes clear the intimate relationship between the rule of law and human rights protections: there can be no rule of law without the adequate protection of international human rights norms and standards in domestic laws.

For the sake of clarity, the UN definition of the rule of law can be broken down into four constituent components: (1) a governance component; (2) a procedural component; (3) a substantive component; and (4) an application of law component. The governance component focuses on the need for separation of powers and for the citizen and the government to be held accountable to the law ('separation of powers', 'accountability before the law', 'supremacy of the law'). The procedural elements address how the law is enacted. The rule of law principle, as defined by the UN requires that laws are 'publicly promulgated'. In addition, the law creation process must be 'legally and procedurally transparent' and it must be a participatory process ('participation in decision-making'). Substantively, the law must be 'consistent with international norms and standards'. It must also be 'legally certain and treat all persons equally'. Finally, in terms of application of the law, this must be done must fairly, equally non-arbitrarily. The next section looks at the many tasks and activities that have been undertaken by the UN in an effort to translate this rule theory into practice in post-conflict states, including through criminal law reform.

Rule of Law and Criminal Law Reform Tasks in Post-conflict States

Of the 60 UN peace operations established to date, over two-thirds of them have encompassed some rule of law field activities. The majority of peace operations with rule of law related tasks – with the exception of the UN peace operations in the Congo, West New Papua and in Cyprus – were established in the post-Cold War era when a rapid expansion of UN peacekeeping heralded newer multidimensional peacebuilding operations.

Rule of law activities, conducted as part of past or present peace operations, involve everything from upholding and enforcing the law to monitoring domestic law enforcement actors, training and rebuilding criminal justice institutions, and reforming the laws that criminal justice institutions are tasked with applying. Involvement in the enforcement of domestic criminal law, whether through international civilian police (CIVPOL), or less frequently through international judges and prosecutors, is relatively rare. The most substantial engagement in this task arose in two UN executive peace operations in Kosovo and East Timor, where the UN was tasked with administering both territories.[25] In the case of the former, military forces engaged in law enforcement functions prior to the deployment of CIVPOL that then assumed an executive policing role.[26] Similarly in East Timor, where faced with the collapse of law and order, the Australian military forces arrested and detained people suspected of committing serious crimes such as murder, grievous bodily harm, weapons offences and kidnapping. Upon their arrival, CIVPOL assumed this law enforcement role.[27]

More commonly in peace operations are capacity-building tasks such as assisting those enforcing the law,[28] monitoring their performance[29] (a task that significantly overlaps with human rights-related monitoring tasks[30]), providing training[31] or assisting in restructuring components of the criminal justice system.[32]

Law reform has been conducted as part of post-Cold War UN peace operations since the peace operation in Namibia, where the UN's mandate included that of repealing discriminatory laws.[33] Much of the focus of law reform efforts in the context of peace operations has been on improving the substantive quality of domestic laws – police laws, criminal laws, criminal procedure laws, civil laws, property law and family laws – and ensuring that they are compliant with international human rights norms and standards. Peace operations in Bosnia, Sudan, Liberia and the UN Mission of Support in East Timor (UNMISET) have all had law reform mandates, albeit in a supportive role to national actors tasked with reforming and promulgating new laws. In East Timor, UNMISET was generally responsible for supporting justice,[34] and in Bosnia, UNMIBH was mandated to 'cooperate with the Council of Europe and the OSCE' in judicial and legal reforms'.[35] Currently, in Liberia and Sudan the UN is providing general rule of law assistance, in reforming their respective legal frameworks.[36]

The impact that the UN can have on the substantive quality of national laws is determined by its mission mandate. In the foregoing examples, the role of the UN is assistance-oriented. Ultimately, the decision on whether to enact a particular law rests with the legislature in the post-conflict state. In three exceptional cases, however, the UN was mandated to reform the laws of post-conflict states, thus assuming a direct role in ensuring they met the substantive element of the rule of law definition outlined above. In East Timor and in Kosovo, UNTAET and UNMIK, respectively, were endowed with law-making powers and functions.[37] In Cambodia, the mandate of the UN Transitional Authority in Cambodia (UNTAC) provided it with law-making powers, subject to the approval of the Cambodian Supreme National Council.[38]

The remainder of the article focuses on criminal law reform in UN peace operations, which aim at fulfilling one aspect of the substantive component of the definition of the rule of law – namely its compliance with international human rights norms and standards. The next section elaborates upon such attempts made by UNTAC, UNTAET and UNMIK in Cambodia, East Timor and Kosovo, respectively. The discussion of these reforms demonstrates the close link between criminal law reform and the protection of human rights in post-conflict societies. It also highlights the challenges faced by the UN in undertaking the task of post-conflict criminal law reform and some of the successes and failures of this process.

The Relationship between Criminal Law Reform and Human Rights Protection

Substantial challenges were faced by UNMIK, UNTAET and UNTAC in enforcing their rule of law and law reform mandates. In all of them, the UN was faced not only with widespread lawlessness in the aftermath of the conflicts but also with shattered and non-existent criminal justice systems, which effectively meant that they had to start from scratch in rebuilding them.[39] Moreover, problems surrounding the designation of the applicable law in Kosovo and East Timor and the laconic state of the law in Cambodia further added to these challenges. As stated in the 'Brahimi Report', 'the law and legal systems prevailing prior to the conflict[s] [in Kosovo and East Timor] were questioned or rejected by key groups considered to be the victims of the conflicts'.[40] In Kosovo, Yugoslavia's criminal laws were considered to have been one of the most potent tools of a decade-long policy of discrimination and repression of the Kosovar Albanian population.[41] Despite widespread popular rejection of these laws, UNMIK promulgated UNMIK Regulation 1999/1 stipulating that the law to be applied in Kosovo was the Serbian Criminal Code which applied prior to 24 March 1999. UNMIK later revoked this executive fiat, in the midst of public consternation and rejection of the designated applicable law by the Kosovar judiciary, and under UNMIK Regulation 1999/24 designated the Kosovo law as it stood in 1989 as the applicable law.[42] In East Timor, too, the Timorese did not welcome the use of the pre-existing Indonesian law. However, based largely on the practical reality that any East Timorese person who received a legal education had done so in Indonesia, it was deemed to be the applicable law pursuant to UNTAET Regulation 1999/1 (Sect.3).

In addition to the political and popular resistance to the use of the pre-existing law in Kosovo and East Timor, these laws were substantively deficient in that they did not fully comply with international human rights standards. To rectify this, under both UNMIK Regulation 1999/24 and UNTAET Regulation 1999/1, international human rights standards were deemed to form the normative framework within which UNMIK and UNTAET should operate. The applicable law was deemed valid insofar as it did not conflict with these standards or subsequently enacted regulations. This applicable law solution followed in both Kosovo and East Timor led to a rather odd law reform strategy, in which UNTAET and UNMIK mandated a judicially-led quasi reform, in which the applicable criminal law was interpreted in light of a heteronymous body of law: international human rights law. Applied in practice, this strategy did not work and often resulted in a confusing and ad hoc process that, in theory, was meant to weed out the domestic criminal laws that were contrary to international human rights norms and standards. It failed to provide immediately applicable 'black-letter law' to which judges, prosecutors, lawyers and police officers could refer to.[43] Furthermore, it also failed to provide one body of black-letter law by which all citizens in East Timor and Kosovo were adjudged. How the law would be interpreted and read depended upon which judge a person came before and their knowledge and expertise in international human rights law – something that was greatly lacking in judges in both East Timor and Kosovo. The strategic aim to integrate international human rights norms and standards into the domestic criminal law framework through judicially-led reform did not succeed. Even if the process had worked, it would still only have resulted in objectionable provisions being removed from the legal framework. Missing elements still had to be added by way of legislative reform.

On a positive note, both UNMIK and UNTAET undertook concrete legal reforms by way of regulations in an effort to ensure that the domestic criminal law comported with international human rights norms and standards. In Kosovo, by reason of the fact that the criminal procedure law did not adequately incorporate the principles for a fair trial, UNMIK enacted UNMIK Regulation 2001/28 on the Rights of Persons Arrested by Law Enforcement Authorities. Other regulations aimed at ensuring basic human rights protections were also enacted.[44] In East Timor, despite designating the applicable criminal procedure law to be that of the Indonesian Code of Criminal Procedure, and charging judges, prosecutors and lawyers with the task of reading it 'through the lens of human rights law', it eventually was deemed defunct.[45] In its place UNTAET promulgated UNTAET Regulation 2000/30, a set of streamlined criminal procedure rules that complied fully with international human rights norms and standards.

The UN faced a somewhat different challenge in Cambodia. Criminal justice actors faced immense difficulties in tackling crime problems in the light of an inadequate legal framework. At the time of the establishment of UNTAC, Cambodia had only a laconic body of criminal law, consisting of only one decree on criminal law with 12 short articles.[46] As a result, an UNTAC-drafted law – the 'Provisions Relating to the Judiciary and Criminal Law and Procedure Applicable in Cambodia During the Transitional Period' – was promulgated by the Cambodian Supreme National Council in 1992. This law set out new rules of procedure, substantive law and laws governing the detention. In addition to the aim of preserving public order, the purpose of the UNTAC laws was to ensure that the criminal law adequately protected the human rights of the citizens of Cambodia.[47]

Previously, in the context of non-executive peace operations, the UN acted only in a technical assistance capacity to law-makers in post-conflict states. It was only when the UN was itself the law-maker that the enormity of the task became apparent. In Kosovo and East Timor, the UN was not only the law-maker but the law-enforcer too, with CIVPOL, international corrections officers, and international judges and prosecutors charged with applying the law. This brought home the inadequacies of the applicable law, not only its practicality and adequacy in terms of ensuring public safety and security, but also its compliance, or lack of compliance, with international human rights standards.

Reflections on Reform in Post-conflict States and the Need for Law Reform Tools

No new executive peace operation, in which the UN has been endowed with law-making powers, has been initiated since the 1990s and the establishment of UNMIK, UNTAET and UNTAC. East Timor, Kosovo and Cambodia had provided the UN with the perfect opportunity to engage in criminal law reforms that domestically implemented international human rights norms and standards in the manner envisaged in the Secretary-General's report. Perhaps if the UN were to be charged with a new executive peace operation in the near future it may fare better than in the past, given the experience accumulated since the 1990s. However, the results of law reform efforts aimed at ensuring domestic law comported with international human rights law in East Timor, Kosovo and Cambodia were mixed to say the least. This is not surprising given the enormity of the task of these missions, the ill-preparedness of the UN to step into this role and a lack of expertise among UN staff members who conducted these efforts.[48] Aside from the criticisms mentioned above in relation to how the UN approached the applicable law question, there were also criticisms of UNMIK in Kosovo regarding its failure to remove legal provisions that violated international human rights law. UNMIK was further criticized on the basis that the laws it promulgated were themselves in violation of international standards.[49] Similar criticisms were raised in relation to law reform efforts in Cambodia and East Timor.[50]

After its experience in Kosovo and East Timor, the UN reflected in the Brahimi Report upon its activities in both executive peace operations, and more generally on other aspects of peace operations. The report examined what proactive steps the UN could take in order to better fulfil its functions in post-conflict states in the future. Noting the difficulties experienced in both peace operations vis-à-vis the applicable law and its enforcement, the report called for the creation of interim criminal codes that could be applied in future executive peace operations by international and national personnel engaged in the enforcement of criminal justice.[51] This solution aimed at circumventing the lengthy process of designating and amending the applicable law that had been mooted on numerous occasions prior to the release of the Brahimi Report with the call for the development of 'justice packages'.[52] The interim criminal codes would be drafted in such a way as to be compliant with international human rights norms and standards, and therefore, no reform of the pre-existing law would be required in the immediate aftermath of the conflict. The report envisaged that the interim codes would apply, pending the long-term reform of the domestic criminal laws. This solution was targeted at future UN executive peace operations. Outside the report, other calls for interim criminal codes envisaged their use in a 'collapsed' or 'failed state' scenario where international actors were being called upon to enforce inadequate or non-existent bodies of domestic criminal law in post-conflict states.[53]

A number of legal, practical and philosophical objections have been raised against the idea of using interim criminal codes in executive peace operations or elsewhere.[54] It is also clear that the idea of completely replacing the domestic criminal law of a post-conflict state with a UN-imposed criminal code has largely fallen out of favour within the UN, given the opposition in the Secretary-General's Rule of Law Report to the imposition of 'foreign models'.[55] This same report however calls for the creation of rule of law tools in the form of codes that could be used, not as interim codes but instead to assist those involved in the law reform process.[56] The need for such a law reform tool is clear when one considers the inadequacies of criminal laws in post-conflict states: 'In post-conflict settings, legislative frameworks often show the accumulated signs of neglect and political distortion, contain discriminatory elements and rarely reflect the requirements of international human rights and criminal law standards'. The Secretary-General further emphasized the 'hard-learned lessons from decades of United Nations experience on the ground' where 'scant attention' was paid to legislative work.[57]

In the current climate of assistance-type peace operations, these tools could assist post-conflict governments in reforming pre-existing criminal laws that are discriminatory or that do not reflect the requirements of international human rights and criminal law standards. In addition, they could assist the work of the UN or other international actors involved in supporting the law reform process. A project has been underway for the past five years to develop a set of model codes that could fulfil this function. The next section discusses this project and how the model codes for post-conflict criminal justice (developed as part of it) may be generally useful in reforming the laws of post-conflict states. It also looks specifically at how the model codes can assist in reform efforts aimed at ensuring that the domestic legal framework adequately protects the human rights of those subject to the law.

The Potential Use of Model Criminal Codes

The Model Codes for Post-Conflict Criminal Justice Project (hereinafter 'Model Codes Project') came into being in August 2001 when the US Institute of Peace and the Irish Centre for Human Rights, in cooperation with the UN High Commissioner for Human Rights and the UN Office on Drugs and Crime, commenced drafting a set of model codes. The original idea behind the project had stemmed from the Brahimi Report recommendation, outlined above, for the creation of a set of interim criminal codes for use in an executive peace operation context. However, the project evolved to focus instead on the creation of a law reform assistance tool.

Space does not permit a full description of the drafting, development and the vetting and consultation process that has been undertaken as part of the project. Much has been written on this elsewhere.[58] The final products of the Model Codes Project are four annotated model codes: a draft penal code, the Model Criminal Code; a draft procedure code, the Model Code of Criminal Procedure; the Model Detention Act, a body of law that regulates procedural and substantive issues relating to pre-trial detention and imprisonment; and finally, the Model Police Act, a draft Police Act.[59] The model codes are in the final stages of completion and are due to be published in mid-2007.[60]

Given the problem of non-compliance of post-conflict laws with international human rights norms and standards, foremost in the drafters' minds was the creation of a set of model codes that are fully compliant with international and regional human rights norms and standards. One of the first tasks undertaken in the Model Codes Project was to research and collate the international human rights norms and standards applicable to the enforcement of criminal justice, policing and public order. Research was conducted on primary documents, the case law of the relevant international and regional human rights bodies and secondary literature. Further research was undertaken on the implementation of human rights standards in the context of past peace operations, and also on the constraints that peace operations faced in implementing such standards in a post-conflict environment, such as a lack of resources or personnel. After this preliminary process, these abstract standards were translated into provisions of criminal law and procedure and police laws by the codes drafters, after which numerous human rights specialists reviewed the provisions as part of the vetting process.

In assessing the sufficiency of the laws in a post-conflict state from the perspective of human rights protection, the model codes thus provide a valuable yardstick against which to judge the pre-existing law and a sort of 'best practice' document that comports with baseline human rights standards. In drafting new laws or in the updating of existing laws in post-conflict states, the model codes represent a useful resource from which to draw. Relevant standards and model provisions on substantive criminal law may be drawn from the Model Criminal Code. Standards relating to the investigation, prosecution, trial and appeal of suspects and accused persons, and other provisions such as international cooperation and extradition, may be sourced from the Model Code of Criminal Procedure. The Model Detention Act is a valuable resource in its articulation of applicable human rights and fair trial standards vis-à-vis detention and imprisonment, while the Model Police Act is as valuable when legislation on police powers and public order is being drafted.

Often it is a difficult endeavour to translate human rights standards into concrete normative provisions of law, even if those involved are well versed in international human rights norms and standards. Whether it is a transitional government or the UN, either directly or indirectly, that is undertaking a reform process aimed at ensuring the compliance of existing domestic criminal laws with international human rights norms and standards, or the drafting of new laws, the model codes may be of great assistance. In addition to the value inherent in providing sample provisions in the model codes, value may also be derived from the commentaries that accompany the provision of each model code. The commentaries serve a variety of functions, one of those being that they provide further explanation and discussion on the nature and scope of the provision it accompanies. In the case of provisions that relate to human rights standards, the commentaries provide a detailed analysis of the particular right, its nature and its scope, thus serving an instructive and pedagogical function.

Conclusion

This article has sought to demonstrate the theoretical and practical linkages between the rule of law, criminal law reform and international human rights norms and standards. It has also attempted to show how the model codes for post-conflict criminal justice could prove a useful tool in future reform efforts aimed at enhancing human rights protections in post-conflict states. Past efforts to fully and effectively integrate human rights protections into domestic criminal legislation have not been entirely successful. In future post-conflict criminal law reform efforts, the model codes may prove a valuable tool in the criminal law reform process. In this way, they may assist in a small, yet meaningful, way in helping post-conflict states move towards the rule of law and more effective human rights protections. One word of caution is merited however. Guido de Ruggiero famously remarked that 'the law of rationalistic simplification ... leads people to think that in the mere technicalities of law they possess the means and the power to effect unlimited changes'.[61] The implication is that law reform efforts are not the end-point of change nor are they a panacea for the realization of human rights protections. Reform actors should be aware that while law reform is an integral part of post-conflict peacebuilding and a good starting point on the road to rule of law and enhanced human rights protections in post-conflict states, it is just that: a start. Much thought should be given as to how laws, once drafted, are effectively enforced and implemented. Criminal law reform is but the first necessary step for post-conflict states on the road towards the rule of law and human rights.

NOTES

1. See, in particular, 'The Rule of Law and Transitional Justice in Conflict and Post Conflict Societies, Report of the Secretary-General', UN Doc. S/RES/616 (2004); Report of the Secretary-General, 'In Larger Freedom: Towards Security, Development and Human Rights for

All', UN Doc. A/RES/59 (2005), paras.133–9; 'A More Secure World: Our Shared Responsibility, Report of the Secretary General's High Level Panel on Threats, Challenges and Change', UN Doc. A/RES/565 (2004), paras.229–30; and 'Strengthening the Rule of Law', UN Doc. A/RES/221 (2003).

2. Kofi Annan, address to the General Assembly, 21 Sept. 2004 (available at www.un.org/apps/sgstate.asp?nid=1088).
3. Jean-Marie Guéhenno, 'Justice and the Rule of Law: The United Nations Role', Security Council Debates, 30 Sept. 2003, UN Doc. S/PV.4833, p.3.
4. 'The Rule of Law' (see n.1 above).
5. See Judith N. Shklar, *Political Theory and the Rule of Law*, in Allan C. Hutchinson and Patrick Monahan, *The Rule of Law: Ideal or Ideology?*, Toronto: Carswell Legal Publications, 1987, p.1.
6. 'The Rule of Law Report' (n.1 above).
7. See Brian Tamanaha, *On the Rule of Law: History, Politics, Theory*, Cambridge: Cambridge University Press, 2004, pp.7–14.
8. See, e.g., Herbert Lionel Adolphus Harte, *The Concept of Law*, Oxford: Clarendon Press, 1961.
9. See Passerin D'Entrève, *Natural Law: An Introduction to Legal Philosophy*, London: Hutchinson, 1970, p.116.
10. See Ronald Dworkin, *Law's Empire*, Cambridge, MA: Belknap Press, 1986 and *Taking Rights Seriously*, Cambridge, MA: Harvard University Press, 1977.
11. See Brian Z. Tamanaha, *A General Jurisprudence of Law and Society*, Oxford: Oxford University Press, 2001, p.96.
12. Ibid., p.98.
13. Lon L. Fuller, *The Morality of Law*, New Haven: CON Yale University Press (rev.edn) 1969, pp.33–94.
14. See Max Weber, *Max Weber on Law in Economy and Society*, in Max Rheinstein (ed.), Cambridge MA: Harvard University Press, 1954.
15. See Jürgen Habermas, *Between Facts and Norms*, Cambridge, MA: MIT Press, 1996.
16. For a further discussion see, Tamanaha (n.11 above), p.102.
17. See David Chandler, 'Imposing the Rule of Law: The Lessons of BiH for Peacebuilding in Iraq', *International Peacekeeping*, Vol.11, No.2, summer 2004, p.326.
18. Ibid.
19. See Aristotle, *Politics*, III, 15, 1286a-16, 1287a, cited in Rachel Kleinfeld Belton, *Competing Definitions of the Rule of Law: Implications for Practitioners*, Carnegie Papers, Washington, DC: Carnegie Endowment for International Peace, 2005; Montesquieu, *L'Esprit des Lois*, 1748.
20. See for example Albert Venn Dicey, *An Introduction to the Study of the Law of the Constitution*, London: Macmillan, 1959, p.110.
21. See for example, the World Bank definition of rule of law in 'Legal and Judicial Reform: Observations, Experiences and Approach of the Legal Vice Presidency', July 2002 (available at www1.worldbank.org/legal/leglr/publications_ljr.html). See also the definition of the UN Development Program (UNDP), available at http://magnet.undp.org/policy.glossary.htm
22. For a discussion on the meaning of 'law and order', see Belton (n.19 above), pp.10–12.
23. 'Justice and the Rule of Law: The United Nations Role', Security Council Debates, 30 Sept. 2004, UN Doc. S/PV.4835.
24. 'The Rule of Law Report' (n.1 above).
25. The UN Mission in Kosovo (UNMIK) was established under Security Council Resolution 1244 (1999) and the UN Transitional Administration in East Timor (UNTAET) was established under Security Council Resolution 1272 (1999). See UNMIK Regulations 2000/6, 2000/57, 2000/64; UNTAET Regulation 2001/11.
26. The power for the military force – KFOR – to act in a law enforcement capacity was provided for in paragraph 9(d) of Security Council Resolution 1244 (1999). The military engaged in this role for approximately one year prior to the reinstatement of civilian authority. See, Capt. Alton L. Gwaltney III, 'Law and Order in Kosovo: A Look at Criminal Justice During the First Year of Operation Joint Guardian', in Larry Wentz (ed.), *Lessons from Kosovo: The KFOR Experience*, CCRP Publication Series, 2002, p.233.
27. See UN Doc. S/RES/1272 (1999), para.2(a).
28. See UN Doc. A/RES/2504 (XXIV) (West New Papua); UN Doc. S/RES/1509 (2003), para.1 (Liberia); See UN Doc. S/RES/1528 (2004), para 6(p) (Côte D'Ivoire); UN Doc. S/RES/1545 (2004), para.7 (Burundi); UN Doc. S/RES/1526 (2004), para.5(a) (Democratic Republic of Congo); UN Doc. S/RES/1289 (2000), para.10(d) (Sierra Leone); UN Doc. S/RES/1542 (2004), para.7(d) (Haiti).

29. See Report of the Secretary-General (Cyprus), UN Doc. S/5697 (1964), in Rosalyn Higgins, *United Nations Peacekeeping 1946-1967. Documents and Commentary Volume III Africa*, Oxford: Oxford University Press, 1980, p.131; Lusaka Protocol Between the Government of Angola and the Uniao Nacional Para a Indepedencia Total de Angola and Annex 5; UN Doc. S/RES/1118 (1997), para.2 (Central African Republic); Comprehensive Agreement on Human Rights, para.19 (Guatamala); UN Doc. S/RES/1509 (2003), para.3(a) (Liberia); UN Doc. S/RES/1545 (2004), para.7 (Burundi).

30. In missions such as the UN Observer Mission in El Salvador (ONUSAL), the rule of law was subsumed within the mandate of a human rights division. See Diego García-Sayán, 'The Experience of ONUSAL in El Salvador', in Alice Henkin (ed.), *Honouring Human Rights and Keeping the Peace*, Washington, DC: The Aspen Institute, 1995, pp.31–55. In current missions, such as Liberia and Burundi, while there are separate human rights units and rule of law units, they both undertake overlapping criminal justice system monitoring roles.

31. See, for example, Agreement on Human Rights (1990), paras.10–14 (El Salvador); UN Doc. S/RES/1063 (1996), para.2 (Haiti); UN Doc. S/RES/997 (1995), para.3(d) (Rwanda); UN Doc. S/RES/1181 (1998), para.8(a) (Sierra Leone); UN Doc. S/RES/1590 (2005), para.4(viii) (Sudan).

32. See, e.g., UN Doc. S/RES/1509 (2003), para.3(a) (Liberia); UN Doc. S/RES/1270 (1999), para.23 (Sierra Leone); UN Doc. S/RES/1590 (2005), para.4(viii) (Sudan); UN Doc. S/RES/1545 (2004), para.6 (Burundi); The General Framework Agreement for Peace in Bosnia and Herzegovina (the 'Dayton Agreement'), Annex 11; UN Doc. S/RES/897 (1994), para.2(d) (Somalia).

33. For a discussion of this role, see *The Blue Helmets: A Review of United Nations Peace-keeping*, New York: UN Department of Public Information (3rd edn), 1996, pp.224–5.

34. See UN Doc. S/RES/1410 (2004), para.4(a).

35. See www.un.org/Depts/dpko/missions/unmibh.background.html

36. See UN Doc. S/RES/1509 (2003), para.3(g) (Liberia); UN Doc. S/RES/1590 (2005), para.4(viii) (Sudan).

37. See UN Doc. S/RES/1272, para.1 and UN Doc. S/RES/1244, para.10.

38. See *Agreement on a Comprehensive Political Settlement of the Cambodia Conflict*, Annex 1, Sect.A, para.1. and Annex 1, Sect.B, para.1.

39. See Organization for Security and Cooperation in Europe, Department of Rule of Law and Human Rights, 'Observation and Recommendations of the OSCE Legal System Monitoring Section Report 1 – Material Needs of the Emergency Judicial System', 7 Nov. 1999; Sidney Jones, 'East Timor: The Troubled Path to Independence'm in Henkin (ed.) (see n.30 above), pp.115–46) and Brad Adams, 'UN Human Rights Work in Cambodia: Efforts to Preserve the Jewel in the Peacekeeping Crown', in Henkin (ed.), p.205.

40. 'Report of the Panel on United Nations Peace Operations', UN Doc. A/RES/502-UN Doc. S/RES/908 (2000), para.79.

41. See Hansjoerg Strohmeyer, 'Making Multilateral Interventions Work: The U.N. and the Creation of Transitional Justice Systems in Kosovo and East Timor', *Fletcher Forum of World Affairs*, Vol.25, summer 2001, p.112.

42. Sec.1. Where there was a gap in the 1989 law, this could, however, be supplemented by the Serbian Criminal Code. The 1989 law was also superseded by any regulations passed by the Special Representative of the Secretary-General.

43. Strohmeyer (n.41 above), p.110.

44. See UNMIK Regulations: 2000/3 (incitement to crime on account of hatred), 2001/4 (trafficking in persons), 2001/20 (witness protection), 2003/1 (sexual violence) and 2003/12 (domestic violence).

45. Strohmeyer (n.41 above), p.112.

46. Dolores A. Donavan, 'Cambodia: Building a Legal System from Scratch', Vol.27, *The International Lawyer*, 1993, pp.445, 448.

47. Ibid., preamble, paras.10–11.

48. See 'Report of the Secretary-General on the United Nations Transitional Administration in East Timor', 26 Jan. 2000, UN Doc. S/2000/53, para.68.

49. OSCE Mission in Kosovo, Department of Human Rights and Rule of Law, 'Kosovo: A Review of the Criminal Justice System – 1 September 2000–28 February 2001', pp.11–12; David Marshall and Shelley Inglis, 'Human Rights in Transition: The Disempowerment of Human Rights-Based Justice in the United Nations Mission in Kosovo', *Harvard Human Rights Journal*, Vol.16, spring 2003, p.142.

50. See Asia Human Rights Commission, 'Adoption of New Laws to Reform Cambodian Police Urged', 1999 (at www.hrsolidarity.net/mainfile.php/1999vol09no02/798/) calling for the Cambodian government to 'adopt a penal code, a criminal procedure code and a law on evidence as soon as possible so that [Cambodia's] police can function according to the standards and norms of a liberal democracy'; Megan A. Fairlie, Affirming Brahimi: East Timor Makes the Case for a Model Criminal Code, *American University International Law Review*, Vol.18, No.5, 2003, p.1059. See also Carla Bongiornio, 'A Culture of Impunity: Applying International Human Rights Law to the United Nations in East Timor', *Columbia Human Rights Law Review*, Vol.22, summer 2002, p.623.
51. See 'Report of the Panel on United Nations Peace Operations' (n.40 above), paras.79–83.
52. See Gareth Evans, *Cooperating For Peace: The Global Agenda for the 1990s and Beyond*, St. Leonards, NSW: Allen & Unwin, 1993; Mark Plunkett, 'Re-establishing Law and Order in Peace-Maintenance', in Jarat Chopra (ed.), *The Politics of Peace Maintenance*, Boulder CO: Lynne Rienner, 1998, p.16.
53. See Michael J. Kelly, *Restoring and Maintaining Order in Complex Peace Operations: The Search for a Legal Framework*, The Hague: Kluwer Law International, 1999, p.231; Plunkett (n.52 above), p.16.
54. See e.g., Bruce M. Oswald, Model Codes for Criminal Justice and Peace Operations: Some Legal Issues, *Journal Conflict & Security Law*, Vol.9, No.2, summer 2004, p.253.
55. 'The Rule of Law' (n.1 above), para.15.
56. Ibid., para.30.
57. Ibid., paras24, 27.
58. See Vivienne O'Connor and Colette Rausch, 'A Toolbox to Tackle Law Reform in Post-Conflict States: The Model Codes for Post Conflict Criminal Justice', *International Peacekeeping: The Yearbook of International Peace Operations*, Vol.10, 2005, p.1.
59. A Police Act is a piece of legislation that would be more familiar to civil law police officers. Most civil law countries, in addition to the criminal code and procedure code, have promulgated such an Act to regulate the organization and discipline of the national police force and police duties and powers outside the realm of criminal investigation.
60. Forthcoming United States Institute of Peace Press, 2007.
61. *The History of European Liberalism (1927)* cited on World Bank website (www1.worldbank.org/publicsector/legal/reforminglaws.htm).

An Assessment of UN Efforts to Address Sexual Misconduct by Peacekeeping Personnel

RAY MURPHY

The sexual exploitation of women and girls by UN and other personnel operating in post- conflict situations is not a new phenomenon, and such activities cover a wide range of behaviour ranging from the solicitation of prostitutes to rape of under-aged girls, to paedophilia.[1] In some countries, payment for sex between adults may be tolerated or even legal. But international personnel working in the field often forget that the local population may be traumatized and extremely vulnerable, and that the situation they find themselves in is anything but normal. Since the early 1990s, sexual exploitation by UN peacekeepers has been documented by the media and human rights organizations in Bosnia and Herzegovina, and later Mozambique, Cambodia, East Timor and Liberia.[2] Such activities have not been confined to UN peacekeepers. In late 2001, a report commissioned jointly by the UN High Commissioner for Refugees and Save the Children UK alleged that sexual violence and exploitation was widespread among the refugee and internally displaced persons in communities in Guinea, Liberia and Sierra Leone.[3] The perpetrators of these abuses were said to include members of UN peacekeeping forces and humanitarian aid workers – the very people who had been designated to protect these vulnerable communities. Linked to this is the issue of peacekeepers who father babies during the mission and then fail to take responsibility for their children. The reality of prostitution and sexual exploitation in this context is all the more disturbing as UN peacekeepers are supposed to facilitate a return to normality in a war-torn society and not to breach the trust placed in it by the local population. The UN presence is intended to protect those most vulnerable, not to exploit them. This article examines the response of the UN to these revelations and argues that more needs to be done to prevent such conduct among UN personnel.

Misconduct by UN Personnel

The publicity surrounding the revelations of misconduct prompted an investigation by the UN Office of Internal Oversight Services (OIOS).[4] Despite efforts to combat such misconduct, including establishing Codes of Conduct, and the adoption of Security Council Resolution 1325 (2000) and the Secretary-General's Bulletin on Special Measures for Protection from Sexual Exploitation and Sexual Abuse (2003),[5] and emphasis on a policy of 'zero-tolerance' towards sexual exploitation and abuse by UN staff, many considered reports emanating from the UN mission to the Democratic Republic of the Congo (MONUC) to be 'the tip of the iceberg'.[6] It was reported in May 2005 that 152 peacekeeping personnel (32 civilians, 3 civilian police and 117 military), and five UN staff members had been summarily dismissed.[7] From 1 January 2004 to 9 December 2005 investigations against 278 peacekeeping personnel were carried out resulting in the dismissal of 16 civilians, the repatriation of 16 members of formed police units and 122 military personnel on disciplinary grounds (including six commanders).[8] Despite these developments, there is a widespread perception that peacekeeping personnel are not held accountable for their conduct, and that there is a de facto tolerance of, and immunity from prosecution for, such behaviour.[9]

In a press release on 19 November 2004, Kofi Annan acknowledged that there was evidence that sexual exploitation and abuse had been committed by MONUC personnel:

> I am afraid that there is clear evidence that acts of gross misconduct have taken place. This is a shameful thing for the UN to have to say, and I am absolutely outraged by it .... We cannot rest until we have rooted out all such practices from MONUC, from any other peacekeeping operation, and indeed anywhere in the Organisation that they might occur. And we must make sure that those involved are held fully accountable.[10]

An OIOS investigation into these allegations was launched in May 2004, and a special investigation team was sent by the Department of Peacekeeping Operations (DPKO) to examine possible further cases. While investigation of such allegations is important, the effectiveness and consequences of the OIOS investigation was seen by many as insufficient.[11]

Unfortunately, dealing with those who engage in such activities is complicated. The UN has no legal authority to prosecute those against whom evidence of wrongdoing is found. At most it can repatriate a peacekeeper to their country of origin, but it cannot ensure the prosecution of that person once they have returned home. Taking action against civilian personnel is more problematic than in the case of the military. UN forces remain subject to their respective national military codes and regulations. Only if these are used properly, can they provide an effective mechanism for holding military personnel accountable.

Human rights are a key issue in guaranteeing consistent and effective peacekeeping, and this seems only to have been recognized in the early 1990s after allegations of human rights abuses by peacekeepers in Somalia.[12] Neither the Status of Force Agreements (SOFAs) nor the participation agreements of states contributing to peacekeeping operations refer to human rights. Nor are human rights expressly mentioned in the model SOFA between the UN and the host state. Violations of human rights and abuse by UN and humanitarian personnel, whether in the form of sexual exploitation or otherwise, should not be tolerated: it violates everything the UN stands for. Anyone employed by or affiliated with the UN must be held accountable and, when the circumstances so warrant, prosecuted.[13] For this reason the report undertaken by the Secretary-General's adviser on sexual exploitation and abuse by UN peacekeepers, Prince Zeid of Jordan, and the investigation by the OIOS into allegations of sexual exploitation and abuse by MONUC personnel in the Congo, provide important analysis and insight into the problem with practical recommendations aimed at eliminating such practices.[14] An understanding of the legal framework under which peacekeepers operate is important for appreciating the constraints imposed when taking disciplinary measures against UN personnel involved in sexual abuse.

The Legal Framework for Peacekeeping Forces

The status of a UN or similar force depends on the underlying authority upon which the force is present in the receiving state, and on the nature and mission of the force.[15] Under existing law, a UN peacekeeping operation is considered a subsidiary organ of the UN, established pursuant to a resolution of the Security Council or General Assembly. As such it enjoys the status, privileges and immunities of the Organization provided for in Article 105 of the UN Charter, and the UN Convention on the Privileges and Immunities of the UN of 13 February 1946.[16] UN staff members are appointed by the Secretary-General and they have the status of officials under the Convention, section 18 of which provides that officials are immune in respect of acts committed by them in their official capacity.

The legal framework for UN forces is usually made up of the following:

- a resolution of the Security Council or the General Assembly;
- a SOFA or Status of Mission Agreement between the UN and the host state;
- an agreement by exchange of letters or memorandum of understanding (MoU) between each of the participating states and the UN;
- the Force Regulations issued by the Secretary-General.

The situation pertaining to UN operations is further complicated by the fact that the majority of contemporary missions may have up to five different categories of participating personnel. The largest group are usually the so-called 'blue helmets' or members of national military contingents supplied to the UN for specified duration (usually six or 12 months). Then there are civilian police from various police forces around the world, civilian staff, UN volunteers, and military observers. The Secretary-General's Bulletin prohibiting exploitation does not apply to all categories. This is unsatisfactory, and the 2003 Bulletin should apply to all categories of peacekeeping personnel without exception.

This was recommended by the Zeid Report but as of mid-2006 has not been implemented.

As UN forces are more often than not deployed in situations of conflict, determining what situations constitute 'armed conflict' under international law, and the laws governing UN and other forces present or participating as combatants in such situations is a vital issue. International humanitarian law will also provide a certain level of protection to UN forces, if and when applicable, depending on the degree of involvement and the nature of the conflict.[17] It also creates certain duties and obligations which are outlined below.

Armed conflict and civil disorder are often characterized by the deliberate targeting of women. Although the 1979 Convention on the Elimination of All Forms of Discrimination Against Women (CEDAW) provides some degree of protection for women,[18] they remain vulnerable to physical and sexual abuse, torture, slavery, rape and other crimes against humanity. Women also constitute the greatest number of refugees, and as refugees they are often vulnerable to violence, discrimination and exploitation.

In addition to the protection provided under CEDAW, Security Council Resolution 1325 of 31 October 2000 on Women, Peace and Security calls on all parties to armed conflict to take special measures to protect women and girls from gender-based violence, particularly rape and other forms of sexual abuse, and all other forms of violence in situations of armed conflict.[19] It further emphasizes state responsibility to end impunity and to prosecute those responsible for genocide, crimes against humanity and war crimes, including those relating to sexual and other violence against women and girls. There is also special protection provided for children under the 1990 Convention on the Rights of the Child and its two Optional Protocols,[20] in addition to that provided under Article 24 of the International Covenant on Civil and Political Rights. The extra-territorial application of these human rights treaties is well established in the jurisprudence of the UN Human Rights Committee.[21]

Investigation into Allegations of Abuse in the DRC

After media reports in early 2004 of the recurrence of acts of sexual exploitation and abuse of Congolese women and girls by UN peacekeepers, the OIOS conducted an investigation in Bunia between May and September 2004. The investigation uncovered evidence of regular and widespread sexual contact by peacekeepers with underage girls. Many of the allegations could not be substantiated owing to their non-specific nature. A combination of the passage of time and the age of victims hindered the investigation of individual cases, but cogent evidence of a pattern of sexual exploitation was found. Many of the victims had been raped during the conflict and their traumas made pressing them for evidence a very delicate matter.

The Report found, *inter alia*, that:

> In many cases of the interviews conducted by the investigation team during its four months of field work, particularly of the younger girls, aged 11 to 14

years, it became clear that for most of them, having sex with the peace-keepers was a means of getting food and sometimes small sums of money. The boys and young men who facilitated sexual encounters between peace-keepers and the girls sometimes received food as payment for their services as well. In addition to the corroborated cases reported ... interviews with other girls and women indicated the widespread nature of the sexual activity occurring in Bunia.[22]

This was consistent with other reports from the region. Human Rights Watch found that MONUC's credibility had been undermined by the exploitative and abusive behaviour of some of its staff.[23] Girls as young as 13 years old had reportedly been raped by MONUC soldiers. Other girls between the age of 12 and 15 had engaged in what is commonly referred to as 'survival sex' – sexual relations engaged in to obtain some food, money or protection. Relations of this nature are inherently exploitative and relatively easy to establish in post-conflict environments where women and girls can find themselves in a vulnerable position.

Codes of Conduct and Bulletins for Peacekeepers

The MONUC Code of Conduct and the Secretary-General's Bulletin on special measures for the protection from sexual exploitation and sexual abuse provide that sexual activity with children (persons under 18) is prohibited regardless of the local age of majority or consent, and that mistaken belief in the age of the child is not a defence. Rule 4 of the Code of Personal Conduct for Blue Helmets and the MONUC code of conduct prohibit sexual exploitation and abuse. The MONUC code of conduct defines an act of sexual exploitation and/or abuse as any exchange of money, employment, goods or services for sex. Any breach of these standards of conduct renders the perpetrators liable to disciplinary action for serious misconduct as defined in section III of the DPKO Directives for Disciplinary Matters Involving Military Members of National Contingents. All troop contributing states recognize the Code of Personal Conduct for Blue Helmets as binding.

The Secretary-General's Bulletin on special measures for the protection from sexual exploitation is binding on all staff of the UN, and its provisions are similar to those contained in the MONUC Code of Conduct.[24] Likewise, the Bulletin prohibits military forces under UN command and control from commit-ting acts of sexual exploitation.[25] These documents expand on the standards found in the Code of Personal Conduct for Blue Helmets. Section 1 of the Bulletin defines sexual exploitation as follows: 'any actual or attempted abuse of a position of vulnerability, differential power, or trust, for sexual purposes, including, but not limited to, profiting monetarily, socially or politically from sexual exploita-tion of another'. Sexual abuse is defined as 'actual or threatened physical intrusion of a sexual nature, whether by force or under unequal or coercive conditions'. Section 2 of the MONUC code of conduct contains similar provisions. It expands on the definition of sexual abuse and provides that abuse and exploitation of this nature includes any sexual misconduct that has a detrimental effect on the image, credibility, impartiality or integrity of the UN.

The Secretary-General's Bulletin on the observance by UN forces of humanitarian law is also relevant.[26] Section 7 governs the treatment of civilians and persons *hors de combat* and prohibits acts of abuse or exploitation. In contains the following express provisions which create a duty to protect women and children from such exploitation:

> Section 7.3 Women shall be especially protected against any attack, in particular against rape, enforced prostitution or any other form of indecent assault.
> Section 7.4 Children shall be the object of special respect and shall be protected against any form of indecent assault.

The UN personnel in the DRC abused the vulnerability of the local population and exploited them for sexual purposes. The conduct was prohibited and it was also a clear violation of the duty to protect the most vulnerable members of Congolese society.[27] The majority of victims were between the ages of 12 and 16 years and were extremely vulnerable. They were very poor and illiterate; many had lost close family members and were traumatized by the sexual and other violence that characterized the conflict. Although the investigation focused on three UN contingents, it could not be assumed that other contingents did not engage in similar activities. Among the factors facilitating a lack of accountability among peacekeepers was the regular troop rotations and the lack of a prevention programme, despite the fact that this was a requirement of the Under Secretary-General for Peacekeeping Operations and the Special Representative of the Secretary-General for MONUC. Few military or civilian staff seemed aware of the directives, policies, rules and regulations governing sexual contact that they were obligated to follow. This was also the case with troops serving with the UN mission in Ethiopia and Eritrea (UNMEE). It was also surprising for the investigation team in Bunia to find evidence of ongoing sexual contact while the investigation was taking place.

While there is a consensus that such conduct is reprehensible and should be prevented, there is also an acknowledgement that it is widespread during UN peacekeeping operations. The Special Representative of the Secretary-General for MONUC provided the following insight into how to deal with such behaviour:

> I believe that emphasis needs to be placed on the accountability of the officers of contingents to which the perpetrators belong, from contingent to company and platoon commanders. It is clearly evident that while there has been no shortcoming insofar as disseminating the code of conduct and the Secretary-General's zero tolerance policy on matters of sexual exploitation and abuse, the same cannot be said for enforcement of this. In certain instances, it is apparent that the feeling of impunity is such that not only have the policies not been enforced, but the command structures have not always given investigators their full cooperation. I also consider it imperative that the results of Member States' actions against

the perpetrators of these abuses be made available to the UN and that the Mission highlight to incoming commanders the gravity and extent of the problem and underscore the commanders' responsibility to prevent similar acts during their mandate. Only such stern deterrents, in my view, will enable us to stamp out sexual exploitation and sexual abuse in the peacekeeping environment.[28]

The OIOS report made several practical recommendations. These included:

- reviewing cases and requesting individual countries to take appropriate action;
- adopting a stringent prevention programme, with emphasis on protecting the most vulnerable (those under 18 years of age), and establishing a rapid-detection programme;
- MONUC managers becoming more involved and demanding accountability from both civilian administrators and contingent commanders;
- enforcing strict discipline over personnel under their command;
- ensuring all military compounds and posts are adequately secured to prevent access and unauthorized trading between troops and the local population;
- strengthening UN and NGO programmes aimed at empowering and protecting the vulnerable population to allow for alternative means of survival;
- DPKO considering a wider application of prevention and detection policies including designating local officials or NGOs to receive reports and the creation of an efficient central reporting system to mission central management. Developing mission-based rapid response teams, and educational programmes employing sanctions for sexual exploitation, and a public name and shame policy, combined with a policy of permanent exclusion from peacekeeping operations both of those who engage in sexual exploitation and abuse and of their contingent commanders.[29]

The Zeid Report

As the UN is not a state, the source of its obligation to observe human rights is not without controversy.[30] Although not a party to the major human rights treaties, it remains a subject of international law. One way around the problem of applying human rights norms to the UN itself is to regard the UN Charter and its accompanying instruments as forming a constitution. In this way the relevant treaties and related instruments govern UN as well as state activities.

The issue of accountability and the conduct of peacekeeping and humanitarian workers has been simmering in the background for years, but in the past ten years it has been acknowledged as a serious problem.[31]Complaints emanated from Cambodia, Bosnia, Macedonia, Mozambique, West Africa, the Democratic Republic of the Congo, Eritrea and Kosovo. Following the publication of several reports, it has emerged that sexual exploitation, rape and trafficking in persons are a common consequence of the deployment of peacekeeping troops and civilian police forces.[32] The response more often than not has been to promulgate codes of practice and revise training programmes and guidelines. Though welcome, such responses are not enough. To be fair, the UN has made repeated calls on troop-contributing states to investigate and prosecute all allegations of human rights violations by peacekeepers and report back to the UN.[33] But the UN itself is bound by the terms of its agreement with troop contributors and the SOFA, and it has no authority to insist on more. The situation is exacerbated in places like Kosovo, where the UN is entrusted with the administration of the entire territory.

The UN has obligations under international human rights law that it has not formally acknowledged until this century. The technical cooperation between the Office of the High Commissioner for Human Rights and the DPKO as part of a policy of 'mainstreaming' international human rights standards into UN activities does not empower human rights components. In order to remove uncertainty surrounding the human rights obligations of UN peacekeeping operations, an explicit and binding commitment to such standards must be made. A broad 'Peacekeeping Bill of Rights' could be formulated and applied selectively to the functions that individual missions undertake.[34]

Another suggestion is the establishment of a UN Ombudsperson. Such tools are indispensable in providing good governance and accountability mechanisms.[35] Such an institution would have to be given real powers to avoid the fate that befell the Ombudsperson Institution established by the OSCE in Kosovo, which was often ignored or merely tolerated rather than supported by the UN. As the UN is not technically a party to the major human rights instruments and treaties, none of the treaty bodies charged with reviewing compliance was ever called to examine the conduct of the UN from a human rights perspective. However, UNMIK was to present a report on the implementation of the International Covenant on Civil and Political Rights (and the International Covenant on Economic Social and Cultural Rights) in Kosovo to the relevant UN committee during 2006. When the Human Rights Committee and the Committee Against Torture had the opportunity to examine the role of the UN in Somalia indirectly through the reports of states whose troops had been involved in violations of international human rights standards while serving in Somalia, no reference was made to the UN's responsibility.

The more specific problem of sexual exploitation has been outlined in the Secretary-General's report on a comprehensive strategy to eliminate future exploitation.[36] Many of the recommendations have merit and should be implemented without delay, especially those relating to individual disciplinary, financial and criminal accountability of all UN staff. One recommendation related to developing an international convention that would subject UN personnel to the jurisdiction of states parties for specified crimes committed by such personnel.[37] Among the difficulties with such a proposal is that it would apply only to the parties to the Convention. Finding consensus in drafting an effective convention could also prove difficult. A worst-case scenario would be the adoption of a convention with inconsistencies and loopholes that created an illusion of protection and accountability, similar to that of the Convention for the Safety of UN Personnel.[38]

However, retaining a system where prosecutions for such actions are 'fortuitous' is unsustainable.[39]

UN Responsibility

The revelations raise the issue of UN responsibility for violations of international law in cases of this nature. While there can be no doubt that the UN is a subject of international law and capable of possessing international rights and duties, an analysis of what the International Court of Justice has stated reveals that it is not possible to give a categorical answer to the question of the legal consequences of personality for international organizations.[40] The UN is, however, a separate legal person from and additional to its member states, and it is not simply an aggregation of those states. Once the existence of international personality and rights is conceded, it is not difficult to infer that this will also entail obligations. In the WHO *Agreement Case* the International Court of Justice specifically referred to the existence of obligations at customary international law for international organizations.[41] There are situations where the UN would be responsible under customary international law for acts of persons or armed forces under its control.[42] In fact, there have been claims by states against the UN arising from violations of international law during the ONUC (Congo) operation that were later settled by negotiation.[43]

The UN has generally accepted responsibility for illegal acts that may have been committed by armed forces (belonging to member states) acting under its control.[44] Imputability to the UN is possible when national contingents become organs of the UN by being placed under its authority and control. This does not happen when a country or countries retain control of a military force, as in the Gulf War, even if acting in the execution of a UN decision. Where national contingents come together to form 'coalitions of the willing' in such cases, but do not become organs of the UN, or fall under its command and control, then the UN cannot be held responsible for their acts.[45] In such cases, the acts of military forces remain the responsibility of the states concerned. However, definitive statements remain problematic due to the linkage with the complex issues surrounding the command and control of UN forces, and a great deal will depend on the facts of a case. In mid-2006 the issue was being examined by the International Law Commission. In the meantime, the control test retains its central role in determining liability and in some cases may even allow for concurrent responsibility because of a limbo status involving an ill-defined form of dual control.[46]

In addition, the UN is not in a position to become a party to the Geneva Conventions or Additional Protocols, as this would entail binding it to detailed provisions that are aimed at states and do not fit the role and function of an international organization.[47] Notwithstanding its international legal personality, the UN is not itself a state and thus, it does not possess the juridical or administrative powers to discharge many of the obligations laid down in the Conventions.[48] The ICRC has been instrumental in obtaining agreement from the UN that international forces acting under UN authority would do so in accordance with the

'principles and spirit' of relevant law.[49] But once a provision to this effect was
incorporated in the Regulations of the Force and in the agreements with troop
contributing states, it did not entail the direct responsibility of the UN to
ensure respect for humanitarian law by members of its forces. In this regard the
relatively recent UN Model Agreement with troop contributing states and the
Model SOFA between the UN and host states now include an express provision
to this effect.[50] Under that provision, the UN undertakes that the operations of
the force in question will be conducted with full respect for the principles and
spirit of the general international conventions applicable to the conduct of
military personnel.

The Secretary-General's Bulletin on the observance by UN forces of humanitarian
law does go some way towards addressing these problems.[51] It adds significant weight
to the ICRC position and it is important in terms of legal certainty by giving obligations
substance. Bulletins of this nature are intended to be legally binding on UN personnel,
in this case UN forces.[52] Section 1 of the Bulletin states that:

> The fundamental principles and rules of international humanitarian law set
> out in the present Bulletin are applicable to UN forces when in situations of
> armed conflict they are actively engaged therein as combatants, to the extent
> and for the duration of their engagement. They are accordingly applicable in
> enforcement actions, or in peacekeeping operations when the use of force is
> permitted in self-defence.

The categorization of UN troops as combatants in certain instances may seem
unusual, especially to troop contributing states. However, this Bulletin must be
judged in the context of the 1994 Convention on the Safety of UN and Associated
Personnel, and there is a problematic overlap in the respective regimes covered.
Both are incompatible because they are based on fundamentally different principles, the objective of the Convention being to protect UN personnel when not
engaged in combat type operations. The remit of humanitarian law is much
broader and respects the combatants' privilege to attack enemy forces once the
general rules of international law are followed. It is based on the cardinal
principle that combat forces are treated equally.

The Bulletin commits the UN to ensuring that military personnel are fully
acquainted with the rules of humanitarian law. It accepts corresponsibility with
the contributing states for this whether or not there is a SOFA. What liability
the UN may be subject to for breach of this duty is unclear. Most important,
however, is Section 4, to the effect that it is the responsibility of the national
courts to prosecute military personnel for violations of humanitarian law. This
means that the UN was not required to establish a special tribunal to consider
violations of humanitarian law by UN troops.[53]

Conclusion

Social and economic history demonstrates that often women have had to rely on
their bodies to support themselves and their dependents. The economic vulnerability of women and girls, and their lack of power in society, have contributed

to the problem. There would be no prostitution without demand.[54] This demand 'has been engendered in a context where masculinity and male sexuality is constructed through sexual prowess and appropriation of the female body, whereas simultaneously, female sexuality is controlled, denigrated and erased'.[55] In many countries the sex trade is increasingly taking on the guise of an ordinary sector of the economy. The UN must not facilitate this process in post-conflict societies where women can be most disempowered. The majority of states have based their public policy initiatives towards combating female sex trafficking on the 'three P's' strategy pioneered by the US government pursuant to the US President's Executive Memorandum of 1998 on Steps to Combat Violence Against Women and Trafficking in Women and Girls.[56] The core elements of the strategy are prevention, the protection of victims, and the prosecution of perpetrators. This too should be the basis of any UN policy adopted.

In order to address the issue of sexual exploitation by UN forces, no further regulations or directives are required. Zero tolerance of this and any related activity must involve holding perpetrators and their superiors responsible. That being said, superior officers cannot be held responsible for all acts of their subordinates, but the principles of command responsibility under international humanitarian law provide a template. Superiors or commanders must be accountable for action when they knew, or ought reasonably to have known, or in the case of civilians, consciously disregarded information which clearly indicated subordinates were engaging in such activities. Failure to cooperate with implementation and investigation should not be tolerated. The Zeid Report made recommendations for action on four broad fronts:

> Rules against sexual exploitation and abuse must be unified for all categories of peacekeeping personnel. A professional investigative process must be established and modern scientific methods of identification must be utilized. A series of organizational, managerial and command measures must be instituted to address sexual exploitation and abuse. A number of recommendations are made to ensure that peacekeeping personnel ... are held individually accountable... and that they are held financially accountable for the harm they have done to victims.[57]

Allegations of sexual abuse of minors and local women were also made against Irish soldiers serving with the UN mission in Ethiopia and Eritrea (UNMEE).[58] These were investigated, and a number of Irish soldiers were disciplined. However, the initial investigation by Italian *Carabinieri* was flawed, and conclusions were made on the basis of unreliable evidence of identification. Allegations of sexual relations with minors proved difficult to prove as it was not possible to establish with certainty the age of the victims. The disciplinary hearings took place in Ireland as the soldiers involved had completed their tour of duty by the time action was taken. This is a common problem with most troop contributing states as witnesses are often reluctant to travel abroad. If soldiers are rotated every six or 12 months, requiring disciplinary hearings to be held in the mission area is not always practical. The procedures put in place to investigate and prosecute wrongdoing must also ensure that the good name and reputation of innocent personnel is protected.

There seems to be little alternative to the present system whereby UN forces are prosecuted by their relevant national authorities. The real problem is to ensure that these do take place. Establishing a central monitoring system adapted to track the process and outcome is one means of addressing this problem. The Secretary-General's 2003 Bulletin on sexual misconduct should be binding on all categories of peacekeepers, and any transgression should constitute 'serious misconduct'. This, and the relevant rules and code of conduct should be made available in the language of all those participating in peacekeeping operations. In order to prosecute successfully, while at the same time respecting the rights of those against whom inaccurate or false allegations may be made, it is of the utmost importance to establish a professional investigative process.[59]

A grey area continues to exist in the nature of personal relationships entered into in the course of peacekeeping operations. In Haiti, many international female personnel became involved in relationships with local men.[60] This was not viewed as an abuse of power or exploitative in nature. UN and other personnel have been known to enter long-term relationships with local women and men, although such relationships may have the additional complication of family or similar commitments back home. This has been recognized in the Secretary-General's Bulletin which permits a Head of Department, Office or Mission to use their discretion where the circumstances justify doing so.[61]

On-site Courts-Martial should be standard. However, regular rotations of military personnel may mean that this is not a practical option. Disciplinary measures should involve financial penalties for transgressions, and the fines should be paid into a trust fund for victims. Although the UN does encounter difficulty obtaining troop contributions from states from time to time, this should not influence the decision to impose conditions on troop contributing countries. The selection process at national level for UN service is often inadequate or non-existent, and this has contributed to problems of corruption and improper behaviour in the mission area.[62]

The Officer of the High Commissioner for Human Rights has developed an important human rights training programme for peacekeepers. This 'training for trainers' is a vital element in promoting the human rights agenda in peacekeeping, and with that an awareness of the broader context of sexual exploitation. Gender awareness training is underfunded and rarely taken seriously by commanders.[63] Training strategies of this nature should be combined with practical measures in the field. In this regard the Zeid report recommended easing the living conditions of those in mission areas with improved access to internet and international telephone facilities, as well as curfews and designating areas to be out of bounds.

Each UN SOFA should contain an express reference to the relevant international human rights instruments. Even the EU SOMA with Macedonia referred to the protection of the environment and cultural heritages while making no mention of human rights.[64] Environments, it seems, outrank people in terms of priority and protection.

It is hard not to see this problem as linked to the overall failure of gender mainstreaming in peace operations and a failure to acknowledge the rights and interests of women in post-conflict situations in general.[65] The accusations of sexual abuse should not be used by those seeking to undermine the role of the UN in general. Human Rights Watch has stated that while it believes the UN needs to take urgent action to deal with those accused of sexual abuse, it is important that the issue not overshadow the important role that MONUC has played in trying to bring about peace in the DRC.[66] Furthermore, one local woman is reported to have said: 'Yes it's true that some girls have been raped by UN soldiers, but so many more have been brutally raped by other armed groups. Please focus on stopping this as it brings us so much pain and suffering'.[67] While UN troops must be held accountable, it is also important to make all perpetrators of sexual violence accountable and keep in mind that it is primarily a human rights issue. Programmes to assist those subject to exploitation are necessary, to include emergency medical care and psychological counselling and advice.

In September 2005 the UN announced it would replace the Ukraine contingent part of the UN force in South Lebanon due to 'significant financial misconduct'.[68] The UN should also name those countries whose troops have been engaged in sexual misconduct and make all internal reports available publicly. The UN is consistently short of peacekeepers for various missions, but this does not mean that it must accept troops whose behaviour is far more serious than financial misconduct. If proper measures are not taken by national authorities to address and prevent such misconduct, then the countries involved must not be allowed act in any capacity that provides an opportunity for further exploitative behaviour.

NOTES

1. Report of the Secretary-General, 'A Comprehensive Strategy to Eliminate Future Sexual Exploitation and Abuse in United Nations Peacekeeping Operations', UN Doc. A/59/10, 24 Mar. 2005 ('Zeid Report'), paras.2–4.
2. 'UN Reforms Aim to End Sexual Abuse by Peacekeepers', *Global Policy Forum*, 10 May 2005.
3. UNHCR and Save the Children UK, 'Sexual Violence and Exploitation: The Experience of Refugee Children in Guinea, Liberia & Sierra Leone', UNHCR Refugee Report, 2002.
4. 'Report of the Secretary General on the Activities of the Office of Internal Oversight Services Investigation in to Sexual Exploitation of Refugees by Aid Workers in West Africa' UN Doc. A/57/465 [3] 11 Oct., hereafter 'OIOS Refugee Report'.
5. UN Doc. ST/SGB/2003/13, 9 October 2003.
6. Interview with UN human rights officer, Kosovo, Aug. 2005.
7. Security Council Press Release SC/8400, 31 May 2005. See also Evelyn Leopold, 'UN turns on the heat in Congo abuse probe', *Reuters*, 21 Mar. 2005; 'UN action over DR Congo abuse', *BBC News*, 21 Mar. 2005.
8. UN Doc. A/60/640 Add 1, 29 Dec. 2005, Implementation of the recommendations of the Special Committee on Peacekeeping Operations, para.42.
9. Zeid Report (n.1 above), para.66.
10. UN Press Release SG/SM/9605 AFR/1069 PKO/115, 19 Nov. 2004.
11. *Global Policy Forum* (n.2 above) and Warren Hodge, 'Report Finds UN Isn't Moving to End Sex Abuse by Peacekeepers, *The New York Times*, 19 Oct. 2005.
12. See *Dishonoured Legacy, Report of the Commission of Enquiry into the Deployment of Canadian Forces to Somalia*, Ottowa, Canadian Government Publishing, 1997; *Africa Rights Report*, 'Somalia – Human Rights Abuses by the UN Forces', London, July 1993.
13. OIOS Refugee Report (n.4 above).

14. Zeid Report (n.1 above) and 'Investigation by the Office of Internal Oversight Services into allegations of sexual exploitation and abuse in the United Nations Organization Mission in the Democratic Republic of the Congo', UN doc., GA, A/59/661, 5 Jan. 2005, hereafter 'OIOS Monuc Report'.
15. See Walter G. Sharp, 'Protecting the Avatars of International Peace and Security', *Duke Journal of Comparative and International Law*, Vol.7, 1996, pp.92–183, at 112–43.
16. In addition, the Secretary-General endeavours to conclude SOFA with the host State governments. This is not always possible, for example, none was concluded in Somalia, and it took nearly 20 years to conclude a Status of Force Agreement in respect of UNIFIL. See generally Dieter Fleck and Michael Saalfeld, 'Combining efforts to improve the legal status of UN peacekeeping forces and their effective protection', *International Peacekeeping* (Kluwer), Vol.1, No.3, 1994, pp. 82–4.
17. This is outlined by Christopher Greenwood, 'International Humanitarian Law and United Nations Military Operations', *Yearbook of International Humanitarian Law*, Vol.1, Dordrecht: Kluwer, 1998, pp.3–34, at 30–31. Art.8, para.2 (d),iii, of the Statute of the International Criminal Court (ICC) also prohibits attacks on peacekeepers 'so long as they are entitled to the protection given to civilians or civilian objects under the international law of armed conflict', see Otto Triffterer (ed.) *Commentary on the Rome Statue of the International Criminal Court*, Baden-Baden: Nomos Verl.-Ges., 1999, pp.277–8.
18. Convention on the Elimination of All Forms of Discrimination Against Women (CEDAW) GA Res 34/180, 34 UN GAOR Supp (No46) 193, UN Doc A/34/46 entered into force 3 September 1981. In December 1993, the UN General Assembly adopted a Declaration on the Elimination of Violence Against Women, the UN has also appointed a Special Rapporteur and the General Assembly adopted an Optional Protocol providing for an individual complaint mechanism.
19. S/RES/1325 (2000). See 'Women, Peace and Security' Study submitted to the Secretary-General pursuant to Security Council Resolution 1325 (2000) and the Declaration on the Protection of Women and Children in Emergency and Armed Conflict GA Res. 3318 (XXIX), 29 UN GAOR Supp (No 31) 146, UN Doc A/9631 (1974).
20. Convention on the Rights of the Child (CRC) GA Res 44/25, 44 UN GAOR Supp (No.49) 167, UN Doc A/44/49 (1989) entered into force 2 September 1990.
21. Human Rights Committee, Comments on United States of America, para.19, UN Doc. CCPR/C/79/Add 50, 1995; John Cerone, 'Reasonable measures in unreasonable circumstances: a legal responsibility framework for human rights violations in post-conflict territories under UN administration', in Nigel D. White and Dirk. Klassen (eds), *The UN, Human Rights and Post-conflict Situations*, Manchester: Manchester University Press, 2005, pp.42–80, at p.46.
22. Ibid., para.11.
23. Human Rights Watch Statement to Committee on International Relations, US House of Representatives, Washington DC, 1 Mar. 2005.
24. The Secretary-General's Bulletin on special measures for the protection from sexual exploitation and sexual abuse, ST/SGB/2003/13, 9 Oct. 2003, hereafter 'Sexual Exploitation Bulletin', Sect.2.1.
25. Ibid., Sect.2.2
26. Secretary-General's Bulletin on Observance by UN forces of international humanitarian law, UN Doc ST/SGB/1993/3, 6 Aug. 1999, hereafter 'Bulletin on IHL'. See Marten Zwanenburg, 'The Secretary-General's Bulletin on Observance by United Nations Forces of International Humanitarian Law: Some Preliminary Observations', *International Peacekeeping* (Kluwer), Vol.5, Parts 4–5, 1999, pp.133–9.
27. OIOS MONUC Report (n.14 above), para.22.
28. Ibid., para.46.
29. OIOS MONUC Report (n.14 above), para.56.
30. Nigel D. White and Dirk Klassen, 'An Emerging Legal Regime', in White and Klassen (eds), (n.21 above), p.7; Boris Kondoch, 'Human Rights Law and UN Peace Operations in Post-conflict Situations', in White and Klassen, p.36.
31. Florian Hoffmann and Frédéric Mégret, 'Fostering Human Rights Accountability: An Ombudsperson for the United Nations? *Global Governance*, Vol.11, No.1, 2005, pp.43–6.
32. See UN Doc. E/CN.4/2001/73, 23 Jan. 2001 and UN Doc. A/51/306, 9 Sept. 1996.
33. UN Doc. A/55/163-/S/2000712, 19 July 2000.
34. Carla Bongiorno, 'A Culture of Impunity: Applying International Human Rights Law to the United Nations in East Timor', *Columbia Human Rights Law Review*, Vol.33, 2002, pp.623–92, at p.679.
35. Hoffmann and Mégret (n.31 above), p.53.

36. Zeid Report (n.1 above).
37. Ibid., para.89.
38. Ray Murphy, 'United Nations Military Operations and International Humanitarian Law: What Rules Apply to Peacekeepers?', *Criminal Law Forum – An International Journal*, Vol.14, No.2, 2003, pp.153–94.
39. Zeid Report (n.1 above), para.88.
40. Chittharajan F. Amerasinghe, *Principles of the institutional law of international organization*, Cambridge: Cambridge University Press, 1996, pp.92–3. See also Brian D. Tittemore, 'Belligerents in Blue Helmets: Applying International Humanitarian Law to United Nations Peace Operations', *Stanford Journal of International Law*, Vol.33, 1997, pp.61–117 at pp.92–5.
41. ICJ Reports, Vol.76, 1980, p.90.
42. Amerasinghe (n.40 above), pp.240–41.
43. See UN Doc A/CN.4/195 and Add.1, 7 April 1967. The principal claimant was the Belgian government. Despite the nature of the authorization to use force in the ONUC operation, the ICJ found that it 'did not involve "preventive or enforcement" measures against any State under Chapter VII', *Advisory Opinion on Certain Expenses of the United Nations*, ICJ Reports, Vol.177, 1962. See David W. Bowett, *United Nations Forces*, London: Stevens, 1964, pp.175–80.
44. Amerasinghe (n.40 above), p.242; René Jean Dupuy (ed.), *A Handbook on International Organizations*, Dordrecht: Martinus Nijhoff, 2nd edn, 1998, p.891. The UN has acknowledged liability for activities carried out by both UNEF and ONUC.
45. Ibid., 243; Finn Seyersted, 'United Nations Forces: Some Legal Problems', *British Yearbook of International Law*, Vol.37, 1961, pp.362, 421.
46. See *Nissan v. Attorney General* [1968] 1 Queens Bench 286, and [1969] 1 All England Reports 629; and Ian Brownlie, 'Decisions of British Courts during 1968 Involving Questions of International Law', *British Yearbook of International Law*, Vol.42, 1968–69, p.217.
47. On the question of treaty making powers, see Amerasinghe (n.40 above), pp102–3.
48. *Reparations Case* [1949] ICJ Rep., p.174.
49. Umesh Palwankar, 'Applicability of International Humanitarian Law to UN Peacekeeping Forces', *International Review of the Red Cross*, Vol.80, 1993, pp.227–40, at pp.229–33. A provision to this effect was incorporated into the UNEF, ONUC and UNFICYP Force Regulations. As no Regulations were adopted in respect of UNIFIL, no such provision exists for that force.
50. Daphna Shraga and Ralph Zacklin, 'The Applicability of International Humanitarian Law to United Nations Peacekeeping Operations: Conceptual, Legal and Practical Issues, *Report on a Symposium on Humanitarian Action and Peacekeeping Operations, June 22–24 Geneva*, Geneva: ICRC, 1994, p.44. The Model Agreement with troop contributors contains the following provision: '[The UN peacekeeping operation] shall observe and respect the principles and spirit of the general international conventions applicable to the conduct of military personnel. The international conventions referred to above include the four Geneva Conventions of 12 August 1949 and their Additional Protocols of 8 June 1977 and the UNESCO Convention of 14 May 1954 on the Protection of Cultural Property in the event of armed conflict. [The Participating State] shall therefore ensure that the members of its national contingent serving ... be fully acquainted with the principles and spirit of the conventions.'
51. Bulletin on IHL (n.26 above).
52. Interview with official, UN Legal Division, New York, Dec. 2000. Bulletins were described as part of the UN 'internal law, binding within the Organization's own legal system'.
53. The Security Council proposed on 22 December 2000 that the Special Court for Sierra Leone have jurisdiction over crimes committed by peacekeepers or related personnel, where the state that had sent the relevant personnel was unwilling or genuinely unable to carry out an investigation or prosecution, see *Amnesty International, Sierra Leone – Renewed commitment needed to end impunity*, 24 Sept. 2001, para.3.6.
54. Norma Hotaling and Leslie Levitas-Martin, 'Increased Demand Resulting in the Flourishing Recruitment and Trafficking of Women and Girls: Related Child Sexual Abuse and Violence Against Women', *Hastings Women's Law Journal*, Vol.13, p.121.
55. Vednita Carter and Evelina Giobbe, 'Duet: Prostitution, Racism and Feminist Discourse', *Hastings Women's Law Journal*, Vol.10, 1999, p.37.
56. US Executive Memorandum, 'Steps to Combat Violence Against Women and Trafficking in Women and Girls', Office of the Press Secretary, The White House, Washington, 11 Mar. 1998.
57. Zeid Report (n.1 above), para.94.
58. Interviews with Irish officers who served with UNMEE, July/August 2005.

59. Zeid Report (n.1 above), paras.90–93.
60. Interview with former UN human rights officer in Haiti, Dublin, May 2005.
61. Sexual Exploitation Bulletin (n.24 above), para.4.5.
62. Interview with senior staff member, DPKO, New York, May 2005.
63. Nadine Puechguirbal, 'Gender Training for Peacekeepers: Lessons from the DRC', *International Peacekeeping*, Vol.10, 2003, pp.113–28; Sandra Whitworth, *Men, Militarism and UN Peacekeeping: A Gendered Analysis*, Boulder, CU: Lynne Rienner, 2004. see also, Louise Olsson and Thorunn L. Tryggestad (eds), *Women and International Peacekeeping*, London: Frank Cass, 2001.
64. 'Agreement between the European Union and the Former Yugoslav Republic of Macedonia on the status of the European Union-led forces in the Former Yugoslav Republic of Macedonia', *Official Journal of the European Union*, 29 Mar. 2003, L 82/46–51.
65. Windhoek Declaration and the Namibia Plan of Action on 'Mainstreaming a Gender Perspective in Multinational Peace Operations, 31 May 2000 and European Parliament resolution on participation of women in peaceful conflict resolution (2000/2025(INI)), A5-0308/2000, 30 Nov. 2000, para.O.
66. Human Rights Watch (n.23 above).
67. Ibid.
68. AFP report, 6 September 2005.

Integration of Human Rights in Peace Operations: Is There an Ideal Model?

KATARINA MÅNSSON

> We have improved coordination to some degree, but with human rights, not as well as we would have liked... Human rights have not been fused as well as they should have been within the mission. It also seems to me that institutions have tended to keep comparative advantages for themselves which has not been good for the mission as a whole.[1]

This statement by a senior official of the United Nations Interim Administration in Kosovo (UNMIK) highlights the challenge of contemporary peace operations to effectively integrate human rights within its various components.[2] Although Security Council Resolution 1244 (1999) identified 'the protection and promotion of human rights' as a main responsibility of UNMIK,[3] the question remains to what extent this has been implemented in practice. The above quotation raises pivotal questions about the conduciveness of UNMIK's institutional design for integrating human rights in the various elements of the mission. The 'integrated' model of UNMIK may have failed with respect to human rights. This is disquieting for two reasons. First, UNMIK has operated as the de facto government in Kosovo since 1999. Second, the 'integrated mission' concept was developed specifically for UNMIK as a means to ensure effective cohesion and division of labour between the UN, Organization for Security and Cooperation in Europe (OSCE) and other actors responsible for implementing Resolution 1244.[4]

The gap between ambitious human rights mandates in Security Council resolutions and the difficulty of operationalizing them implies that any examination of the integration of human rights in peace operations must consider the integration processes unfolding at both the *macro* (decision-making) and *micro* (operational)

levels and the (lack of) synergy between the two.[5] This interplay has been referred
to as the 'human rights trail': human rights must be discernible 'from the legal
principles of UN law, through the mandates, down to the promotion and protection of human rights on the ground'.[6]

Integration of human rights in peace operations has developed in parallel to
the concept of 'integrated missions'. 'Integration' has been hailed as the
'guiding principle' of UN peace operations and a recent UN document defines
an integrated mission' as follows:

> An Integrated Mission is one in which there is a *shared vision* among all UN
> actors as to the strategic objective of the UN presence at country level [...].
> An Integrated Mission is one in which the structure is derived from an
> *in-depth understanding* of the specific country setting; of the evolving secur-
> ity, political, humanitarian, *human rights* and development imperatives in
> that particular country...[7]

At the UN Secretariat, this first found expression in the integrated mission task
forces (IMTF), recommended by the Brahimi Report as 'the standard vehicle
for mission-specific planning and support'.[8] The task forces were intended to
remedy the absence of an integrated planning or support cell in the Department
of Peacekeeping Operations (DPKO) where those in charge of issues such as political analysis, military operations, civilian police, electoral assistance, and human
rights were represented.[9] The first application of the IMTFs occurred in the
context of the United Nations Assistance Mission in Afghanistan (UNAMA) in
2001.[10] Assessments suggest that this and later task forces never fully realized
their potential, beset by similar problems as the Integrated Mission Planning
Process set up internally within DPKO.[11]

It remains a tremendous challenge to get human rights to penetrate peace operations because the issue is imbued with political sensitivities and institutional
hurdles. This article outlines the advances from the 1990s made in this endeavour,
without claiming to measure the extent to which peace operations have failed or
succeeded in protecting or promoting human rights.[12] Here, the working definition of integration refers to policies or structures put in place to ensure that
human rights concerns are considered within a mission. The article starts by
exploring the legal and political framework relevant to the legitimate role of
human rights in UN peace operations. An analysis of the extent to which
human rights have been considered at the macro (UN Headquarters) and micro
(field) levels of peace operations then follows. The role played by the Office of
the High Commissioner for Human Rights (OHCHR) will be examined throughout the discussion – in line with its mandate as the 'lead agency' on human rights
issues within the UN system.

The Legal and Political Setting

Two instruments in the UN context particularly are relevant to the integration of
human rights in peace operations: the UN Charter and the Office of the High
Commissioner for Human Rights.

The UN Charter

The UN Charter is a key document and starting point in considering the integration of human rights in UN peace operations. According to the Charter, three of the UN's purposes are:

1(1) To maintain international peace and security, and to that end ... to bring about by peaceful means, in conformity with the *principles of justice* and *international law*, adjustment or settlement of international disputes or situations which might lead to a breach of the peace;

1(2) To develop friendly relations among nations based on respect for the principles of equal rights and *self-determination of peoples*, and *to take appropriate action to strengthen universal peace*;

1(3) To achieve *international co-operation* ... in *promoting and encouraging respect for human rights* and for fundamental freedoms for all without distinction [emphasis added].

Interpreted broadly, these purposes constitute a 'constitutional requirement' of the UN to integrate human rights considerations in all activities, in particular those related to peace and security.[13] Paragraph 1(1) may be read as an obligation of the UN to ensure that the deployment, conduct and activities of peace operations *comply* with international human rights law; paragraph 1(2) as the obligation of peace operations to facilitate the *implementation* of the right of peoples to self-determination;[14] and 1(3) as an obligation of peace operations *to act* for the promotion and respect for international human rights law. Read in conjunction with Art 55 of the Charter, which sets out that the UN shall promote universal respect for and observance of human rights with a view to create peaceful relations among states, the Charter accords the UN both a moral and legal mandate to integrate human rights in peace operations.

Article 1(3) deserves particular attention. It suggests that peace operations may not only advance respect for individual human rights but also enhance international cooperation. Human rights-sensitive peace operations can, and should, further the common understanding of human rights as universal legal entitlements and, as a consequence, improve inter-state relations. This reasoning holds that there is a direct link between equal rights of nations (a principle of the UN) and individual rights (a purpose of the UN): universal rights are not feasible without international social, economic and political equality among nations.[15]

The requirement of the UN to integrate human rights within peace operations stems also from the inherent nature of human rights and the delegation of responsibility from member states to the UN.[16] Closely related is the issue of applicability of international human rights law to UN operations and the legal responsibility and accountability of UN military and civilian personnel deployed in a post-conflict situation.[17] Of interest here, however, is the evolution through which human rights have gradually come to be incorporated in peace operations and to analyse whether different institutional structures of integration may affect substantive integration of human rights.

The High Commissioner for Human Rights and UN Reform Process

Two processes have been essential in furthering the cause of human rights in peace operations: The establishment of the UN High Commissioner for Human Rights, including the creation of OHCHR (as the High Commissioner's Office merged with the UN Centre for Human Rights in 1997), and the UN reform process. The 1993 Vienna Declaration and Programme of Action proposed the creation of a High Commissioner and recommended increased coordination in support of human rights within the UN system.[18] The *traveaux préparatoires* of the Vienna Conference indicate that some delegations favoured an active role for the UN Centre for Human Rights in the field of peace and security.[19] The Vienna Declaration gave effect to the proposal:

> *Recognizing* the important role of human rights components in specific arrangements concerning some peacekeeping operations, recommends that the Secretary-General take into account the reporting, experience and capabilities of the Centre for Human Rights and human rights mechanisms, in conformity with the Charter of the United Nations.[20]

When the General Assembly shortly thereafter established the mandate of the High Commissioner, no explicit authority was bestowed upon the Commissioner to ensure that human rights would permeate all activities of the UN. Nor were matters related to peace and security mentioned. Recognition of the mutually reinforcing relationship between human rights and peacekeeping had, however, been made in *An Agenda for Peace* one year earlier. This stressed the need for all functional elements of the UN to share the responsibility of the Security Council in the maintenance of international peace and security since 'each has a special and indispensable role to play in an *integrated approach* to human security'.[21] It also identified that efforts to promote human rights were essential to the consolidation of peace.[22] While Boutros-Boutros Ghali later reaffirmed the importance of integrating human rights in peacebuilding processes, he was initially opposed to the idea of a High Commissioner for Human Rights.[23] The choice of diplomat José Ayala-Lasso as first High Commissioner reflected the Secretary-General's caution.[24] Mirroring a non-confrontational approach to human rights, one of Ayala-Lasso's priorities was to increase cooperation within the UN system in order to ensure a 'coherent, coordinated and complementary approach' to human rights. Human rights were, as a result, included as a separate item on the agenda of the Administrative Committee on Coordination for the first time in 1994.[25] Ayala-Lasso was furthermore instrumental in launching the first major OHCHR human rights field operation in support of a peace operation, the Human Rights Field Operation in Rwanda (HRFOR).[26]

If Boutros-Ghali laid the foundations for human rights integration in peace operations, Kofi Annan entrenched it. Under his leadership, human rights were made a cross-cutting issue to be mainstreamed within the primary strategic areas of the UN, including peace and security.[27] Annan mandated OHCHR to 'stimulate and coordinate action for human rights throughout the UN system'.[28] He commissioned the Brahimi Report, which recommended that OHCHR coordinate and institutionalize human rights fieldwork in peace operations.[29] These achievements culminated in the landmark report *In Larger Freedom* in 2005 which acknowledged the interrelationship between development, security and human rights.[30] The report underlined the need for the High Commissioner to play a more active role in the deliberations of the Security Council, particularly regarding the implementation of relevant provisions in Security Council resolutions.[31] Later at the 2005 World Summit, all UN member states resolved to 'integrate the promotion and protection of human rights into national policies and to support the further mainstreaming of human rights throughout the UN system, as well as closer cooperation between the Office of the High Commissioner for Human Rights and all relevant United Nations bodies'.[32] Louise Arbour, present High Commissioner, referred to this commitment as 'the first clear, broad-based, and high-level intergovernmental mandate for mainstreaming human rights throughout the UN system'.[33] Political will, resources, and expertise, however, are required to give effect to this mandate. According to OHCHR staff, the Brahimi recommendations were made 'without the institutional limitations of the Office in mind'. And while OHCHR's initial response to the recommendations by OHCHR was positive, any importance attached to the Brahimi proposals appears to have vanished after 2002. The posts originally intended for OHCHR to give effect to the recommendations were then: 'basically situated ... in DPKO and the person in that post will [first] look after the interests of DPKO and [second] after the interests of OHCHR'.[34] According to another staff member of the Office, 'mainstreaming human rights within the UN system has asked the OHCHR to spread itself so thin to be able to do everything so that it will be able to do very little'.[35] The latter view embraces a key conundrum of human rights integration: which human rights will be integrated and within which actors in the UN system? Who decides on areas of priority? How do we measure whether integration is successful or not? Should one develop a list of indicators to this aim?

The importance attached to human rights in the field of peace and security by Annan came to fruition in November 2005 when his Policy Committee issued a decision on 'Human Rights in Integrated Missions'. It set out that all UN entities have a responsibility to ensure that human rights are promoted and protected through and within their operations in the field.

Integration at UN Headquarters (Macro level)

The following section explores how human rights have been taken into account in the main decision- and policy making bodies concerned with matters of peace and security at UN Headquarters. Focus here is on the Security Council, the DPKO, the Department of Political Affairs (DPA), the Executive Committee on Peace and Security (ECPS), and the Special Committee on Peacekeeping Operations, though others are also involved.[36] Corresponding efforts at the field level will subsequently be discussed.

The Security Council

The inclusion of human rights provisions in Security Council resolutions is pivotal in two respects. First, it determines the human rights mandate of a peace operation. Second, it renders peace operations an interesting tool by which the status of international human rights law in international politics can be assessed. Of relevance to both aspects is that the Council consistently avoids referring to international human rights law *per se*. The Council has repeatedly condemned violations of international humanitarian law and authorized reporting on such violations since early 1990s.[37] With respect to '*international* human rights law', however, it is silent. Resolution 1181 (1998) establishing United Nations Observer Mission in Liberia (UNOMSIL) serves as an interesting illustration. This was the second time that the Council explicitly provided a human rights mandate in a resolution establishing a peace operation.[38] Resolution 1181 decided that UNOMSIL should:

> report on violations of *international humanitarian law* and *human rights* in Sierra Leone, and, in consultation with the relevant UN agencies, to assist the Govt of Sierra Leone in its efforts to address the country's human rights *needs* [and demanded] ...that all factions and forces in Sierra Leone strictly respect the status of UNOMSIL personnel ... and that they respect *human rights* and abide by applicable rules of *international humanitarian law*.[39]

Subsequent Council resolutions establishing multidimensional peace operations use similar language.[40] Improvement has been made compared to the early 1990s when reference to human rights was avoided altogether,[41] and since 1998 the Council does refer to 'human rights law'. Such references, however, are made only in conjunction with the one or two (or both) of the other bodies of international law concerned with the protection of the individual: international refugee law and international humanitarian law. A recurring formula is that of 'Reaffirming the need for both parties to fulfil their obligations under international law, including international humanitarian, refugee and human rights law.'[42] This could reflect an inclination of the Council to accord international human rights law equal status as to that of international humanitarian law. But in condemning violations of human rights, or calling for adherence to human rights, the Council still avoids the use of explicit legal language. Why: is it a sign that state sovereignty still trumps the protection of individual rights, or does the Council attempt to avoid accountability, for instance in missions like UNMIK and UNTAET? The importance of referring to international human rights obligations and standards resides in the fact that it leaves no doubt as to which rights are intended. Express provisions of international human rights law also provide a legal framework for both UN and local actors and can, in addition, constitute an important incentive for the ratification of international human rights instruments.

The inclusion of express provisions on 'human rights' in Security Council resolutions since 1998 occurred in tandem with its official recognition of the importance of including peacebuilding elements in the mandates of peacekeeping operations.[43] In 1998, the Executive Committee on Peace and Security endorsed a set of guidelines on the integration of human rights in conflict prevention, peacemaking, peacekeeping, peacebuilding, and humanitarian activities.[44] These events can be construed as constituting a basis for Security Council resolutions to formally outline the mandate for human rights components. Prior to 1998, the Council often merely endorsed and approved the report of the Secretary-General as a means of determining the mandate of a peace operation, including its human rights responsibilities. This appears to signal an enhanced role for the Security Council and a weaker role for the Secretary-General and the UN Secretariat in determining the scope and responsibilities of peace operations. When comparing, for instance, the Secretary-General's suggestions as to the tasks of a peace operation in Burundi and the subsequent Security Council resolution establishing the UN Operation in Burundi (ONUB) in 2004, one finds that several tasks of high importance to human rights protection were omitted by the Council: to monitor human rights; advocate and intervene with local and national authorities to protect civilians and vulnerable groups; provide training for peacekeepers and the civilian police component; and, importantly, integrate human rights and protection of civilians into the overall work of the mission.[45]

Briefings by the High Commissioner for Human Rights for members of the Security Council constitute another important aspect of human rights integration. Initiated during Mary Robinson's tenure in office,[46] this practice has been institutionalized into monthly briefings by OHCHR before the Council. An interesting example of how briefings by the High Commissioner can result in concrete measures in the field relates to the situation in the Democratic Republic of the Congo (DRC). After a call directed to the High Commissioner in a Presidential Security Council statement, the High Commissioner's field office in the DRC undertook a joint mission with the UN Mission in the Congo (MONUC) to investigate the circumstances of the Kisangani massacres of May 2002.[47] Following a second briefing by the High Commissioner, the Council authorized MONUC to assist the Congolese parties in investigating serious violations of international humanitarian law and human rights.[48] This provided the basis for MONUC's multidisciplinary human rights investigation missions in cooperation with OHCHR. An example in 2005 was the call by Louise Arbour for urgent action by the Security Council in Sudan after the findings of the International Commission of Inquiry on Darfur and the subsequent establishment of UNMIS.[49]

The DPKO and the DPA

Prior to the establishment of DPKO and DPA in 1992, peace operations were serviced in an ad hoc manner by the old service bureaucracies for the General Assembly and the Security Council.[50] The formal division of responsibilities between the two departments today is such that DPA focuses on preventive diplomacy, conflict prevention and peacemaking as the lead department for political and peacebuilding while DPKO focuses on the design, deployment and day-to-day operational aspects of all peacekeeping operations.[51] Both are headed by an Under-Secretary-General, tasked to advise the Secretary-General, liaise with member states, vet reports on peace operations for the Secretary-General's approval, and brief the Security Council.[52]

Given that DPKO is 'the operational arm of the Secretariat for all UN peace-keeping operations',[53] it is surprising that DPKO still has no staff tasked to deal specifically with human rights. Instead, DPKO relies on OHCHR for support on human rights issues, as set out in the Memorandum of Understanding (MoU) from 1999.[54] This stresses that 'a unified United Nations approach [to human rights and peace and security] is essential to the fulfilment of these two Charter-mandated areas'. Rwanda remains a tragic case where the lack of such unified approach resulted in catastrophe. The Independent Inquiry on Rwanda was critical of the ignorance of the UN Assistance Mission in Rwanda (UNAMIR) of a report by the UN Special Rapporteur on Extrajudicial, Summary or Arbitrary Executions that had warned of imminent genocide.[55] In this respect, the Inquiry considered that 'responsibility for this oversight in the planning of UNAMIR [lay] with the parts of the UN Secretariat concerned, in particular the Centre for Human Rights and DPKO'.[56]

The MoU provides a framework for cooperation and coordination between DPKO and OHCHR in the areas of planning, design and establishment of human rights components, reporting and public statements, administration and funding, training, information exchange, and joint activities.[57] Among its more important provisions is the participation of OHCHR in the integrated mission task forces and in DPKO preparatory missions. Far-reaching also is the provision that sets out that 'the SRSG or Head of the peace-keeping operation shall ensure that all staff of the operation – whether military or civilian – are aware of, and abide by, international human rights and humanitarian law standards'.[58] A serious flaw is that the MoU fails to address the question as to how these ambitious arrangements materialize in operations with no human rights components. Such operations then lack an agreement to ensure human rights training to all mission staff or that reports are copied both to both OHCHR and the SRSG.

The calls for system-wide attention to human rights are likewise lost in oper-ational structures as those of UNMIK, where the human rights component is run by a regional organization and NATO in charge of the peacekeeping troops. Fur-thermore, it leaves unsaid how implementation of the MoU is enforced and updated. Due to these shortcomings, a designated human rights unit within DPKO could greatly improve integration.[59] Another solution may be the second-ment of OHCHR personnel to DPKO or, as suggested by OHCHR staff, a stand-ing committee with members of DPKO and OHCHR meeting regularly. Although the UN Secretariat by January 2006 had expertise in gender, HIV/AIDS and dis-armament, demobilization and reintegration, human rights still does not figure as a cross-cutting substantive issue.[60] Interviews with OHCHR staff who have served in peace operations suggest, however, that desk officers at DPKO at times provide more support and feedback to the field than OHCHR Headquarters in Geneva. Personal contacts and information sharing thus appear to constitute, in mid-2006, a primary means of integrating human rights within UN departments such as DPKO.

No corresponding MoU has been concluded between OHCHR and DPA.[61] While there seems to be a general acceptance in DPA of the mutually reinforcing relationship between peace and human rights, its lack of a formal human rights policy runs contrary to the recognition of human rights as part of peacebuilding (*An Agenda for Peace*) and of the nexus between development, security and human rights (*In Larger Freedom*). Such omission becomes even more obsolete in view of the call to the High Commissioner to play an active role in the newly created Peacebuilding Commission.[62]

Two other factors stress the need for a human rights-sensitive DPA. First, DPA is responsible for assisting the Secretary-General 'in the discharge of his responsibilities under the Charter relating to the maintenance and restoration of peace and security'.[63] Second, the Head of DPA also chairs the Executive Committee on Peace and Security. If given a formal human rights mandate, DPA could, in this capacity, enhance integration of human rights in strategies and policies with respect to peace and security-related activities of the UN.

The Executive Committee on Peace and Security (ECPS) and the Special Committee on Peacekeeping Operations

While the Special Committee on Peacekeeping Operations has a long-standing history in the UN Secretariat since its establishment in 1965, the Executive Committee on Peace and Security (ECPS) is a child of Kofi Annan's reform process in 1997. Four executive committees were then established to facilitate coherence in the five core activities of the UN, human rights being the cross-cutting activity.[64] Human rights issues are formally integrated in ECPS through the active participation of OHCHR.[65] OHCHR is mandated to assess the work carried out on human rights issues in the Executive Committees and to regularly participate in every stage of the Organization's activities in relation to actual or potential conflict or post-conflict situations that have a human rights situation.[66] This role of OHCHR was highlighted as 'one of the objectives' of the reorganization of the UN Secretariat.[67] The first task force created by ECPS, in 1998, was indeed on the integration of human rights into efforts for conflict resolution, peacemaking, peacekeeping and peacebuilding, which endorsed the guidelines on integration of human rights referred to earlier.[68] Importantly, they set out that substantive guidelines on human rights 'should be developed between OHCHR, DPKO and *DPA* for the reporting by human rights components or advisers within peacekeeping or political missions'.[69]

The Special Committee on Peacekeeping Operations is mandated to undertake annual comprehensive reviews of the whole question of peacekeeping operations in all their aspects. It is the sole universal body providing recommendations to the Secretary-General, UN Secretariat, DPKO and member states on issues and policy relating to peacekeeping operations.[70] With this in mind, the Special Committee maintains a highly conservative view on human rights: 'Peacekeeping operations should not be used as a substitute for addressing the root causes of conflict. Those causes should be addressed in a coherent, well-planned, coordinated and comprehensive manner, using political, social and developmental instruments'.[71] This position goes hand in hand with the Committee's emphasis on sovereignty, territorial integrity and political independence of States and non-interference as principles crucial to the success of peace operations.[72] The Committee has supported the idea of dedicated capacities in DPKO for gender issues and disarmament, demobilization and reintegration, public information, humanitarian affairs and safety and security – but not human rights.[73] Closer interaction between OHCHR and the Special Committee could be beneficial to address such an omission. Judging from the lists of briefings received at the Committee's substantive sessions, no visits by the High Commissioner or her Office have been made. This is yet another argument why OHCHR urgently needs to reinforce its New York presence which could compensate for its geo-political confinement to Geneva.

Integration in the Field (Micro level)

Since the beginning of 1990s, the meaning of integration of human rights in peace operations has moved from that of physically deploying human rights experts within missions ('structural integration') to the expectation that all activities of peace operations are human rights compliant and pro-active ('substantive integration'). The difference is significant, particularly when considering that states still seem to prioritize certain principles of the UN (non-interference in domestic affairs) before certain purposes (promotion of human rights). Until the integrated mission concept was officially embraced, human rights figured at the operational level of peace operations primarily through four guises: human rights field operations, civilian police components, human rights components and human rights experts. UNMIK and UNAMA have added a fifth dimension: Senior Advisers on Human Rights to the SRSG. These models will be discussed briefly below.

Human Rights Field Operations

While a number of operations fall under this definition,[74] the meaning here relates to deployments that started as 'stand alone' human rights missions, but which later merged with or operated in parallel to multidimensional peace operations or international military forces. The UN Observer Mission in El Salvador (ONUSAL, 1991–95), the International Civil Mission in Haiti (MICIVIH, 1993–98) and the UN Human Rights Verification Mission in Guatemala (MINUGUA, 1994–99), the Human Rights Field Operation in Rwanda (HRFOR, 1994-98) and the human rights field operations in Bosnia and Herzegovina (BiH) constitute the main human rights field operations to date.[75] MICIVH, HRFOR and the operations in Bosnia operated in parallel to the military operations throughout their deployment.

Civilian Police Components

The UN Observer Mission in Mozambique (UNOMOZ, 1992–95) encompassed no human rights field officers; instead a civilian police component was mandated to monitor respect for political and civil rights, as part of its responsibility to ensure the holding of free and fair elections. Complaints of violations by

Mozambique police or security forces were investigated by CIVPOL and forwarded to a National Police Affairs Commission.[76] Reflecting the significance attached to this task, Mozambique was first to benefit from in situ training for UN peacekeepers by the UN Centre for Human Rights.[77] The International Police Task Force (IPTF) in Bosnia, constituting the main component of the UN Mission in BiH (UNMIBH), also had specific human rights tasks.[78]

Human Rights Experts

Some peace operations during the 1990s did not encompass distinct human rights components, but included experts dedicated to protect and promote human rights. The UN Observer Mission to Liberia (UNOMIL, 1993–97) appears never to have exceeded three human rights officers tasked with investigative, reporting and capacity-building functions.[79] The human rights monitoring mandate of the UN Confidence Restoration Operation in Croatia (UNCRO, 1995–96) was undertaken by four human rights action teams led by the UN Centre for Human Rights.[80] The only specific human rights element of the UN Protection Force (UNPROFOR, 1992–95) consisted of six human rights officers, also fielded by the Centre for Human Rights for the purpose of assisting the UN Special Rapporteur on the human rights situation in the former Yugoslavia.

Human Rights Components (Units/Sections/Offices/Divisions)

As mentioned above, ONUSAL and MINUGUA later evolved into multidimensional peace operations inclusive of human rights components working alongside the military and police. The UN Transitional Administration in Cambodia (UNTAC, 1991–92) was the first peace operation to include a human rights component alongside other substantive components at the outset. In this sense, UNTAC preceded contemporary operations in that it embodied the most common institutional formula of integrating human rights within peace operations. Regrettably, peace operations also appear to have inherited UNTAC's restricted number of human rights officers. Compared to the more than 100 officers deployed in Rwanda and Haiti, UNTAC initially encompassed ten human rights officers. This decision was, paradoxically, justified in the name of integration: 'The number of human rights officers required may be modest, since all UNTAC staff, operating in all areas of the mandate, would be charged with carrying out human rights functions, as an integral part of their primary duties'.[81] Varying in name, scope and operational set-up, human rights offices/sections/units/divisions/departments have been established as part of peace operations or observer missions in Somalia, Angola, Georgia, Eastern Slavonia, Sierra Leone, Kosovo, East Timor, DRC, Ethiopia/Eritrea, Afghanistan, Côte d'Ivoire, Burundi, Haiti and the Sudan.

Senior Adviser on Human Rights

One of the latest development in the quest for human rights integration is the establishment of Senior Advisers on Human Rights to the SRSG. First tried out in UNMIK,[82] the concept is best known from Afghanistan. UNAMA's unified structure under the leadership of the SRSG, supported by a Senior Adviser on Human Rights, would ensure that 'a rights-based and gender-sensitive approach ... be integrated fully into the UN activities in Afghanistan'.[83] Today, however, all heads of human rights components also act in the capacity as senior human rights advisers to the SRSG as well as representatives of the High Commissioner.[84]

Given this plethora of institutional designs, the attendant question is: what model serves human rights best? In other words, what structural integration serves substantive integration in the mission best? Does structure matter at all? At a general level, this is virtually an unanswerable question. First of all, each mission operates in its own unique circumstances, necessitating unique responses. Second, external as well as internal factors influence the degree to which human rights concerns will permeate an operation. Some operations benefit from operational support from stand-alone OHCHR field offices (ONUB and MONUC). Some police or military components have more substantial human rights predeployment training than others. In addition, recent operations also include specific expertise on the rights of children and women as well as on the rule of law and HIV/AIDS. One conclusion, however, may be that if a human rights field presence is deployed it should constitute an integral part of the peace operation, excluding operations such as HRFOR in Rwanda. According to a OHCHR employee: 'Of course you pay a price in becoming part of the operation, but in my view the price can never be too high if this entails that you have influence. Therefore it is better to be inside than outside'.[85] More difficult is whether the human rights component model or the Senior Adviser model is more conducive to substantive human rights integration. On the one hand, you risk the Kosovo experience where human rights become sidelined as 'the task of the OSCE'. On the other hand, the Afghanistan model may result in a 'fragmentation of duties that has effectively deprived human rights of a strong institutional advocate within the mission'.[86] Does the answer reside in a merge between the two, as was originally attempted in Kosovo? Field research in Kosovo suggests that a clear disadvantage of not having a Senior Adviser after 2000 was that human rights were 'dilut[ed] between different actors involved, none of them having a clear focus on universal human rights.'[87] A stronger mandate and role for OHCHR, as the only international agency focusing solely on human rights, may have addressed some of these shortcomings.

Regardless of the structure, the personality of the SRSG appears key to whether integration of human rights will be successful or not. A women's rights activist in Kosovo was firm in her view: 'The Government is now looking at UNMIK as a model. Until Søren-Jessen-Petersen (SRSG in Kosovo 2004–2006) there was no model. Now there is'.[88] Also, the degree to which human rights will be taken into account by military peacekeepers, for example, may depend on whether the security components (military and police) are under UN command or not. Since delegation of peacekeeping responsibilities to regional organizations (in particular the African Union, the EU and NATO) is and will continue to be a main characteristic of peace operations, this aspect requires further analysis.

Concluding Remarks

While how best to ensure integration of human rights in peace operations raises more questions than answers, a few tentative conclusions can be drawn. First, the importance of OHCHR cannot be understated. During a symposium in 2003 on the occasion of the tenth anniversary of the High Commissioner, a keynote speaker stated:

> I ... was never able to figure out precisely what the role of the UN High Commissioner's Office was in Kosovo. They were there; they were working away, but it never appeared that their work was effectively integrated with what the OSCE was doing. This will be particularly important in transitional societies.[89]

My field research in Kosovo casts doubt on this statement. OHCHR, despite its minimal presence, was one of the most appreciated human rights actors in Kosovo. Not only did all OSCE human rights personnel interviewed indicate a good relationship with OHCHR; it was also generally felt that OHCHR had a comparative advantage over the OSCE due to its vested authority and independence. OHCHR was perceived to possess political leverage in lobbying for policy recommendations. For instance, a major report on the conditions of holding cells in Kosovo addressed by UNMIK's Inter-Pillar Working Group on Human Rights would not have been possible 'without the moral backing of OHCHR'.[90] OHCHR does play a key role, the most important perhaps being that its work is based on international human rights law. Subsequently, greater integration of human rights in peace operations requires that member states honour their commitment to double OHCHR's regular budget funding over the next five years.[91]

The policies adopted at headquarters level remains a necessary aspect for effective integration in the field. The Security Council should take on board explicit language on the need to integrate international human rights law throughout a mission. If military peacekeepers were explicitly endowed with a mandate to protect and promote human rights in Security Council resolutions, their human rights role would be less ambiguous. Such provisions would, according to military personnel, 'give [us] a clear mandate to intervene and prevent human rights violations' because 'we tend to hide behind [the mantra] "it is not in my mandate" in dealing with human rights violations'.[92] This is not likely to happen in the near future. It took almost 50 years for human rights to formally be integrated into peace operations. Today's challenge may be simply to keep human rights on the peacekeeping agenda and enhance efforts to make local authorities accept and embrace international human rights standards. A first step in this direction is to reach a common understanding among both civilian and military peacekeepers and between them and the local population of what human rights protection and promotion entails and how to best put it into practice.

NOTES

1. Interview UNMIK staff, Pristina, 19 Dec. 2005.
2. A wide definition of peace operations is used throughout the article, encompassing observer missions, transitional administrations and peace operations authorized under Chapters VI and VII.
3. UN Doc. S/RES/1244 (1999), para.11(j).
4. Espen Barth Eide, Anja Therese Kaspersen, Randoph Kent, Karin von Hippel, *Report on Integrated Missions: Practical Perspectives and Recommendations*, Independent Study for the Expanded UN ECHA Core Group, May 2005, p.12.
5. See also the statement by Kofi Annan in *Implementation of the Recommendations of the Special Committee on Peacekeeping Operations*, Report of the Secretary-General, UN Doc. A/59/608, 15 Dec. 2004, para.7.
6. Nigel D. White, 'Towards a Strategy for Human Rights Protection in Post-Conflict Situations', in White and Dirk Klaasen, *The UN, Human Rights and Post-conflict Situations*, Manchester: Manchester University Press, 2005, p.486.
7. Report of the Secretary-General, 'Implementation of the recommendations of the Special Committee on Peacekeeping Operations', 29 Dec. 2005, UN Doc. A/60/640, para.25. See United Nations, *Integrated Mission Planning Process (IMPP), Guidelines Endorsed by the Secretary-General on 13 June 2006*, p.3 (emphasis added) and *Implementation of the Recommendations of the Special Committee on Peacekeeping Operations*, Report of the Secretary-General, 29 Dec. 2005, UN Doc. A/60/640, para.25.
8. *The Report of the Panel on United Nations Peace Operations* [hereafter the Brahimi Report], 21 Aug. 2000, UN Doc. A/51/950-S/2000/809, para.217.
9. Ibid., para.198.
10. See *A Review of Peace Operations: A Case for Change*, The Conflict, Security and Development Group, International Policy Institute, London: King's College, 2003, p.341.
11. See William Durch, Victoria K. Holt, Caroline R. Earle, Moira K. Shanahan, *The Brahimi Report and the Future of UN Peace Operations*, Washington: Henry Stimson Center, 2003, pp.75–6.
12. For an overview of human rights considerations in peace operations deployed during the Cold War, see Katarina Månsson, 'The Forgotten Agenda: The Protection and Promotion of Human Rights During the Cold War', *Journal of Conflict and Security Law*, 2005, Vol.10, No.3, pp.379–403.
13. Karen Kenny, 'Fulfilling the Promise of the UN Charter, Transformative Integration of Human Rights', *Irish Studies in International Affairs*, Vol.10, 1999, p.44.
14. The UN Transition Assistance Group in Namibia (UNTAG, 1990–91), and UN Transitional Administration in East Timor (UNTAET, 1999–03), can both be considered to fall within this category.
15. Dag Hammarskjöld (UN Secretary-General 1953–61) was a strong proponent of this line of thought. See Katarina Månsson,'Dag Hammarskjöld – Vördnad för livet genom internationell tjänst' ['Dag Hammarkjöld – Respect for life through international service'] *Nordic Journal of Human Rights*, Vol.23, No.4, 2005, pp.440–41.
16. Karen Kenny, 'UN Accountability for its Human Rights Impact: Implementation through Participation', in White and Klaasen (n.6 above).
17. See, for instance, Boris Kondoch, 'Human Rights Law and UN peace Operations in Post-conflict Situations', in ibid., pp.33–41.
18. *Vienna Declaration and Programme of Action* (hereafter the *Vienna Declaration*), A/Conf. 157/23, 12 July 1993, Annex II, para.1.
19. See in particular the position paper of the European Community and its Member States, UN Doc. A/CONF.157/PC/87, para.23.
20. *The Vienna Declaration* (n.18 above), Annex II, para.97.
21. *An Agenda for Peace: Preventive Diplomacy, Peacemaking and Peace-keeping*, Report of the Secretary-General, 17 June 1992, UN Doc. A/47/277-UN Doc. S/24111, para.16 (emphasis added).
22. Ibid., para.55.
23. *Supplement to An Agenda for Peace*, Position paper of the Secretary-General on the occasion of the Fiftieth anniversary of the United Nations, 25 Jan. 1995, UN Doc. A/50/60, para.22; Philip Alston, 'Neither Fish nor Fowl: The Quest to Define the Role of the UN High Commissioner for Human Rights', *European Journal of International Law*, Vol.8, No.2, p.324.
24. The Vienna Declaration, para.4, sets out that the High Commissioner shall be 'under the direction and authority of the Secretary-General'.

25. Markus Schmidt, 'What Happened to the "Spirit of Vienna"?', *Nordic Journal of International Law*, Vol.64, No.3, 1995, p.613.
26. See Roberto Ricci, *One Year of Human Rights Monitoring with the UN High Commissioner for Human Rights in Rwanda: Afterthoughts*, Papers in the Theory and Practice of Human Rights, No.21, Human Rights Centre: University of Essex, 1998.
27. *Renewing the United Nations: A Programme for Reform*, 14 July 1997, UN Doc. A/51/950, para.274.
28. *Organization of the Office of the High Commissioner for Human Rights*, 15 Sept. 1997, UN Doc. ST/SGB/1997/10, paras.2.1(d) and 10.2(e).
29. *The Brahimi Report* (n.8 above), para.244.
30. *In Larger Freedom: Towards Development, Security and Human Rights for All* (hereafter *In Larger Freedom*), Report of the Secretary-General, UN Doc. A/59/2005, 21 Mar. 2005.
31. Ibid., para.144.
32. 2005 World Summit Outcome, A/RES/60/1, 24 Oct. 2005, para.126.
33. Statement by the High Commissioner for Human Rights at the 60th Session of the General Assembly Third Committee, New York, 25 Oct. 2005.
34. Interview, OHCHR staff, Ireland, May 2005.
35. Interview, OHCHR staff, Geneva, May 2005.
36. The General Assembly and the Office of Legal Affairs (OLA) are also of particular importance. The Assembly was instrumental in establishing two of the first human rights field operations (MICIVIH in Haiti and MINUGUA in Guatemala). It also authorizing certain periods of the Observer Mission in El Salvador (ONUSAL). Since the Assembly has not established any operation since 1999, its activities are excluded here. OLA, for instance, reviews and approves all draft UNMIK regulations.
37. See, for instance, UN Doc. S/RES/771 (1992) on UNPROFOR, UN Doc. S/RES/866 (1993) on UNOMIL, UN Doc. S/RES/1181 (1998) on UNOMSIL.
38. The UN Transitional Authority in Eastern Slavonia (UNTAES) was the first, see S/RES/1037 (1996), para.12. It should be noted that several operations, for instance UNOMIL, adjusted the mandate later on in the mission to include human rights tasks. See UN Doc. S/RES/1020 (1995), para.2(f).
39. UN Doc. S/RES/1181, paras.8(b),12 (emphasis added).
40. See UN Doc. S/RES/1244 (1999); UN Doc. S/RES/1272 (1999); UN Doc. S/RES/1291 (1999); UN Doc. S/RES/1320 (2000); UN Doc. S/RES/1410 (2002); UN Doc. S/RES/1509 (2003); UN Doc. S/RES/1528 (2004); UN Doc. S/RES/1542 (2005); UN Doc. S/RES/1545 (2005).
41. The Council used other wording to describe human rights violations. See, for instance, UN Doc. S/RES/693 (1991): 'the persistence of and the increase in the climate of violence in El Salvador, which seriously affects the civilian population'; UN Doc. S/RES/751 (1992) *'Deeply disturbed* by the magnitude of the human suffering' (Somalia).
42. See UN Doc. S/RES/1320 (2000); UN Doc. S/1369 (2001); UN Doc. S/1398 (2002); UN Doc. S/RES/1446 (2003).
43. UN Doc. S/PRST/1998/38, 29 Dec. 1998.
44. Bertrand Ramcharan, *A UN High Commissioner for Defence of Human Rights*, Leiden: Nijhoff, 2005, p.28.
45. *Report of the Secretary-General on Burundi*, 16 March 2004, UN Doc. S/2004/210, para.84.
46. See Hurst Hannum, *Human Rights in Conflict Resolution: The Role of the Office of the High Commissioner for Human Rights in UN Peacemaking and Peacebuilding*, Centre for Human Rights and Conflict Resolution, The Fletcher School of Law and Diplomacy, Tufts University, 2005, p.8.
47. Briefing by the High Commissioner for Human Rights to the Security Council, Report on the 14–15 May Events in Kisangani – the DRC.
48. UN Doc. S/RES/1468, para.7.
49. See in particular SC Resolution 1590, 24 Mar. 2005, para.17.
50. See, for instance, William J. Durch, 'Structural Issues and the Future of UN Peace Operations', in Donald C.F. Daniel and Bradd C. Hayes, *Beyond Traditional Peacekeeping*, London: Macmillan, 1995, p.157.
51. *Strengthening of the United Nations: An Agenda for Further Change*, UN Doc. A/57/387, 9 Sept. 2002, para.126.
52. *The Brahimi Report* (n.8 above), para.186.
53. Ibid., para.18.

54. Available at OHCHR website: www.ohchr.org. The MoU was revised in 2002.
55. *Report of the Independent Inquiry into the Actions of the UN during the 1994 Genocide in Rwanda*, UN Doc. S/99/1257, 15 Dec. 1999.
56. Ibid., part II, III, conclusions, sect.2.
57. MoU between OHCHR and DPKO (n.54 above), Annex.
58. Ibid, para.12.
59. David Marshall and Shelley Inglis, 'The Disempowerment of Human Rights-Based Justice in the United Nations Mission in Kosovo', *Harvard Human Rights Journal*, Vol.95, 2003, p.145, and Steven Ratner, 'The United Nations in Cambodia and the New Peacekeeping', in D. Warner, *New Dimensions of Peacekeeping*, Dordrecht: Martinus Nijhoff 1995, p.61.
60. UN Doc. A/60/640 (n.7 above), para.8.
61. Hannum (n.46 above), p.16.
62. *In Larger Freedom* (n.31 above), para.144.
63. UN Doc. A/55/977, Annex L, p.87.
64. Peace and security; economic and social affairs; development cooperation; humanitarian affairs and human rights. See *Renewing the United Nations* (n.27 above), para.28.
65. As of 2003, there were 21 members, among them the Under-Secretaries-General for Peacekeeping Operations, Legal Affairs, Humanitarian Affairs, Disarmament Affairs, High Commissioner for Refugees and Administrator of UNDP (www.un.org/Depts/dpa/prev_dip7fr_preventive_action.htm#ecps).
66. *Renewing the United Nations* (n.28 above), para.201.
67. Ibid., para.199.
68. Ramcharan (n.44 above).
69. See reproduced by Bertrand Ramhcaran, 'The Human Rights Field Operation in Partnership for Peace', in Michael O'Flaherty (ed.), *The Human Rights Field Operation: Law and Practice* (forthcoming).
70. *Report of the Special Committee on Peacekeeping Operations and its Working Group at the 2005 substantive session*, UN Doc. A/59/19, 1 Mar. 2005, para.23.
71. This view is repeated in all annual reports of the Special Committee since 2000.
72. UN Doc. A/59/19 (2005), (n.70 above), para.29.
73. *Report of the Special Committee on Peacekeeping Operations*, 11 Mar. 2002, UN Doc. A/56/863, para.69.
74. For instance, OHCHR's country-specific and stand-alone field offices in Colombia, Nepal and Cambodia and other countries.
75. See Alice Henkin (ed.), *Honoring Human Rights and Keeping the Peace*, Washington: The Aspen Institute, 1995; Henkin (ed.), *Honoring Human Rights, From Peace to Justice*, Washington: The Aspen Institute, 1998. The operations in the former Yugoslavia include the Human Rights Field Operation in Former Yugoslavia (HRFOFY) of the OHCHR, the Human Rights Office of UNMIBH, and the operations of the Organization for Security and Cooperation in Europe (OSCE), carrying the main human rights monitoring mandate.
76. *The United Nations and Mozambique, 1992–1995*, New York: United Nations Department of Public Information, 1995, pp.45–6. It should be added that the Police Commission never acted on the complaints forwarded by ONUMOZ police.
77. See Cees Rover and Anne Gallagher, 'Human Rights Training for United Nations Peacekeepers: Lessons from Mozambique', *The Netherlands Quarterly of Human Rights*, Vol.13, No.3, 1995, pp.217–35.
78. See Claudio Cordone, *Bosnia and Herzegovina: The Creeping Protectorate*, in Alice Henkin, *Honoring Human Rights under International Mandates, Lessons from Bosnia, Kosovo and East Timor*, Washington, DC: The Aspen Institute, 2003, pp.36–7.
79. *Nineteenth Report of the Secretary-General on the United Nations Observer Mission in Liberia*, UN Doc. S/1996/858, para.33.
80. *The Blue Helmets, A Review of United Nations Peace-keeping*, New York: UN Department of Public Information, 1996, p.553.
81. *Report of the Secretary-General on Cambodia*, 19 Feb. 1992, UN Doc. S/23613, para.21.
82. The position was discontinued after six months and replaced by various units. It was finally replaced by the Inter-Pillar Working Group on Human Rights.
83. A human rights section now exists in UNAMA, but was not originally planned for.
84. See The UN High Commissioner for Human Rights, *Strategic Management Plan 2006–2007*, p.37 and Secretary-General's Decision No. 2005/24, para.(ii) c.
85. Interview, OHCHR staff, Geneva, May 2005.
86. *The Brahimi Report* (n.8 above), p.347.

87. Interview UN staff, Pristina, Dec. 2005.
88. Interview, Pristina, 9 Dec. 2005.
89. Harold Hongju Koh, 'A Job Description for the UN High Commissioner for Human Rights', *Columbia Human Rights Law Review*, Vol.35, No.3, Summer 2004, p.499.
90. Interview, Human Rights Officer, OSCE, Gnjilane, 8 Dec. 2005.
91. 2005 World Summit Outcome (n.33 above), para.124.
92. Questionnaire distributed to participants of the United Nations Training Course on Human Rights for Trainers of Military Personnel of Peace Operations, UN Training School Ireland, 28 Feb.–4 Mar. 2005.

Human Rights Aspects of EU Crisis Management Operations: From Nuisance to Necessity

HADEWYCH HAZELZET

'If we are threatened by a child soldier, can we shoot back?' This was one of the human rights related issues identified in the preparation for the first EU-led operation in the Democratic Republic of Congo (DRC) in 2003. Asking for an ID to check the age of the armed opponent might not be the most appropriate action in a threatening situation.

Should human rights monitors in Aceh, Indonesia, look into abuses of the past? NGOs pushed for this the very first time the EU sent human rights monitors to the field in August 2005. As soon as the human rights dimension got more attention, the first reaction was to clarify the scope of the mandate so as not to endanger the fragile peace agreement.

An EU policeman witnesses the discovery of a mass grave in Darfur. Should they report it and if so to whom? Could they become an accomplice in the destruction of evidence of potential relevance to the International Criminal Court (ICC)?

EU police forces in the Balkans get information on trafficking in human beings. NGOs are up in arms. What is the EU policy on countering this?

Would putting a certain rebel group on the EU terrorist list, for instance the Tamil Tigers in Sri Lanka, have a positive or a negative impact on an ongoing peace process?

Suppose the African Union appoints a high-level General to lead an operation which is heavily funded by the EU. The General has a notorious human rights record in his country of origin. Can or will the EU object? Should the EU pose conditions to funding an AU-led peace operation or is 'African ownership' a higher value?

This book is written in a personal capacity and does not reflect EU positions.

These are examples of aspects of past and ongoing EU operations relevant to human rights. Some questions are perhaps more hypothetical than others, but they could well become reality in the near future. To what extent have human rights issues been integrated thus far into EU peace building initiatives, in particular into crisis management operations, and how can we do better? How can we move from a perception where calling attention to human rights aspects is perhaps seen as a nuisance which threatens to destabilize peace negotiations or a strictly defined mandate, to a perception where human rights aspects are seen as a necessary ingredient to make a success of crisis management operations?

This article will first explain the decision-making process on EU involvement in crisis management operations and outline the instruments at the disposal of the EU with a particular focus on human rights policy. Second, it provides an overview and analysis of current and past crisis management operations and points to ongoing developments. The article concludes with suggestions for better integrating human rights in future crisis management operations.

Decision-making Process

What activities will a pending crisis or potential peace initiative trigger in Brussels? In a nutshell: the first step is to analyse the situation.[1] The EU disposes of various early-warning tools, in particular the reports prepared on the basis of 'watch lists' by the Policy Unit and the Situation Centre as well as regular country reports by Heads of Mission.

In case of a crisis situation, at the request of the UN, the initiative of one of the member states, the Commission, the EU Presidency or High Representative for Common Foreign and Security Policy (CFSP), the Political and Security Committee (PSC) will discuss whether, and in what way, the EU could contribute to stabilize the situation, either alone or together with other international or regional actors. Then the PSC will ask the relevant Council Working Groups to prepare an advice, namely the Committee on Civil aspects of Crisis Management (CIVCOM), the Politico-Military Group (PMG), and External Relations Councillors who deal with the financial aspects of CFSP. The Situation Centre reports daily on the situation. Meanwhile, the Council Secretariat, which includes military and civilian staff, plans the operation and seeks coordination of civilian and military operational instruments and structures. Member states will internally discuss how they could contribute to an EU-led operation, through expertise, offering headquarters to lead the operation, personnel, equipment or financing.

Furthermore, the Commission will look at the possibility of flanking measures, paid for from Community instruments or the European Development Fund for such situations. The Council Secretariat and the Commission, possibly with experts from member states, will send a joint fact-finding mission to the spot and produce recommendations on the possible risks and type of operation. Finally, the PSC reconsiders the advice and various reports and recommends to the Council whether or not to launch a military and/or civilian crisis management operation. A Joint Action is prepared for adoption by the Council, and an operational plan with all the details on who does what and when, and rules of engagement if appropriate. A head of mission/operation is appointed and member states start sending their contributions. Within five days after the Council decision, the EU can be present on the ground. A clear exit strategy could be designed so that the UN or a regional organization could take over the operation in the near future.

Only a few years ago such a rapid reaction seemed like a distant dream. Even if the EU had started to declare its intentions to become an international actor of importance, implementation of its lofty words seemed far from reality. Meanwhile, the EU is and has been involved in about a dozen different operations, and for each operation lessons are identified in order to do better in the future.

The EU's Human Rights Toolbox

What tools does the EU have at its disposal to react to human rights crisis situations, and is it willing and capable of using them? Although the EU is still very good at issuing declarations, it has learned to walk, not just talk.[2] Crisis management has only been squarely on the agenda since 1999 when the High Representative/Secretary-General (HR/SG) Javier Solana placed crisis management tasks at the core of the process of strengthening the CFSP.[3] The EU seems well placed to address complex crisis situations and it is getting better in reducing obstructions between the various policy domains previously dealt with in relative isolation by the various Council working groups.

It has tools at its disposal in the fields of trade, development, diplomacy, humanitarian aid, sanctions, and the possibility – if need be at short notice – to send in police officers, rule of law experts or military personnel.[4] These instruments help to prevent conflict, to stabilize a crisis situation and to build up long-term sustainable solutions. Many conflicts are regional in character. The EU is also well equipped and connected to work with countries through a regional approach.[5] Through diplomacy, the HR/SG plays a very important role in mediation and the facilitation of conflict resolution. The EU has also extended its diplomatic arsenal with the appointment of EU Special Representatives for certain regions or countries, many of them with a UN or Organization for Security and Cooperation in Europe (OSCE) background. In January 2005 Solana also appointed a Personal Representative for Human Rights. In addition, various 'headline goals' indicate EU capabilities for civilian and military crisis management and increasing the 'peacebuilding' component of the CFSP.[6] The EU works increasingly closely with international and regional organizations, the International Committee of the Red Cross (ICRC) and international NGOs. EU states are important actors in the UN and are behind many UN Security Council Resolutions (such as those on children and armed conflict). Eight EU states figure in the top 35 of blue helmet providers.[7] The EU and its member states are among the largest financial contributors to various UN bodies, and EU co-operation with the UN has been strengthened since 2003 with the adoption of an EU–UN declaration. Through its extensive network of trade and development (or partnership) agreements, the EU has bilateral contacts and mechanisms to react throughout the world. These agreements include human rights clauses since 1995, as well as provisions on political dialogue and some on conflict resolution (notably the Cotonou Agreement). Country and Regional Strategy Papers which form the basis of development cooperation now also include provisions on conflict resolution and human rights, rule of law and democracy. There are funds to address systemic issues. The EU and its member states are the biggest donors of development and humanitarian aid in the world (US$30 billion a year in Official Development Assistance (ODA) – 56 per cent of the global total) and spends €200 million a year directly promoting democracy and human rights, notably through the European Initiative for Democracy and Human Rights (EIDHR). Finally, the external dimension of Justice and Home Affairs facilitates EU discussions on, for instance, the functioning of the judiciary system and possibilities for cooperation with third states.

But to what extent have human rights been incorporated into the European Security and Defence Policy (ESDP)?[8] Human rights policy provides a number of hooks: the various EU Human Rights Guidelines are all of potential relevance: death penalty (1998), torture (2001), children and armed conflict (2003), human rights defenders (2004), and human rights dialogues (2001).[9] Human rights aspects, in particular gender issues and child protection, have now been incorporated into many key documents, such as the EU guidelines on the protection of civilians (2003), the EU training concept (2004), and standards of behaviour (2005). Also useful are the human rights fact sheets prepared by Heads of Mission on virtually every country in the world that are regularly updated. COHOM, the Council Working Group on Human Rights, is responsible for the articulation of EU human rights policy *vis-à-vis* third states and in the UN context (in particular the UN Commission on Human rights and the General Assembly Third Committee). At expert level, the human rights desks of the Council Secretariat as well as a number of member states are increasingly involved in the planning, review and follow-up to operations. OSCE and Council of Europe (CoE) fall under the responsibility of a separate working group (COSCE) through which the EU is an active player in OSCE and CoE activities with regard to, for instance, election observation, legal reform and implementation of the European Convention on Human Rights.

Under which conditions is the EU willing and capable of using these instruments? It is important to understand what the EU is, in order to understand its policies, its strengths and its weaknesses. The EU itself is a community built on the rule of law, on treaties, in many areas working on the basis of consensus. Its often-mentioned weakness ('lengthy decision making procedures') is thus also a strength (broad support and credibility by consensus).[10] The enlargement process itself is often seen as the main peacebuilding success of the EU, and each enlargement has brought new expertise to the EU of relevance for conflict prevention. The Copenhagen criteria and their cross-references to OSCE recommendations linked benefits and potential membership to performance in protecting human rights.

The fact that the EU is represented by many countries and its image of a 'soft power' gives it a unique status in the world. Its strong belief in a rules-based order and effective multilateralism stands in sharp contrast to other powers that tend to believe more in military solutions.[11] 'Speak softly but carry a big carrot', it is often jokingly said within the EU, but not without a certain truth to it, and not without results. There is a strong belief that effective multilateralism, a central element of the 2003 European Security Strategy, is not 'just a method' but the best way to solve conflicts in a sustainable manner.[12]

Analysis of Current Operations

The EU has been actively involved in addressing certain crisis situations, but not others. Sometimes its members are bilaterally involved, other times they operate under the EU or NATO or UN flag. Under what conditions is the EU likely to intervene? And how is the EU's capacity evolving? The appendix provides an overview of past and current operations since 1999, all of which are part of a more comprehensive approach towards the countries in question.

One thing most of the operations have in common is that many were post-conflict operations. In Macedonia, the mission was preventive in character. In Aceh, there was a window of opportunity to settle the conflict during a temporary ceasefire following the Tsunami in 2004. In the DRC the conflict was ongoing when the first EU operation took place in 2003. The EU actively contributed to finding solutions to the crises before monitoring peace agreements. In most cases, but not always, they were carried out with one or more other international partners (NATO, UN, AU, ASEAN). In all cases, the governments in charge were willing to accept an international presence to monitor the situation or to contribute actively to a process of transition.

What made the EU intervene in these cases and not in others? More research on this would be interesting and useful. It is difficult to escape the impression that these operations were decided on an ad hoc basis. In some cases dedicated individuals skilfully used windows of opportunity to put the European Security and Defence Policy (ESDP) into practice. The decision at EU level to get involved was then the result of a combination of a strong personality pushing for an operation, backed up by at least one delegation with a stake in the matter, followed by other delegations for their own motivations, perhaps because they foresaw the need for others' support in the future.

Still, one can perhaps point to three factors, interests, norms and institutions that can largely explain the conditions which have led the EU to intervene in the past two to three years.[13] These factors played a varying role per operation and one can delineate some trends that help explain the conditions under which the EU is likely to decide on an ESDP operation.

Interests

The European Security Strategy (ESS), published in 2003, gave a push to a more active international role for the EU: 'the EU is inevitably a global player ... it should be ready to share in the responsibility for global security'. It also spoke of the 'need to develop a strategic culture that fosters early, rapid and when necessary, robust intervention'.[14] Not coincidentally 2003 was also the year of disagreement over Iraq. As the US was keen to withdraw troops from the Balkans for use elsewhere, the EU was keen to show it was up to the job.

Why the Balkans? According to Solana: 'the importance of continued EU engagement in the Balkans cannot be over-stated. More than any other region in the world, this is a European responsibility. Simply put, we cannot afford to fail'.[15] Why Gaza/Ramallah? The EU and its member states have long been the largest donor to the Palestinians (€500 million annually in emergency support and medium-term assistance to institution building projects). The EU has also been an active player in the peace process, in the so-called Road Map.[16] In the case of Iraq, the EU was looking for a modest way to restore some EU co-ordination in its approach towards conflict and show its major ally that it was prepared to assist in reconstruction and stabilization. However, interests alone cannot explain all EU interventions, because there are clearly bilateral historic ties or economic or strategic interests in countries where the EU did not intervene through a civilian/military operation (albeit sometimes through other instruments in its toolbox).

Norms

The ESS also spoke of the EU's responsibility for 'building a better world'. The EU is 'committed to upholding and developing international law', and 'establishing the rule of law and protecting human rights are the best means of strengthening the international order'.[17] Promotion of human rights is one of the key objectives of CFSP and development policy as laid down in the Treaty. Without genuine concern about human rights violations and the humanitarian situation in these crises situations, intervention would have been unlikely. Many of these countries are not the biggest trading partners or of strategic importance to the EU.

If interests were the only factor behind intervention, one would expect the EU to focus on its own backyard. Yet, it intervened in countries as far afield as the DRC, Sudan and Aceh. These areas were however among the worst humanitarian situations at the time. Also, if pure interests were at stake, the EU would be primarily interested in raising its flag. Yet, it has operated in a rather low-key way with the prime aim being to get the job done. Darfur is probably the best example of EU involvement to stop atrocities and contribute to peace by assisting the African Union. Yet, the limited scale of its involvement compared to the scale of the tragedy also shows that norms alone cannot explain EU operations.[18] Therefore, like interests, norms are a necessary but not a sufficient condition – since of course there are many other areas of concern where the EU has not yet intervened.

Institutions

One cannot understand the outcome of EU decisions if one does not understand its institutions, its decision-making process. Therefore, the institutional argument can be marked as a necessary condition comprising internal and external institutional factors. In terms of its internal decision-making process, it is easier for the EU to agree on positive than on negative measures. Qualitative majority voting rules the EU's trade and development policies; unanimity rules CFSP and ESDP. Therefore, 'robust intervention' is usually the last option, since one country is enough to block an initiative. Externally, as an institution built on treaties, the EU also institutionalizes its relations with other actors. It is easier for the EU to intervene where there are already NATO or UN structures in place, or when the UN asks for help. The involvement of the wider international community, preferably underpinned by a UN Security Council resolution, enhances legitimacy. Also, member states would not have engaged in any of these operations alone, even if some of them have closer ties with the countries involved than others.

Why the DRC and Aceh? When MONUC was looking for a quick and temporary solution to stabilize the situation there as a bridge to a UN operation, the UN asked the

EU to intervene. In reply, some EU delegations pushed successfully for EU involvement.[19] Since this involvement had already evolved extensively over time, it was difficult for other delegations not to go along. This scenario repeated itself in March 2006 when the UN was again looking for additional security back-up in the run-up to the elections in DRC.

Perhaps Aceh is a good illustration of interests, norms and institutional factors at work. The post-tsunami situation offered a window of opportunity to solve a long-standing conflict and state of emergency. A former president of an EU country brokered a peace deal and got EU support. Of course the area is also of strategic interest (in terms of trade, military and the fight against terrorism). At least one EU state had historic ties with the country. Moreover, Indonesia was unwilling to allow a major UN role after East Timor – but could accept an EU role, especially together with ASEAN. By contrast, in other cases where the EU did not intervene it seems that the right mix of norms, interests and institutions was not present or the conditions were not ripe for any international involvement.

Security versus Human Rights

Where is human rights protection in all this? The human rights component is not necessarily included in the 'normative' factor; one could argue that it is a matter of perception whether it is in line with someone's moral convictions or whether it is in someone's 'interest' to stop human rights atrocities. The very aim of peace-building and crisis management initiatives is to create stability and foster a safe environment in which people are respected and free. Contributing to the rule of law and an independent judiciary system through civilian missions clearly fosters human rights protection. In theory, developing military capacity should also enable the EU to deploy quickly to prevent human rights catastrophes unfolding as in Rwanda. However, human rights should become a greater part of the decision making and planning process for operations.

In three years time the EU will show that it can rapidly deploy a civilian and/or military operation, either autonomously, with recourse to NATO common assets and capabilities or in the context of a UN operation. Military and civilian experts have learned to plan operations together; the various institutions and member states have worked effectively together in time-bound, clearly defined operations. The 'walls' between security and development have started to be torn down; more could be done to breach the wall between security and human rights. Kofi Annan's vision that there is no security without development and no enjoyment of human rights without either security or development will be a catalyst for peacebuilding. We can no longer deny the linkages; one is a condition for the other.

References to human rights are by now included in most of the key documents. How to implement them? Bringing crisis management in line with human rights policy is the area where the EU should – and is expected to – be active. The questions posed at the beginning of this essay allude to both limitations and development. Human rights monitors in Aceh only monitor human rights violations linked to the monitoring mission's mandate and to the Memorandum of Understanding between the Indonesian government and the Movement for Free Aceh (GAM). Human rights conditions have not yet been imposed on AU cooperation. But standards of behaviour were developed for EU troops following accusations in Bosnia and following UN-wide developments in this direction. And steps have been taken for ongoing operations in the framework of cooperation with the UN as well as in relation to civil society.

First, initiatives have been taken on various fronts. The EU has built up considerable experience in terms of structures, procedures and rapid reaction for civilian and military personnel, alone and together with others.[20] In line with the Brahimi report, lessons are identified for each operation.

The EU sent human rights monitors to Aceh for the first time, and human rights advice was prepared for the mission for the first time. The Brussels task force assisting the mission also included a human rights expert. Also ground breaking, one of the deputies to the Head of Mission was responsible for human rights issues and amnesty matters. As part of the overall mission there are about 40 human rights monitors in teams in Aceh. The Commission is financing 'flanking measures' to assist in the creation of a truth and reconciliation commission, a human rights court, reintegration of the GAM fighters and monitoring of elections. It will be very important to identify lessons from this mission for future operations, ideally by also including independent assessments. Human rights aspects were therefore an important part of the first review. Also, significantly, the Indonesian government agreed to adhere to the International Covenant on Civil and Political Rights (ICCPR) and the International Covenant on Economic, Social and Cultural Rights (ICESCR) as part of the peace agreement. Such adherence could be tied to EU involvement in other missions.

The ESDP operation to the DRC includes a gender and a human rights adviser in the headquarters in Potsdam. The EU is working with DRC on improving police and military payment systems to counter corruption and increase professionalism. This assistance is deemed absolutely necessary as part of efforts to break the cycle of violence and conflict. The EU now has a small team of human rights experts on reserve as part of a crisis response team. The EU planning team for a possible EU crisis management operation in the field of rule of law in Kosovo indicates that, in conformity with UNSCR 1325, the EU strives for improved gender balance in ESDP operations. The Civilian Response Teams that are currently being trained as a pool of rapidly deployable experts also include human rights experts.

More generally, a number of 'awareness raising' measures have been taken within the EU. For the first time human rights aspects have been part of the Presidency's programme in the field of crisis management in 2006. Following this mandate a seminar was organized for the Political and Security Committee on transitional justice. Also various UN officials together with the Personal Representative for Human Rights were invited for an informal exchange of views with the civilian and military committees dealing with ESDP operations, and, vice versa, high-level staff responsible for the operations have been invited to the COHOM.[21] There are also efforts to integrate the concepts of transitional justice into EU planning and operations.

All EU Special Representatives have the promotion of respect for human rights and the rule of law in their mandate and therefore they need to report on their activities in this field to the Council. They have all been made aware of the EU Human Rights Guidelines, and the EU special representative for Afghanistan has a human rights expert in his team. A mainstreaming or awareness raising campaign has been launched by two consecutive Presidencies and the Personal Representative for Human Rights to inform all geographical working groups in the Council of the guidelines and the fact sheets.

Human rights experts have started discussions with the military staff and the civilian–military cell on the possibilities to effectively cover human rights aspects in future operations. There is an awareness that human rights incidents will be detrimental for the image, credibility or success of any operation. Managing operations means having very clear operational plans and a well-defined mandate and exit strategy. There is a need to operationalize human rights requirements and translate them in a clear and practical way for the people in the field. As a first step, a clear human rights dimension was included in the 2006 simulation exercise in which UN organizations participated, through a scenario which includes child protection issues.

Second, in the context of cooperation with the UN, numerous other initiatives have been taken. The EU drafted a strategy on the implementation of UN Security Council resolution 1325 on peace, women and security, which is taken into account by planners and others (doc. 11932/2/05). Contacts have been undertaken with the UN and others: DPKO, UNICEF, Save the Children, OHCHR, the Secretary-General's Special Representative on Children and Armed Conflict, and the ICRC on issues such as 'best practice', child protection, scenario planning and training. Cooperation in the field should be further intensified on the basis of identified lessons of the past. These organizations, as well as NGOs, are willing to provide training materials and assist in giving training to EU personnel. Since this is mainly done at national level, limited progress has been made in this respect, but various training institutes now include at least child protection issues in their courses. A high-level EU–UN staff-to-staff steering group meets twice a year to discuss cooperation, best practice, planning, training, communication and exercises.

In the context of the UN reform process, the EU lobbied hard to get agreement at the UN Summit and thereafter for the establishment of a Peacebuilding Commission, acknowledgement of the Responsibility to Protect, a Human Rights Council, doubling of the OHCHR budget and mainstreaming of human rights throughout the UN. The EU will play an active role implementing the agreements on these new bodies.

Third, NGOs have played an important role in these developments. They have been actively involved since the beginning of the guidelines on children and armed conflict (CAAC), as well as on human rights defenders. NGOs played an invaluable role in the disarmament, demobilization and rehabilitation (DDR) programmes in DRC in cooperation with Operation *Artemis*.[22] A lot remains to be done to implement the action plan on the CAAC guidelines, but Heads of Missions have prepared reports on a dozen priority countries, the Community and member states have given an overview of their funding activities in this field to seek more synergy, and closer cooperation with UN country teams is sought in line with UN Security Council resolution 1612 on this topic. The review of the guidelines set out various concrete steps for a more active approach. The civilian and military committees were involved in drawing up the guidelines and attempts made to involve them more in the implementation. Civil society groups are also actively pushing the EU to follow up on Security Council resolution 1325, for instance in Kosovo.[23]

How to Do Better in the Future

How will the EU react in the future to a pending crisis or opportunity to foster peace? Several steps should be included.

First, human rights aspects will be included from the start, in the fact-finding missions, in developing the operational plans and concepts and in the agreements with host states. Lessons identified from past operations show that expertise that was not included in the beginning was difficult to make up for later. All EU staff – be they military, police or civilian – will be trained in international human rights standards and international humanitarian law as well as EU human rights policy. Heads of Mission reports on the human rights situation in the countries, regularly updated human rights fact sheets and the EU human rights guidelines will be duly taken into account. The EU and its member states will be particularly active in 'priority' countries in the field of children and armed conflict. The EU will be proactive rather than reactive to NGO reports.

More generally, raising human rights with civilian and military staff will no longer trigger alarm bells. It will be understood that the human rights situation is part of the problem, and thus of the solution, that the search for justice does not impede the search for peace but has to be an integral part of any sustainable solution. To a large extent due to an EU initiative, tackling impunity was a priority in the establishment of the ICC, and in April 2006, the EU and the ICC signed a cooperation and assistance agreement.[24]

Also, a human rights expert should be part of the civilian and military staff, the civilian military cell and the EU Special Representative teams. Each operation should include human rights expertise and a contact point at headquarters. Human rights departments could be reinforced to provide expert advice to other relevant parts in the EU institutions in this area. The pool of national experts on rule of law could also be complemented with more human rights experts who can be sent to the field. Expertise and responsibility for this domain should be present in Brussels as well as in capitals, not least with a view to continuity and lessons learned. The EU should seek to cooperate closely with international organizations that have relevant expertise, in particular the Office of the High Commissioner for Human Rights.

What changes could be envisaged at an institutional level? For instance, what role could or should the COHOM play?[25] It should get more involved in setting out the policy on the protection of human rights in crisis management operations. It should be involved in giving input to the decision-making process in Brussels, especially as long as human rights 'mainstreaming' is not fully achieved. The human rights advice on the Aceh monitoring mission could serve as a basis for more general and operational advice on how human rights should be taken into account in crisis management operations. On the other hand, operations need practical experience, which should be effectively covered by experts within the Secretariat and the Commission. As it is not yet a reflex to include human rights protection in these operations, human rights experts (perhaps both internal and external) should be invited to provide input throughout the process and to be involved in the lessons learned processes.

One important element is operating in line with the international obligations of EU member states, also in cooperation with third states and regional organizations. For instance, prisoners should not be handed over to authorities of a country where they risk the death penalty, an unfair trial or torture. EU relations with third states should be tied to support for the Convention on the Rights of the Child and its Optional Protocols. International humanitarian law should be upheld among other parties, especially as the so-called 'war on terror' challenges the Geneva Conventions. As one step in that direction, the EU adopted guidelines on IHL at the end of the 2005.[26] They should now be implemented. Promotion of regional and national capacity building and adherence to, and observance of, international standards remain important. In this regard Asia lags behind: it is the only region in the world without a regional human rights body, and China and India among others will need to be convinced that a rules-based international system is in their interest.

Finally, in terms of how the EU organizes itself: whatever happens to the draft Constitutional Treaty, the need for coherence between political, economic and military instruments has not weakened, nor has the need for a more effective diplomatic representation of the EU. Indeed, Solana has remarked that CFSP has a role to play in reconquering public opinion in favour of the European project.[27]

How can member states, third countries (in particular those taking part in EU-led operations), national human rights institutions, NGOs and universities help? They can reinforce the message by raising the importance of human rights protection as a key part of crisis management and peacebuilding initiatives. They can come forward with concrete suggestions as to how to translate international obligations into the operational plans, concepts, training and standard operating procedures. More independent research on lessons identified will be very important, in particular looking at past missions, results of specific ESDP actions, the conditions under which EU operations are likely to be initiated, or key factors for their success.

Finally, for future ESDP operations the question should not be 'how do we react when we are faced by a child soldier?' but 'how do we prevent children from recruitment in the first place?' The EU should not be content that operations are not prepared and conducted only by men; but should ensure that women are active participants in these processes. Human rights need to be seen as the solution, not the problem. One of the HR/SG's visions for the EU's international stance is to be 'engaged and result-oriented'. Human rights protection as part of EU crisis management operations fits into that vision.

ACKNOWLEDGEMENTS

An earlier version of this article was first presented at a conference, organized by the Irish Centre for Human Rights, in Galway on 30 September 2005. The author is grateful to colleagues who provided comments and insights on this topic during various discussions.

APPENDIX

TABLE A1:
EU CIVILIAN AND MILITARY CRISIS OPERATIONS AND ASSISTANCE TO AU/UN OPERATIONS (2003–06)

Operations	Aims	Reference	Year	International cooperation	Staff
Civilian					
Bosnia & Herzegovina	Help local authorities fight organized crime, promote EU standards. First civilian EU mission.	EUPM–EU Police Mission	2003 (Joint Action 2005/824/CFSP) – (ong).	Follows from UN International Police Task Force, over 30 countries contribute	€38 million, 532 police, 400 support staff
DRC	Assist in setting up an integrated police unit to ensure protection of state institutions and reinforce internal security apparatus;	EUPOL Kinshasa, follow up to operation ARTEMIS (2003)	2005 (ongoing)		30 staff
fYROM	Help local authorities fight organized crime, promote EU standards	EUPOL Proxima police mission, followed up by EU police advisory team (EUPAT) in Dec. 2005	2003 (ongoing)		200 staff (Proxima), 30 police advisors (EUPAT)
Georgia	Support and assistance in reforms of criminal justice system. EU support in follow-up to implementation strategy for reform criminal system.	EUJUST Themis – rule of law mission	June 2004–May 2005	In addition to existing EU assistance and other international activities	€2 million, 10 staff

(Continued)

Operations	Aims	Reference	Year	International cooperation	Staff
Indonesia	Monitor implementation of MoU	AMM – Aceh Monitoring Mission	2005 (ongoing)	Cooperation with ASEAN, NW, SW	240 staff
Iraq	Training in management and criminal investigation of senior officials and executive staff from judiciary, police, penitentiary	EU Just Lex	2005 (ongoing)	UNSCR 1546 (2004)	€10 million
Moldova and Ukraine	Assistance in creation of an international customs control arrangement and effective border monitoring mechanism on Transnistrian segment of the Moldova–Ukraine State border; training and advice to Mold/Ukr officials; Strengthen crossborder cooperation; appointment EUSR	EU border assistance mission	2005 (ongoing)	Border police and customs officials from 16 EU member states	69 experts seconded, 50 local support staff

Palestinian Authority–Gaza/Ramallah	Palestinian Civil Police Development Programme (PCDP); police and security reform	2005 (ongoing)	EU Coordinating Office for Palestinian Police Support (COPPS), follow up mission EUPOL-COPPS in Jan. 2006	Road map, coordination with Palestinian Civil Police and US Security Coordinator	33 police and civilian experts seconded and 2 local staff
Palestinian Authority–Rafah	EU border assistance mission for the Rafah crossing point: Monitors, verifies and evaluates PA border control; PA capacity building; Liaison between PA, Israeli and Egyptian authorities	2005	EU BAM Rafah	Established pursuant to the Agreement on Movement and Access between Israel and Palestinian Authority (PA) in Nov. 2005	Approximately 70 personnel
Sudan	Support to military component of African Union-led operation AMIS II and support to police (CIVPOL) component of AMIS II – planning and technical experts, material support, training, assistance and advisory teams, appointment of EU Special Representative	2004 (ongoing)	Contribution to AU/UN lead operation AMIS I–II	UNSC 1590, support to African Union, cooperation notably with UN, US, Canada, Norway, NATO	€89.2 million (I +II), add. €70 m. considered. Bilat. over €30 m., +/– 40 staff

(Continued)

Operations	Aims	Reference	Year	International cooperation	Staff
Military fYROM	Prevent civil war, build environment favourable to identification and implementation of political settlements	Concordia, EUFOR mission	March–Dec. 2003	UNSC 1371, NATO. Over 27 countries contribute.	€6.2 m. 350 staff.
DRC	Facilitate a successful transition, stop rapid deterioration involving massive HR violations.	ARTEMIS	2003	UNSC 1484, first military deployment outside EU without NATO	2000 staff
DRC	Advice and assistance to military authorities for security sector reform, contribute to integration army.	EUSEC DR Congo (2.4 million)	2005 (ongoing)		50 staff
DRC	Bridging operation to provide additional security in run up to elections	On 23 March 2006 the Council approved the concept for a possible EU support to the UN mission in the Democratic Republic of Congo (MONUC) during the electoral process and decided to start military planning and preparation on that basis.	2006	At the request of UN	Deployment of an advanced element to Kinshasa of circa 400–450 military personnel and the availability of a battalion-size 'on-call' force 'over the horizon' outside the country

				6,200 troops
Bosnia & Herzegovina	Maintaining stable and secure environment, ensure continue compliance with Dayton/Paris Agreement, assist ICTY; support international community's High Representative and local authorities ia in fighting organized crime	EUFOR ALTHEA (uses NATO assets and capabilities) – transition from NATO's SFOR mission	2004 (ongoing)	Transition NATO-led SFOR. UNSCR 1575 (2004) and UNSCR 1639 (2005), UN Chapter VII mandate. Troops from 22 EU and 12 third countries.

Source: Inter alia: www.consilium.europa.eu/foreign policies/security and defence.

123

NOTES

1. This article does not go into the detail of EU decision-making procedures in the area of CFSP but focuses only on crisis management situations.
2. The International Crisis Group asked whether the EU could walk or just talk. See, *EU Crisis Response Capability Revisited*, Europe report No. 160, 17 Jan. 2005.
3. EU states were involved bilaterally in UN operations before and after 1999. See, Roel von Meijenfeldt, *At the frontline for human rights. Final Report. Evaluation of the EU participation in the human rights field operation in Rwanda of the United Nations High Commissioner for Human Rights*, Brussels, European Commission, Oct. 1995.
4. International Crisis Group (n.2 above) and EU/EC websites give further details on these tools.
5. E.g., through the Neighbourhood Policy, the Barcelona process, the Cotonou Agreement.
6. Of the total CFSP budget (€2 million), 5.4 million goes to crisis management operations, 30.7 million to conflict resolution, 12 million to emergency aid, 6.5 to EU Special Representatives and 7.2 million to non-proliferation and disarmament (cf the UN's DPKO budget of US$3.5 billion). In April 2006, agreement was reached with the European Parliament to increase the CFSP budget to €80 million, not least to finance increasing crisis management demands.
7. EU member state personnel comprise about 10 per cent of DPKO contributions, compared to 1 per cent from the United States: Peace and Security Section, UN Department of Public Information in consultation with DPKO, background note, 31 Aug. 2005, DPI/1634/Rev.51, Sept. 2005).
8. Academic literature does not yet cover human rights aspects of EU crisis management operations. On human rights aspects of other policy areas. See Philip Alston, *The EU and Human Rights*, Oxford: Oxford UP, 1999; Barbara Brandtner, and Allan Rosas 'Human Rights and the External Relations of the E.C.: an Analysis of Doctrine and Practice', *European Journal of International Law*, Vol. 9, No. 3, 1998, pp.468–90.
9. The EU Human Rights Guidelines and papers on their implementation are at www.consilium.europa.eu/human-rights/.
10. Under the pressure of events the EU has been able to overcome its 'lengthy decision making procedures'. The Aceh mission was decided, framed and launched within three weeks. Operation *Artemis* in the DRC was deployed two weeks after Kofi Annan's first phone call to Solana.
11. The US defence budget almost totals that of the rest of the world (US$420 billion), and US ODA is among the lowest for OECD countries (US$10 billion scheduled to increase to $15 billion). EU member states also spend more on defence than on aid. See *Meeting new challenges*, UN Department of Public Information, DPI/2350/Rev.1 – July 2004 – 5M, 2005.
12. Javier Solana, speech at the Institute for Security Studies, Paris, 26 Sept. 2005.
13. See Hadewych Hazelzet, 'Carrots or Sticks? EU and US reactions to Human Rights Violations (1989–2000)', unpublished PhD thesis, European University Institute, San Domenico di Fiesole 2001; Hazelzet, *Suspension of development cooperation: an instrument to promote human rights?*, European Union Development Policy and Management Institute (EUDPM), Maastricht/Brussels, 2005; H. Hadewych, *Carrots or Sticks? EU and US reactions to Human Rights Violations in the nineties and beyond*, The Hague: Institute for Multiparty Democracy, 2004.
14. European Council, *A Secure Europe in a Better World – The European Security Strategy*, Brussels, 12 Dec. 2003, drafted under the responsibilities of the EU High Representative (www.consilium.europa.eu/foreign policy/european security strategy).
15. Solana (see n.12 above).
16. Ibid.
17. European Council (see n.14 above).
18. In Sudan, an additional factor is the wish that the AU takes the ownership and lead in the operation, reflecting its unwillingness to accept further international involvement, in particular Western troops.
19. These historic ties have engaged the EU for a long time through the Lomé and Cotonou Agreements, to which mainly former colonies are a party and beneficiary. See Hazelzet 2001 and 2005 (n.13 above); Frank Hoffmeister, *Menschenrechts- und Demokratieklauseln in den vertraglichen Außenbeziehungen der Europäischen Gemeinschaft*, [Human Rights and Democracy clauses in External Agreements of the European Community], Berlin, 1998.
20. Solana (n.12 above).
21. COHOM's mandate is at www.consilium.europa.eu/human-rights/.
22. Eventually the EU contributed €20 million to DDR programmes in the DRC with a focus on children.

23. See, e.g., Antonia Potter, *We the Women: Why conflict mediation is not just a job for men*, Centre for Humanitarian Dialogue, October 2005 (www.hdcentre.org/datastore/We%20the%20Women.pdf).
24. Available at www.iccnow.org.
25. COHOM unites the human rights directors of all EU member states and meets on average once a month in Brussels to prepare and develop EU human rights policy.
26. See www.consilium.europa.eu/policies/foreign policy/international humanitarian law.
27. Solana (n.12 above).

Peace versus Justice: Creating Rights as well as Order out of Chaos

HURST HANNUM

Perhaps because we wish that it were true, advocates working in fields that might very broadly be called 'peace' (conflict resolution, conflict management, diplomacy) and 'justice' (human rights, transitional justice, accountability) often assume that peace and justice are always compatible and complementary. While this may be true with respect to ultimate goals – we all want both – the short-term goals and strategies of practitioners in the two fields may differ fairly dramatically. Recognition of those differences is a necessary first step to ensuring that the theoretically compatible goals of peace and justice may be pursued with the least possible tension, whether in the short or long term.[1]

The potential contradiction of pursuing peace and justice simultaneously is a particular challenge in the context of large-scale conflicts, whether internal or international. The peacemakers generally have a clear idea of their immediate task, which is to stop the violence and pave the way for negotiations. But where does human rights fit in negotiation, mediation or conflict resolution strategies? More specifically, how do human rights norms affect issues such as who comes to the table, whether human rights must be included as part of any formal peace agreement, how human rights will be monitored in the post-agreement period, where human rights fit into post-agreement capacity-building, and how human rights affect long-term rule of law issues?

Who Comes to the Table?

One of the significant advances in international law and politics in the past decade has been the increased attention focused on 'international' crimes, particularly genocide, war crimes and crimes against humanity. Initially reflected in the special tribunals created by the UN Security Council to deal with the former Yugoslavia and Rwanda, respectively, this concern found its clearest expression in the creation of the International Criminal Court (ICC) in 1998; approximately 100 states are now party to the ICC Statute. Additionally, special tribunals with at least some international component are found in Sierra Leone and Cambodia.

If one takes international criminal accountability seriously, this poses obvious problems for negotiators or mediators who believe that the only way to achieve peace is to create a setting in which all of the parties to violence can participate, no matter how vicious their crimes. Sadly, the worst perpetrators are often significant military and/or political actors, and threatening them with criminal sanctions is unlikely to get them to the bargaining table. Unfortunately, such sanctions also seem to have had little deterrent effect, although the proponents of expanding international criminal law often assume without proof that such deterrence exists.[2]

The standard view of mediators is perhaps expressed in a publication by Conciliation Resources, a London-based NGO: 'It seems obvious that third parties should work to ensure that the parties to the conflict operate in ways that maintain humanitarian standards... But in the midst of conflict the issues become very difficult. Seldom does any party have "clean hands" and they have all fallen short of accepted humanitarian standards'.[3] The same organization implicitly prioritizes its own work as follows, putting itself firmly on the side of 'peace' rather than 'justice': 'While engagement with armed groups by states can involve complex issues of international law, state sovereignty and national interest, the issue is fundamentally about improving the lives of the local populations who are the victims of conflict.'[4]

Until 1999, the United Nations had no specific policy with respect to amnesties for crimes committed during conflict, and it is not difficult to think of countries in which new governments preferred not to investigate the past; Mozambique, where atrocities were widespread during its civil war, comes readily to mind. However, as some UN officials and NGOs became increasingly uncomfortable with the impunity enjoyed by former combatants for even the most horrific crimes, a set of guidelines was eventually developed under the leadership of long-time senior UN diplomat Alvaro de Soto and promulgated as an informal document in 1999.[5] These guidelines formed the basis of the UN's formal rejection of the amnesty that was included in the July 1999 Lomé Agreement on Sierra Leone.[6] At least one of the guidelines has been reiterated publicly and demarcates one of the normative boundaries of UN engagement: 'United Nations-endorsed peace agreements can never promise amnesties for genocide, war crimes, crimes against humanity, or gross violations of human rights.'[7] This principle has been scrupulously followed by UN representatives. Thus, the United Nations has adopted at least a negative norm: It will not lend its approval to impunity for international crimes, even if all parties to a conflict wish to do so.[8]

Thus far, no observer seems to have suggested that rejecting blanket amnesties means that mediators should not talk with suspected war criminals or invite them to participate in negotiations or any subsequent peace process. Given the unfortunate likelihood that widespread crimes will be committed in most of today's wars, any other option would require that the international community pick a side and create peace, not just broker it, and actively seek to punish perpetrators. However, since an outside mediator usually becomes active only when neither side is likely to 'win', such an approach would be highly problematic even if there were sufficient political will to adopt it – which is clearly not the case in the present international environment.

The Thorny Issue of Accountability

It should first be clarified that individual criminal accountability per se does not constitute part of the main corpus of international human rights law, although many have argued strenuously that it should do so.[9] Human rights norms are primarily applicable to states, and their violation contravenes international law; such violations do not automatically (or even frequently) carry with them individual criminal sanctions. Although the persistent refusal of a state to safeguard rights through a policy of benign or deliberate neglect (for example, by refusing to conduct serious enquiries or institute prosecutions in situations of political disappearances or widespread spousal abuse) would constitute a human rights violation, discretion in the prosecution and punishment of crimes normally falls within a government's 'margin of appreciation'.[10]

Despite this fact, the issue of criminal accountability for past 'human rights' crimes is thought by many to be the essence of 'transitional justice' and human rights in post-conflict societies.[11] The major international human rights NGOs dedicate significant efforts to promoting such accountability, and calls for trials of (usually only the major) perpetrators of war crimes and crimes against humanity have been raised in nearly every large-scale conflict since the early 1990s. The New York-based International Center for Transitional Justice was founded in 2001 (with a reported budget of $25 million over five years) to promote accountability for 'past mass atrocity or human rights abuse' through criminal prosecutions and other methods, such as truth commissions.[12] These calls are based on demands for 'retributive justice', but the claim also is made that prosecuting war criminals and their ilk will serve as a deterrent against similar conduct in future armed conflicts, that it responds to legitimate demands by victims, and that it is a necessary component of healing or reconciliation processes that must occur in order to ensure meaningful long-term peace.

Demanding criminal accountability is very different from the formal UN position of simply refusing to endorse any peace agreement that provides for blanket amnesty or impunity for international crimes. Neither the UN guidelines for mediators referred to above nor subsequent UN practice clarifies whether mediators should actively seek prosecution or some kind of truth commission arrangement to document past atrocities.

In 1997, French expert Louis Joinet submitted a final report on impunity to the UN Sub-Commission on Prevention of Discrimination and Protection of Minorities, which included a set of principles for the protection and promotion of human rights through action to combat impunity.[13] Several years later, another independent expert, US law professor Diane Orentlicher, was appointed by the

UN Commission on Human Rights to update the principles; her report, with an updated set of principles, was submitted to the Commission in 2005.[14]

These principles have been cited as constituting 'best practice' in the area of accountability, and they set an extremely high standard for states to follow.[15] As potential international norms, however, they certainly reach far beyond the current state of the law. The principles include an 'inalienable right to know the truth about past events',[16] and an obligation on states to 'ensure that victims do not again have to endure violations of their rights'.[17] This latter obligation requires that states 'undertake institutional reforms and other measures necessary to ensure respect for the rule of law, foster and sustain a culture of respect for human rights, and restore or establish public trust in government institutions'.[18]

Although Orentlicher claims that her report 'chronicle[s] remarkable advances in national and international efforts to combat impunity',[19] her enthusiasm is warranted only if one focuses on 'efforts' rather than 'achievements'. It is clearly too soon to determine on the basis of any objective evaluation whether criminal accountability is always necessary or even conducive to a sustainable peace settlement, however much human rights advocates would like to believe this to be the case. With respect to international tribunals, for example, Helena Cobban observes: 'The idealists who supported the ICC's creation hoped that it would help check the power of governments and improve the well-being of much-abused people. There is little to suggest that it will do either'.[20]

In this context, one also might consider the decision of the East Timorese government not to pursue prosecutions against perpetrators of the massacres in that country in 1999 and to opt instead for a Commission on Truth and Friendship. 'What's more important for us?' said Nobel Peace Laureate, Jose Ramos-Horta, East Timor's foreign minister, 'That democracy slowly is consolidated in Indonesia? Or the blind pursuit of justice at the expense of stability in Indonesia?'[21] Another analysis of accountability efforts in Southeast Asia concludes: 'For now, the jury should stay out on whether the various permutations of the transitional justice industry will be taking East Timor, Indonesia and Cambodia back into the fire or out to safety', although the author does observe that 'to date, the accountability efforts have not caused major disruption or destabilization in any of the three countries.'[22]

One possible way of reconciling the need for accountability with the necessity of overlooking many, if not all, crimes in the course of negotiating a peace settlement and establishing a transitional government may be found in the concept of 'sequencing'.[23] Sequencing allows criminal actions against perpetrators to be delayed until some later date, when they are out of power and/or the state itself is more stable. These subsequent investigations and prosecutions require either non-adoption or annulment of broad amnesty provisions and are perhaps best exemplified by the attempts to institute criminal prosecutions in countries such as Argentina, Chile and Cambodia decades after the crimes occurred. Of course, sequencing (or avoiding difficult decisions) may violate the maxim that 'justice delayed is justice denied', but it may be the only realistic option in many situations.

This approach is implicitly reflected in the following September 2003 statement to the Security Council by the UN Secretary-General:

> Ending the climate of impunity is vital to restoring public confidence and building international support to implement peace agreements. At the same time, we should remember that the process of achieving justice for victims may take many years, and it must not come at the expense of the more immediate need to establish the rule of law on the ground ...

> We also know that there cannot be real peace without justice. Yet the relentless pursuit of justice may sometimes be an obstacle to peace. If we insist, at all times, and in all places, on punishing those who are guilty of extreme violations of human rights, it may be difficult, or even impossible, to stop the bloodshed and save innocent civilians. If we always and everywhere insist on uncompromising standards of justice, a delicate peace may not survive.

> But equally, if we ignore the demands of justice simply to secure agreement, the foundations of that agreement will be fragile, and we will set bad precedents.[24]

The Role of Human Rights in Peace Agreements

Concluding an examination of peace versus justice in the UN context in late 2004, this author observed that empirically testing the relationship between the inclusion of human rights provisions in peace agreements and their impact on both the course of negotiations and ultimate implementation of the agreement 'is long overdue'.[25] Since that time, at least one new study, by the Geneva-based International Centre for Human Rights Policy (ICHRP), has partially filled that gap;[26] the study's primary author, Christine Bell, is also the author of one of the few earlier studies devoted to this topic.[27]

Most contemporary peace agreements do include reference to human rights principles, if only through a general promise by all parties to respect human rights in the future. However, as Bell notes: 'General rights frameworks often do not threaten the interests of the parties.... Agreement on basic human rights principles framed in general terms can mask and postpone disagreement in the application of human rights in practice.'[28] Nonetheless, there seems to be little harm in including a commitment to guarantee human rights in the future, even if the guarantee is more symbolic than substantive.

The key issue, of course, is the implementation of the human rights (and other) provisions found either in initial ceasefire or interim agreements or in more comprehensive powersharing or transitional arrangements for post-conflict governance. Here, the details become important, and any role for the 'international community' in monitoring the agreement is likely to be crucial. Vague political commitments to human rights are unlikely to be enforceable, and differing interpretations of such commitments (for example, to protect 'minority rights' or establish 'democracy') may actually make implementation more difficult. Even broad incorporation of the international norms contained in major multilateral treaties may mean little, in the absence of any mechanism for monitoring, reporting or enforcing their provisions.

On the other hand, where human rights violations were at the core of the conflict itself – for example, in El Salvador or Guatemala – international human rights norms help to legitimize the inclusion of both general and situationally specific human rights provisions in peace agreements. In some instances, particularly where these norms set at least minimum standards that govern minority–majority relations or participation in the political process, obtaining agreement to specific provisions may also resolve some (although certainly not all) of the differences that lay at the basis of the conflict.

One must be careful not to push parties too far beyond their real willingness to compromise or change tactics, but mediators might also encourage inclusion of meaningful human rights provisions by promising to provide financial and/or technical assistance to ensure that they are implemented. New institutions devoted to aspects of human rights protection and promotion are frequently created in peace agreements, even though this does not guarantee that they will be politically relevant in the post-settlement phase.

Outsiders must be wary of adopting an overly reactive approach to human rights, in which provisions in peace agreements are designed primarily to ensure monitoring and enforcement, as opposed to a partnership approach in which the promotion of human rights will be achieved by building government institutions. Tonya Putnam has been particularly critical of this approach, arguing that tactics such as gathering information about violations, expressing formal protests, pressuring the government, and using the justice system to enforce individual accountability are doomed to fail, 'because they assume the functionality of the very institutions that peace implementation operations are tasked to help bring into existence'.[29]

One also should guard against using the opportunity of drafting wide-ranging human rights provisions in peace agreements or new constitutions in order to promote particular agendas (no matter how worthy) unrelated to the conflict itself. For example, while one cannot disagree with the substance of the ICHRP recommendation that 'the particular needs of women and of vulnerable groups should be specifically addressed in human rights frameworks',[30] the inclusion of such issues where they are not directly relevant to the conflict (women's rights per se, for example, were hardly a major concern in conflicts such as Northern Ireland or Sri Lanka) simply expands an already long list of human rights obligations that are likely to be extremely difficult to meet.

Bearing in mind the difficulty of determining causation in any complex post-settlement situation, we are left with insufficient evidence to conclude that the mere inclusion of human rights provisions in peace agreements, without institutional change and/or significant capacity-building, makes reaching an agreement easier or more successful in the short or medium term. At the same time, the (re)assertion of human rights norms is an appropriate goal in and of itself, and there is no evidence that including human rights provisions makes it more difficult either to reach agreement or to implement peace settlements.

Peacemakers often undervalue the concept of justice (excluding the issue of criminal accountability) in fashioning a viable agreement, but it may be an essential tool in attempts to achieve balance among parties with different degrees of power. In addition, internationally recognized human rights norms set a floor for negotiations and may favourably constrain some negotiation options (for example, by rendering impossible a consideration of any agreement by the most powerful factions that would wholly exclude less powerful groups). At the same time, human rights advocates should not let the best be the enemy of the good, by insisting that only complete adherence to international 'best practice' is acceptable.

Monitoring and Protecting Human Rights in the Immediate Post-agreement Period

Once accountability is dealt with, and assuming that some human rights provisions are included in a peace agreement, how careful should one be about ensuring that human rights abuses do not continue? While the answer may appear obvious – of course, human rights abuses must cease – reality again rears its ugly head. The dilemma is that there are great pressures to give the benefit of the doubt to transitional or coalition governments, many or all of whose partners may have been guilty of gross human rights violations during the conflict, because of the fear that public criticism of that government on human rights grounds may undermine the carefully constructed coalition and lead to instability. The dilemma is even more acute when there is no history of responsible, rights-protecting government in the past, and the expectations of human rights advocates and civil society groups may be wildly unrealistic, in light of a country's history. One cannot pretend that post-conflict society is likely to live up to normal peacetime human rights norms, particularly when such norms were not respected before the conflict. There is a difference between pre-Pinochet Chile, a country with a long history of constitutionalism and rule of law, and pre-genocide Rwanda, a country wracked by massacres and authoritarian government from its inception. Such differences must be taken into account by both negotiators and human rights practitioners.

One somewhat technical way around the dilemma might be to rely on the concept of states of emergency, during which the temporary derogation from many normal human rights norms is permitted. Even though open armed conflict has ceased, a fragile country recovering from massive violence might certainly be able to make a legitimate case for restricting some rights that would otherwise be guaranteed. The key to adopting this approach, however, is to ensure that such derogations or exceptions are subject to a meaningful degree of oversight, preferably by both national and international bodies. International norms regarding permissible derogations are strict, requiring that any suspension of rights be only 'to the extent strictly required by the exigencies of the situation . . . not inconsistent with . . . [states'] other obligations under international law and do not involve discrimination solely on the ground of race, colour, sex, language, religion or social origin.'[31] In practice, this means that a derogating state must justify the specific derogation in terms of its being both necessary and proportionate to ensuring a legitimate goal. And, of course, any derogation must be temporary.[32]

Whatever the human rights standard to which the parties agree, continuing abuses will undermine the legitimacy of any government and lead the population to believe that little has changed since the end of the conflict, except for the presence of new (sometimes along with the old) and equally corrupt leaders. Whatever the decision with respect to accountability for past abuses, it is essential that future abuses not be tolerated. Such a position is not inconsistent with granting a relatively broad 'margin of appreciation' to a new government, so long as that deference does not include turning a blind eye to abuses or attempting to excuse them by arguing that meaningful criticism might destabilize a carefully crafted transitional regime.

Finally, although the focus in the immediate post-agreement period is usually on physical security and political rights, the rapid implementation of economic, social, and cultural rights also will tend to support any peace accord. Many conflicts stem from economic and social inequities (whether real or perceived), and progress towards the non-discriminatory, equitable distribution of resources is essential. Such human rights issues go well beyond the lip service normally given to 'development', and foreign economic assistance in the short term should be directed at satisfying basic rights and needs.

Rule of Law and Long-term Capacity Building

Much of human rights is about procedural fairness, where the government acts as a neutral arbiter and follows the agreed-upon rules of the game so that solutions to past and future problems can be determined in a manner that the population generally perceives as fair.[33] In many countries, incompetent or inadequate police forces, biased or corrupt courts, and inhumane prisons not only perpetuate human rights violations but also undermine attempts to introduce stability and accountability to newly formed governments.

The scope of 'rule of law' is clearly beyond that of any single international entity, and one challenge of peacebuilding is to coordinate activities designed to promote the rule of law in a manner that is both efficient and sustainable.[34] The breakdown or absence of the rule of law often leads to violence, since aggrieved parties believe that they cannot receive a fair hearing in administrative or judicial fora. Given the stresses in any post-conflict society, improvement in equality and procedural fairness is even more essential in ensuring that an often fragile peace agreement or societal accommodation does not disintegrate. This need not only extends to politically sensitive issues, such as the treatment of minorities or freedom for political parties, but is equally required with respect to ordinary civil disputes, the treatment of individuals by the government bureaucracy, land issues, non-political criminal justice, training of correctional officers and similar issues.

Reform of criminal justice, police, and judiciary must be seen as concepts which go beyond the basics of courts and institutional structures . . . . Property disputes, birth registrations, juvenile justice, citizenship/statelessness, and Disarmament, Demobilisation and Reintegration (DDR) can all be essential to insuring an end to conflict and establishing the rule of law. While consti-tutional courts are often a focus of reform, it is often at the lowest court level, or through the actions of police, that the most marginalised and excluded find themselves denied access to justice.[35]

Establishing the rule of law should not be confused with the more visible or external indicators of democracy, such as elections. Several studies have noted problems in holding early elections, such as those in Bosnia and Herzegovina soon after the 1995 Dayton Agreement, which may have the effect of consolida-ting existing ethnic and other divisions. Roland Paris warns against rapid attempts to democratize and introduce market reforms into post-conflict situations as follows: 'What is needed in the immediate post-conflict period is not quick elec-tions, democratic ferment, or economic "shock therapy" but a more controlled and gradual approach to liberalization, combined with the immediate building of governmental institutions that can manage these political and economic reforms.'[36] The danger of this kind of gradualist or institutionalist peacebuilding is that it may ignore or downplay the implementation of fundamental human rights norms that are essential for even short-term stability, although the caution against quick-fix elections and economic restructuring may well be valid.

Long-term capacity building is often the biggest carrot available to outside mediators, because international donors are enamoured of the concept and are often willing to support institution building with financial assistance. However, institution building also provides an opportunity for squabbling over the 'spoils' of war (and international assistance), and the creation of civil society groups and NGOs often becomes the quickest way to relative riches in a post-conflict environ-ment. And if one must prove one's civil society credentials by constantly criticizing the government, the risk is that criticism may displace the collaboration among government, civil society and individuals that is essential to (re)building a viable country.

No one would dispute that long-term capacity building and establishing the rule of law are essential to sustainable peace. At the same time, however, both mediators and human rights advocates must recognize that, in many cases, neither governmental capacity nor reliable justice ever existed in countries emer-ging from widespread conflict. Thus, the task is the *creation* of such institutions and attitudes, not merely their reconstruction.

Similarly, although the international community regularly calls for particular attention to be paid to women and other disadvantaged or marginalized groups, this cannot be accomplished to the detriment of more pressing needs of the whole population of the state. Ingrained cultural norms and prejudices often take gene-rations to change; while a peace process may offer an opportunity to raise these issues, they are rarely central to the causes of the conflict and may not be central to the resolution of that conflict either. Of course, in some situations, discrimination against particular regions or ethnic groups are at the heart of the conflict, and redressing such discrimination will be essential to creating a stable peace. However, general discrimination against women or the marginalization of the poor are quite different issues. Such problems must be addressed as soon as possible as part of any meaningful campaign to promote and protect human rights, but they should not be linked to wider issues of peacemaking or stabilization.

Flowing from these observations, it is likely to be counterproductive for the international community to promise more than it (or the country itself) can deliver in the medium or long term. Populations should not be promised that, in only a few years, their societies will become economically prosperous, politically open, ethnically tolerant and free of corruption and discrimination. Of course, these should be the ultimate goals of international intervention, both short-term and long-term. However, raising expectations too high in situations where reality will almost inevitably fall short will only put greater pressure on an often tenuous new government and make it easier for 'spoilers' to highlight the apparent failures of any peace agreement.

It is worth bearing in mind the following admonition from former Special Representative of the Secretary-General Lakhdar Brahimi:

> [Peacekeeping is becoming more difficult because] our expectations and agendas are not getting any more realistic. Instead, they have become more ambiguous and multifaceted, seeking to promote justice, national reconciliation, human rights, gender equality, the rule of law, sustainable economic development and democracy – all at the same time, from day one, now, immediately, even in the midst of conflict.[37]

Conclusions

The goals and expertise of the human rights advocate are different from the goals and expertise of the mediator or diplomat.[38] The normative and often adversarial approach of human rights professionals does not generally involve taking into account the views of all sides in a dispute, and neutrality is seen as inappropriate in the face of human rights violations. On the other hand, the mediators zealously guards neutrality as a essential attribute of their job, and the core conflict resolution principles of participation, inclusion, empowerment, cultural sensitivity and equity are quite different from the normative demands of human rights law.

At the same time, human rights practitioners and mediators share the values of impartiality and independence, which are essential to their tasks. Each discipline is concerned with ensuring that the less powerful are adequately protected and represented. Neither group should be tolerant of injustice, although they may disagree on the definition of justice and the degree of relevance it may have at various stages of negotiations.

What has become abundantly clear in the past decade is that neither 'negative peace' (the absence of violent conflict) nor an exclusive focus on human rights protection is sufficient to assist societies in moving from human rights violations and conflict to a fairer, more peaceful life. The positive attributes and focuses of *both* disciplines must be promoted, alongside the efforts of other actors (ethicists, religious figures, intellectuals) who foster values such as humanitarianism, tolerance, generosity, and fairness.

Although they are rather prosaic, the conclusions of the ICHRP report are probably valid:

> Neither an attempt to impose human rights standards as abstract principles, nor the jettisoning of such standards in the search for a cease-fire, is likely to produce lasting solutions. Rather, the best approach to 'peace v. justice' dilemmas may simply be to view them as on-going dilemmas which require to be managed in pursuit of a just and sustainable peace.[39]

Human rights norms and standards provide a floor of justice below which no attempt at conflict resolution should go. This is not an exceptional statement – all mediators have a moral 'bottom line' that prevents them from, for example, facilitating the settlement of a conflict between two parties by condoning genocide against a third party. Conflict resolution practitioners should be aware of human rights norms in the same way that they are aware, in a purely domestic context, of any laws that might limit the scope of potential solutions to the conflict with which they are dealing (this is sometimes referred to as operating within the 'shadow of the law').

At the same time, very few international human rights norms are absolute, and there is legitimate room for taking local conditions into account when one attempts to translate general international norms into specific domestic practices. Neither peace agreements nor their implementation can reflect only global norms without ensuring their relevance to the particular situation at hand. One example is the post-1994 situation in Rwanda, when some international human rights NGOs condemned the use of the informal village-based *gacaca* process to deal with those involved in the genocide as incompatible with international fair trial norms. While *gacaca* may be flawed, insistence on 'fair trials' for over 100,000 detainees in a country without a functioning judiciary is ludicrous and counterproductive.

Human rights advocates are often adversarial in their approach, but this is not necessarily bad. As in the domestic context, reason and compromise do not always prevail, and there is room for attempting to protect rights 'the old fashioned way', through courts, adverse publicity, and public pressure. Such pressure may even be useful to mediators, as a means of narrowing distasteful options that might otherwise make it more likely that notorious criminals or corrupt officials are able to retain a major share of power in a post-settlement situation.

Similarly, conflict resolution techniques can be valuable at any stage of a conflict or potential conflict, whether or not human rights norms are also involved. The basic conflict resolution principles of neutrality, fairness, inclusiveness and 'a level playing field' are essential in helping to encourage adversaries to better understand their options. Human rights advocates need to understand that the goal is not to 'win' debates about violations but to change government practices and attitudes. This change may often be brought about more readily through dialogue, consensus building and flexibility, rather than the 'naming and shaming' that is the stock-in-trade of most major international NGOs. At the same time, not every situation can be honestly described as 'win-win', and mediators must be more forthright when they attempt to persuade parties that this is possible. One of the goals of effective conflict resolution should be to articulate what 'losing' for one side might mean – and the human rights guarantees available to potential 'losers' might be not only relevant but reassuring.

Human rights norms were developed in the post-1945 era in large part as preventive tools to constrain governments from mistreating their own citizens. The goal was not only humanitarian but also to ensure international security; while the maxim that democracies do not go to war with one another may not apply in every situation, the notion that rights-respecting states whose populations are generally treated fairly are less likely to be outwardly aggressive rings true. Thus, human rights rely on peace for their effective implementation and contribute to ensuring that peace exists.

Unrealistically forcing peacetime human rights norms into a context of widespread violence or even into the fragile environment of post-conflict settlements may do a disservice to both human rights and peace. Other norms, such as refugee law and the laws of war, are of more immediate relevance. There is also scope for purely humanitarian activities, in addition to the imposition of law. At the same time, 'peace at any cost' often has a very high cost indeed, one borne on the backs of ordinary people who may see their rights sacrificed to appease those who began the conflict in the first place. Neither justice nor sustainable peace can be built on such a scaffold.

In the end, both mediators and human rights advocates could use more humility and less arrogance. Neither group can create world (or even local) peace by itself, and each must recognize that there are other morally and politically legitimate concerns that might have an impact on the way in which they do their work. Collaboration or at least mutual appreciation is certainly possible, and one should hope that it increases as we gain more knowledge about how to make our interventions more effective.

Perhaps there are still lessons to be learned from what purports to be an old Irish proverb, which is frequently found on tea towels and plaques in souvenir stores: 'May I be given the serenity to accept the things that I cannot change, the courage to change the things that I can, and the wisdom to know the difference between them.' Neither human rights nor conflict resolution practitioners – nor the 'international community' – can change everything, and we need to understand the limits as well as the possibilities of what outside intervention can accomplish.

NOTES

1. There has been relatively little scholarship specifically devoted to examining the relationship between human rights and conflict resolution. In addition to references cited elsewhere in this essay, see Eileen F. Babbitt and Ellen Lutz (eds), *Human Rights and Conflict Resolution in Context* (forthcoming, 2007) [examining the cases of Colombia, Northern Ireland, and Sierra Leone]; Carnegie Council on Ethics and International Affairs, *Human Rights Dialogue* (Special

Issue on Integrating Human Rights and Peace Work), Winter 2002; Hurst Hannum and Eileen F. Babbitt (eds.), *Negotiating Self-Determination*, Lanham, MD: Lexington Books, 2006; Michelle Parlevliet, 'Bridging the Divide: Exploring the Relationship between Human Rights and Conflict Management', *Track Two* Occasional Paper, Vol.11, No.1, Centre for Conflict Resolution, University of Cape Town, 2002, pp.1–52; Joe Saunders, 'Bridging Human Rights and Conflict Resolution: A Dialogue Between Critical Communities,' report of Carnegie Council workshop, 16–17 July 2001 (available at www.cceia.org).

2. To offer only two examples, the existence of the ICTY obviously had no deterrent effect on the actions of Serb forces either in Srebrenica in 1995 or in Kosovo in 1999. The existence of neither the ICTR nor the ICC appears to have had much impact on the scale of atrocities in Africa, from Darfur to the Democratic Republic of Congo, although, in fairness, it is possible that meaningful and timely prosecutions by the ICC of those responsible for crimes in Sudan and Uganda could have an impact on conflicts in the future.

3. Clem McCartney, *Engaging Armed Groups in Peace Processes: Reflections for Practice and Policy from Colombia and the Philippines*, Conciliation Resources: London, 2005, p.7.

4. Robert Ricigliano, 'Introduction: Engaging Armed Groups in Peace processesP, in Ricigliano (ed.), *Choosing to Engage: Armed Groups and Peace Processes*, London: Conciliation Resources, 2005.

5. Guidelines for United Nations Representatives on Certain Aspects of Negotiations for Conflict Resolution. This is an internal, quasi-confidential document that guides UN mediators in a number of areas, particularly with respect to human rights and accountability for violations of international humanitarian law.

6. Peace Agreement between the Government of Sierra Leone and the Revolutionary United Front of Sierra Leone, Lomé, 7 July 1999 (www.usip.org/library/pa/sl/sierra_leone_07071999_toc.html).

7. *Report of the Secretary-General on the Rule of Law and Transitional Justice in Conflict and Post-Conflict Societies*, UN Doc. S/2004/616 (2004), para.10 (Rule of Law Report); cf. Michael O'Flaherty, 'The Sierra Leone Peace Process: The Role of the Human Rights Community, *Human Rights Quarterly*, Vol.26, No.1, 2004, pp.29–62.

8. Contrast this position with the following, which is discussed under the heading 'Difficult Issues and International Law': 'Questions of amnesty, human rights, treatment of prisoners, torture, maintenance of 'no-go' zones, laying of mines, etc. will arise at an early stage in most negotiated settlements to armed conflict. The mediator's responsibility is to draw the parties' attention to the appropriate international law provisions, while conceding that the terms of the agreement will ultimately be the responsibility of the parties themselves. With issues of amnesty in particular, the mediator may simply point out that such provisions will have limited applicability outside their territories and may serve to undermine their status and international support.' N. (Fink) Hayson, 'Engaging Armed Groups in Peace Processes: Lessons for Effective Third-party Practice', in Ricigliano (see n.4 above).

9. See, e.g., Diane Orentlicher, 'Settling Accounts: The Duty to Prosecute Human Rights Violations of a Prior Regime', *Yale Law Journal*, Vol.100, 1991, pp.2539–615.

10. The phrase is taken from the jurisprudence of the European Court of Human Rights and many other international bodies.

11. For a discussion of the problematic nature of the term 'transitional justice', see Hurst Hannum, 'Human Rights in Conflict Resolution: The Role of the Office of the High Commissioner for Human Rights in UN Peacemaking and Peacebuilding, *Human Rights Quarterly*, Vol.28, No.1, 2006, pp.36–7.

12. See International Center for Transitional Justice Mission Statement, available at www.ictj.org/aboutus.asp.

13. UN Doc. E/CN.4/Sub.2/1997/20/Rev.1 (1997); the set of principles is contained in Annex II of the report.

14. UN Doc. E/CN.4/2005/102 and Add.1 (2005).

15. International Council on Human Rights Policy, *Negotiating Justice? Human Rights and Peace Agreements*, Geneva: ICHRP, 2006 (draws on case studies of Bosnia-Herzegovina, Burundi, Cambodia, El Salvador, Guatemala, Mozambique, Northern Ireland, and Sierra Leone), p.96.

16. Orentlicher (see n.9 above), Add.1, Principle 2.

17. Ibid., Principle 35.

18. Ibid. Adequate representation of women and minority groups is considered to be 'essential' to the achievement of these aims.

19. Orentlicher, para.70.

20. Helena Cobban, 'Think Again: International Courts', *Foreign Policy*, March/April 2006, issue 53, pp.22–8. The subtitle of the article (perhaps not Cobban's words) reads: 'Criminal tribunals in places such as Rwanda and the former Yugoslavia were supposed to bring justice to oppressed peoples. Instead, they have squandered billions of dollars, failed to advance human rights, and ignored the wishes of the victims they claim to represent. It's time to abandon the false hope of international justice.' Also see Cobban, *Amnesty after Atrocity?: Healing Nations after Genocide and War Crimes*, Boulder, CO: Paradigm Press, 2006.

21. Ellen Nakashima, 'East Timor massacre survivors pursue justice', *Boston Globe*, 18 Sept. 2005, p. A14.

22. Suzannah Linton, *Putting Things into Perspective: The Realities of Accountability in East Timor, Indonesia and Cambodia*, Baltimore: University of Maryland School of Law, 2005 (Maryland Series in Contemporary Asian Studies, No.3, 2005, pp.88, 82.

23. See, e.g., *Negotiating Justice?* (n.15 above), pp.90, 113.

24. Press Release, Secretary-General, 'Secretary-General Expresses Hope for New Security Council Commitment to Place Justice, Rule of Law at Heart of Efforts to Rebuild War-Torn Countries', UN Doc. SG/SM/8892, SC/7881, 25 Sept. 2003.

25. Hannum (n.11 above), p.46. For an early exchange on the topic, compare Anon., 'Human Rights in Peace Negotiations', *Human Rights Quarterly.*, Vol.18, 1999, pp.249–58, with Felice Gaer, 'UN-Anonymous: Reflections on *Human Rights in Peace Negotiations*', *Human Rights Quarterly.*, Vol.19, 1997, pp.1–8.

26. *Negotiating Justice?* (n.15 above); also see Cobban (n.20 above). Although they are not empirical studies, cf. an April 2006 speech by the Norwegian Minister of Foreign Affairs, Jonas Gahr Støre, 'The Role of Human Rights in Peace Agreements – Norway's facilitation of peace processes' (http://odin.dep.no/ud/english/news/speeches/minister_a/032171-090557/dok-bn.html), and Amnesty International's '15-Point Programme for Implementing Human Rights in International Peace-keeping Operations' (http://web.amnesty.org/pages/aboutai-recs-peace-eng).

27. Christine Bell, *Peace Agreements and Human Rights*, Oxford: Oxford University Press, 2005. Another quasi-empirical study is Tonya L. Putnam, 'Human Rights and Sustainable Peace', in Stephen J. Stedman et al. (eds.), *Ending Civil Wars: The Implementation of Peace Agreements*, Boulder, CO: Lynne Rienner, 2002.

28. *Negotiating Justice?* (n.15 above), p.40.

29. Putnam, p.238. Contrast Bell's recommendation that 'human rights frameworks should have clear enforcement mechanisms which meet international standards', *Negotiating Justice?* (n.15 above), p.48.

30. *Negotiating Justice?* (n.15 above), p.48.

31. The quoted language is from art. 4 of the Covenant on Civil and Political Rights; other international instruments have similar provisions.

32. On derogations and states of emergency, see generally J. Fitzpatrick, *Human Rights in Crisis: The International System for Protecting Rights During States of Emergency*, Philadelphia: University of Pennsylvania Press, 1994; Anna-Lena Svensson-McCarthy, *The International Law of Human Rights and States of Exception: With Special Reference to the Travaux Preparatoires and Case-Law of the International Monitoring Organs*, The Hague: Kluwer, 1998.

33. Rule of Law Report (n.7 above), paras. 2, 4.

34. See generally Rule of Law Report (n.7 above); Hannum (n.11 above), pp.41–3.

35. *Negotiating Justice?* (n.15 above), p.105.

36. R. Paris, *At War's End: Building Peace After Civil Conflict*, Cambridge: Cambridge University Press, 2004, pp.7–8.

37. B. Crossette, 'The U.N.'s Top Envoy Speaks Out, But Who's Listening?' *UN Wire*, 19 July 2004. Others have reached similar conclusions: 'Democratisation efforts ... are premised on the idea that the democratic state functions as an entity in which the population participates. However, the fact that most populations have never experienced a democratic state or that their immediate experiences are not based on liberal-style democratic principles appears to have been overlooked.' Conflict, Security and Development Group, King's College London, *A Review of Peace Operations – A Case for Change* [Overall Introduction and Synthesis Report], London: King's College, 2003, para. 84, available at http://ipi.sspp.kcl.ac.uk/rep002/index.html.

38. See generally E. Lutz, E.F. Babbitt, and H. Hannum, 'Human Rights and Conflict Resolution from the Practitioners' Perspective', *Fletcher Forum of World Affairs*, Vol. 27, Winter/Spring 2003, pp.173–93.

39. ICHRP, p.113.

Peacekeeping, Observers and Human Rights: Challenges for the Future

BERTRAND G. RAMCHARAN

Introduction

The challenge that still remains for Governments, regional and international organizations, NGOs and the human rights movement at large, is to help develop adequate and effective arrangements for the protection of human rights in the face of continuing onslaughts on the human rights of people across the globe. Genocide, ethnic cleansing, crimes against humanity, and war crimes are, alas, far too prevalent in our contemporary world. These acts have been recognized as international crimes, and the International Criminal Court, International Criminal Tribunals for the Former Yugoslavia and Rwanda, the court for Sierra Leone and the court for Cambodia will hopefully have a deterrent effect.

As we look to the future, however, it is important to strive for approaches and methods that would prevent violations before they come to the stage where they necessitate the intervention of the International Criminal Court. We must try to prevent atrocities from taking place to begin with. Prevention is a crucial challenge.[1]

To date, discussion of peacekeeping and human rights has focused on the human rights components of peacekeeping operations and on relations between the UN Department of Peacekeeping Operations (DPKO) and the Office of the UN High Commissioner for Human Rights (OHCHR). There is in existence between the two offices a Memorandum of Understanding on practical cooperation on the ground. There is much of value that has taken place that one should applaud. But the discussion of peacekeeping and human rights cannot remain there. It must become a discussion of how peace forces can be used pro-actively in preventive, containment, protective and settlement modes to head off dangers and to protect people before they become the victims of atrocities. We have in view not only peacekeeping, but also observer forces, deployed flexibly according to need. The discussion of the human rights role of peace forces must not be locked in the past but must look to the future, mindful of contemporary and future security challenges.

Security and Protection Challenges of the Future

In *Contemporary Conflict Resolution*, Ramsbotham, Woodhouse and Miall suggest that 'peace and conflict research is part of an emancipatory discourse and practice which is making a valuable and defining contribution to emerging norms of democratic just and equitable systems of global governance'.[2] This is an apt perspective from which to approach the preventive role of peace forces. Under the category of deep or structural prevention, they discuss issues such as democracy and conflict, governance and conflict, development as prevention, inequality and conflict, abuse of human rights and conflicts and preventive peacebuilding. Under the category of light or operational prevention, they identify a wide range of policy options that 'are in principle available'.

Their assessment is that 'It is generally recognized that when it comes to conflict prevention in practice, there is a long way to go in translating rhetoric into reality. This is especially the case as far as the UN is concerned, where the resources available for preventive programmes are meagre'.[3] It is a tough assessment but it is close to the mark.[4]

According to Cameron Hume, the most urgent threats to international peace and security, Hume thinks, are not identical to those of greatest concern when the Charter was written.[5] The world of the present is affected by the phenomena of state failure, transnational threats and international terrorism.

State failure, Hume argues, 'will be the breeding ground for threats to international peace and security, including terrorism, narcotics, trafficking, infectious diseases, the spread of weapons of mass destruction, and other transnational problems'.[6] He also cites transnational threats such as refugees, famine, arms trafficking, and terrorist sanctuaries.

The traditional tools of diplomacy as cited in the Charter language of 1945, he further argues, and the innovations of third party intervention by the Secretary-General, peacekeeping forces and coalitions of the willing, have not been adequate to deal with these challenges. The years ahead will test the capacity of a significant number of States to govern and to conduct their relations with other States. Population pressures, resource constraints, and uneven economic growth will present real challenges to the ability of the international system to preserve peace and security. The Security Council will have to confront the problems of failing states and of transnational threats. It will have to confront the challenges of rogue states and weapons of mass destruction.

Hume advocated four new approaches for the Security Council. First, in dealing with transnational threats, such as terrorism or the spread of weapons of mass destruction, the Council will need to demonstrate the capacity to make new rules and to make their implementation operational. Second, the Council must lead the way to improved coordination on problems such as refugees, famines and plagues. Third, the Security Council must work with regional organizations and coalitions of the willing. Fourth, the Security Council, working most often with the Secretariat, must expand its capacity to deal with non-state actors, positively and negatively. Hume considers that the post 11 September 2001 National Security strategies of the US have some of these issues in mind, particularly the need for new rules to deal with new problems.

Gregory Fox has noted that the Security Council has been recognizing the importance of democratic governance to further the general welfare of the society of States on whose behalf it acts in matters of peace and security.[7]

The US National Security Strategy, as reported on 17 March 2006, has the spread of democracy as its overarching theme: 'In the cause of ending tyranny and promoting effective democracy we will employ the full array of political, economic, diplomatic and other tools at our disposal.'

Such is the world of the present and the foreseeable future. What, then, should one aim for when considering the future contribution of Peace Forces to the protection of human rights? Let us, to begin with, look at parts of the intellectual history of UN Peace Forces.

The Intellectual History of UN Peace Forces

Peace observation goes back to the time of the League of Nations.[8] Early on in the UN, Trygve Lie, the first Secretary-General, called in 1948 for the establishment of a corps of UN Guards who could be deployed as needed to a variety of tasks. In the Introduction to his Third Annual Report, Lie advocated a force of 1,000 to 5,000 personnel, which could be used for guard duty with the UN, in the conduct of plebiscites under supervision of the UN and in the administration of truce terms. It could be used as a constabulary under the Security Council or the Trusteeship Council during the establishment of international regimes. It might also be called upon for provisional measures to prevent the aggravation of a situation threatening the peace.[9]

In explaining, developing, and eventually modifying his idea for the establishment of a corps of UN Guards, Lie envisaged them performing, *inter alia*, five sets of functions relevant to the discussion of preventive approaches and strategies. They might, he thought, have been called upon by the Security Council under Article 40 of the Charter, which provides for provisional measures to prevent the aggravation of a situation threatening the peace.[10] Second, they might have carried out observation functions.[11] Third, they might have carried protection functions.[12] Fourth, they might have supported commissions of inquiry, conciliation, or mediation.[13] Fifth, when Secretary-General Lie modified his idea to that of a Technical Field Service he added the concept of a panel of field observers, a list of names of qualified persons to be available on call by the Security Council or the General Assembly.[14]

Lie's idea of a corps of UN Guards did not come to fruition in his time but he did see, already in 1948, the UN deployment of observers in sensitive situations, a concept that would subsequently be taken forward and built upon by his successor, Dag Hammarskjöld. His intellectual and policy partner, Lester Pearson's great idea, elaborated in the Reith Lectures over the BBC in 1957, was for the establishment of an international police force that could be rapidly deployed in diverse situations, depending on the need. It was an idea that had in view prevention, containment, settlement, and transformation, core elements of conflict resolution as presented by Ramsbotham, Woodhouse and Miall.[15]

The preventive role of peace observation and peacekeeping forces in the history of the UN needs to be emphasized because it has not only historical significance but crucial relevance to the future of the UN, of peacekeeping, and of the contribution that peacekeeping and peace observation can make to human rights. Peacekeeping, in its first and second generations, had containment and preventive effect on the situation where they were deployed. Nowadays, in what is deemed the third generation of peacekeeping operations, or peace support operations, there is explicit recognition of a more pronounced preventive dimension.

The British doctrine of peace support operation, for example, states the issue thus:

> For the foreseeable future United Kingdom (UK) foreign policy is likely to underpin its conflict prevention activities with the regeneration or sustainment of fragile states. The UK Government usually undertakes such operations as a part of UN (UN) led operations or as part of multilateral endeavours ... The generic title of Peace Support Operations (PSOs) is given by the military to these activities. Typically, the UK's Armed Forces are given responsibility for preventing or suppressing any conflict so that others can undertake activities that will alleviate the immediate symptoms of a conflict and/or a fragile state. Usually, there are associated activities to ensure stability in the long term.[16]

The importance of the preventive role of UN peacekeepers and observers in the future gives particular significance to the preventive deployment in the Former Yugoslav Republic of Macedonia. The author worked personally on the initiative for this preventive deployment and, in the section that follows, relates how this idea came about.

Preventive Peace-keeping: Macedonia

The initiative for a preventive deployment first came from the Co-chairman of the International Conference on the Former Yugoslavia. They had discussed this idea with President Kiro Gligorov who, in turn, wrote to the Secretary-General of the UN on 11 November 1992 asking for such a preventive deployment. In a letter of 18 November 1992, to the UN Secretary-General, drafted by this author, the Co-chairman told the Secretary-General that there was growing need to take preventive measures to avoid the outbreak of violence in Macedonia and Kosovo. They recalled that they had warned the Security Council a few days earlier, on 13 November 1992, that a tragedy of dreadful proportions could occur if conflict were to break out in Macedonia and Kosovo, engulfing the neighbouring countries.

Elaborating upon their idea, the Co-chairman stated that in terms of preventive diplomacy it would be desirable to put the UN personnel, under the aegis of UNPFOFOR, into Macedonia so as to provide a calming influence for all sides and give a sense of stability. They suggested to the Secretary-General:

> The deployment of a contingent of UNPROFOR personnel within Macedonia, who could have their headquarters in Skopje and be distributed in the main population centres, as well as on the Macedonian borders with Serbia (including Kosovo) and Albania. Their efforts would be

complemented by those of the CSCE, which already had a small 'spill-over' mission in Skopje.

Upon receipt of the Co-chairman's recommendation, Secretary-General Boutros Boutros-Ghali advised the Security Council that he would be sending an exploratory mission to the Former Yugoslav Republic Macedonia to look into the possibility of establishing a preventive deployment of UN peace-keepers in the country. Following its visit, the exploratory mission made the following recommendations:

(a) That a small UNPROFOR presence be established on the Macedonian side of the Republic's borders with Albania and the Federal Republic of Yugoslavia (Serbia and Montenegro) with an essentially preventive mandate of monitoring and reporting any developments in the border areas which could undermine confidence and stability in Macedonia or threaten its territory;
(b) That a small group of Untied Nations civilian police be deployed in the border areas to monitor the Macedonian border police.

The rationale for the deployment was that incidents arising from illegal attempts to cross the border had led to increased tension on the Macedonian side. The Mission believed that the presence of a small UN civilian police detachment would have a calming effect.

The Secretary-General reported to the Security Council on the findings of the exploratory mission, together with his recommendations[17] and, on 11 December 1992, the Security Council authorized the Secretary-General to establish a presence of the UN Protection Force (UNPROFOR) in the Former Yugoslav Republic of Macedonia. The Council requested that the Secretary-General deploy immediately the military, civil affairs, and administrative personnel he had recommended in his report, as well as police monitors.

The first UN Civilian Police (UNCIVPOL) monitors arrived on 27 December 1992. They were eventually deployed along the northern and western borders. On 7 January 1993, a Canadian company arrived in the country pending the arrival of a joint battalion from Finland, Norway and Sweden. On 18 February, the Nordic battalion took over the operation from the Canadian company. At the beginning there were 19 UN Military Observers (UNMOs) in the area of operations. The western border south of Debar was covered solely by UNMOs.

From early January 1993, the northern border and the western border north of Debar were constantly monitored from observation posts and by regular patrols, with a view to reporting any activities that might increase tension or threaten peace and stability. The UNMOs conducted regular patrols in their area of operations to monitor the situation. They also carried out a programme of visits to border villages aimed at gaining the confidence of their inhabitants and assisting in defusing possible inter-ethnic tensions. While carrying out their border visiting programme, the UNMOs were approached by representatives of different ethnic groups who lodged various complaints about discriminatory practices by the authorities. In those cases where the complaints were relevant to the mandate of the mission, they were brought to the attention of the appropriate authorities. Some were also brought to the attention of the competent international bodies, such as the International Conference of the Former Yugoslavia.

UNCIVPOL also conducted regular patrols to specific crossings, and the border areas in general, on a daily basis. In the course of doing so, it received through local mayors a number of complaints concerning the local border police. In those cases where there appeared *prima facie* to be a basis for the complaint, UNCIVPOL took up the matter with the relevant police authorities.

The Civil Affairs component of the mission established, from the outset, an information programme to explain the role of UNPROFOR in the country. UNPROFOR maintained close coordination with the CSCE mission in the country.

By the middle of 1993, UNPROFOR's assessment was that it had been successful in its preventive mandate in the country. It was concerned however, about the internal situation and the possibility of instability should there be an increase in the inter-ethnic tensions, a possibility which, it reported, was repeatedly mentioned by local and international sources. A related concern of UNPROFOR was about the deterioration of the economic situation stemming from the implementation of sanctions which, it was felt, could contribute to heightened inter-ethnic tensions.

At the beginning of the deployment, and well before a human dimension was explicitly authorized by the Security Council, members of the Nordic battalion had given a spectacular example of the human dimension through voluntary service. On a visit to the Nordic troops on the northern border with Kosovo, one saw the troops on a mountain overlooking Kosovo and some Macedonian Albanian villages connected by dirt roads. In the rainy seasons these roads became impassable and the villages were almost cut off from one another. Members of the Nordic battalion undertook Operation Mongoose as a private initiative: in their spare time they constructed proper roads linking the villages so that they would not be isolated during the rainy seasons. During the time of our visit one could see from their high observation post the roads they had already built and those they were continuing to work on. In the author's three and a half years with the peace operations in the Former Yugoslavia this was one of the proud moments he felt for the UN and for the power of goodness.

By September of 1993, the Secretary-General reported to the Security Council that the FYROM Command of UNPROFOR consisted of 1,190 military and civilian, including UNCIVPOL, personnel. UNPROFOR reported: 'The first venture in the field of preventive peace-keeping on the part of UNPROFOR continues to be successful, and to enjoy an excellent cooperative relationship with the FYROM Government, and to be fully supported by the people of the country.'

The leadership of the preventive deployment would come to conclude that 'the increasing internal instability in the FYROM could prove to be more detrimental to the stability of the country than outside threats'. UNPROFOR would therefore need 'to consider what its role should be, if any, in the event that internal stability results in some form of civil conflict'.[18]

Thus it was that the deployment developed the second of its three pillars, as presented by Sokalski, good offices and political action, alongside troop deployment and the human dimension. As Sokalski has written, the mission developed and maintained active contacts with political forces and ethnic groups in the country as a means of promoting domestic stability. Efforts were made to reduce the level of mistrust among the country's political and ethnic actors, and UNPREDEP set in place a dialogue on questions regarding the rights of ethnic communities and national minorities. Sokalski's assessment was that:

> UNPREDEP was recognized as a significant instrument for facilitating dialogue, restraint and practical compromise between the different segments of Macedonian society. UN troop patrols along the northern and western borders of the country effectively complemented such activities; this outreach had a calming and stabilizing effect throughout the area. The contingent of UN military observers and the team of civilian police monitors rendered equally invaluable services.[19]

The preventive deployment in the Former Yugoslav Republic of Macedonia worked effectively – externally as well as internally. The model of UN observers patrolling sensitive areas where ethnic tensions were high, receiving complaints, transmitting them to the authorities, and serving as an intermediary and confidence builder, is one that clearly has great relevance to situations of ethnic and religious tension in situations where there are minority populations, or in other situations where internal strife or conflict could result in gross violations of human rights.

Other Preventive Deployments

In his 2001 report on conflict prevention, Secretary-General Kofi Annan, noted that while all peacekeeping operations could be said to have a preventive function in that they were intended to avert the outbreak or recurrence of conflict, their preventive role had been particularly clear where they had been deployed before the beginning of an armed internal or international conflict. This had taken place three times over the past decade, with UNPREDEP, the UN Mission in the Central African Republic (MINURCA) and a succession of operations in Haiti. Apart from the shared feature that their host countries had not been involved in a violent internal or international conflict, the common features included the possibility, or even the likelihood, of armed conflict, consent of the States concerned to the peacekeeping operations as the form of prevention, and the authorization of the operation by the Security Council.

The rarity of preventive deployment, the Secretary-General commented, suggested that the international community had been reluctant to expend the political and financial capital required for a peace operation without the clear case for deployment that is made by open conflict. However, while success in a preventive mission was by definition hard to measure with precision, it was clear that there were circumstances in which preventive deployment of a peacekeeping operation could save lives and promote stability. The fact that conflict did not erupt within the host country during the above deployments strongly suggested that a UN preventive deployment operation, a symbol of the international community's interest and as a source of leverage to promote its aims, might make a crucial contribution.

In preventive deployment as in other forms of peacekeeping, a multi-dimensional approach would be required to address the root causes of conflict. It was also clear that, as with all peacekeeping, the ability of preventive deployment operations to contribute to lasting peace depended ultimately upon the readiness of the parties to take advantage of the opportunity before them.

In light of the close relationship between peacekeeping and peace-building, the Secretary-General welcomed the recognition by the Security Council of the value of including, as appropriate, peace-building elements in the mandates of peace-keeping operations. In light of the civil conflicts typical of the post-cold war world, particular emphasis needed to be given in this regard to civilian police, who had played an increasingly important preventive role in UN peacekeeping. Their contribution had been to restore public support to the local forces of law and order, whether by training the local police, monitoring their performance or assisting with the restructuring and reform of police institutions.

Preventive Observation: South Africa

As South Africa tackled the dismantling of the apartheid regime and the introduction of democratic governance, the struggle for ascendancy among its political parties presented serious dangers of a descent into anarchy and violence. One such moment occurred in July-August 1992 when the African National Congress (ANC) and its supporters launched a series of 'mass actions' in different parts of the country to show its strength and support among the population at large.

Fearing a descent into the abyss, Nelson Mandela and Frederick de Clerk jointly asked Secretary-General Boutros Boutros-Ghali to send UN observers to South Africa to observe the mass action campaign with a view to heading off violence. Within a matter of days, the Secretary-General sent ten UN staff members, including this author, to South Africa. There was no opportunity of being briefed or given guidance beforehand. We had to make up the rules as we went along.

This author was assigned to the most violent area, Natal-Kwazulu. Observation contributed to calming a violent situation, as the following excerpt from the author's daily reporting cables shows:

Thursday 6 August

> Observation party started today by visiting Durban township of Fulwenimet local police chief (Kwazulu police) who provided list of five recent deaths. Visited scene of one death and spoke to neighbours. Spoke to another man whose home had been attacked with shots and petrol bombs and whose wife had died and his child injured. He identified one of his assailants. Visited third home where man had been shot dead and wife injured. Two young children (about 12 and 8) were living alone. Also visited four homes which had recently been fire-bombed.
>
> . . .

Then overflew Esikhaweni where large crowd had assembled before police station. ANC representative Radebe proposed to land. IFP [Intakha Freedom Party] representative objected, saying agreed ground rules provided for landing only in event of violence-related incidents. I upheld ground rule and said we would not land. ANC representative entered a reservation.

Then flew to Pietermaritzberg where IFP and ANC manifestations had led to two large gatherings involving blockage of buses. Overflew 'PM' and observed that gatherings were dispersing. Landed at airport then set off in van draped with UN markings. Showed the UN flag by visiting downtown 'PM' police reported that city had been in chaos during the day.

Eight other UN colleagues were similarly deployed in other areas of South Africa. There is no doubt that the UN presence helped control the situation and reduce the risk of clashes between ANC and IFP supporters. This mission would subsequently be followed by an Observer Mission, UNOMSA, which arrived with 13 staff members on 13 September 1992, after the settlement process had run into problems.[20] UNOMSA grew to 100 observers in its first year and rose to 2,500 people in the final election stage of its operation. It was deployed first to the spots with greatest violence, the Vaal, Johannesburg and Kwazulu/Natal. The mission eventually spread to 45 locations. Its mandate was carried out by teams of two and sometimes three in various locations all over the country in daily contact with headquarters in Johannesburg.

The presence of international observers did not end political violence but it created favourable conditions for democratic transition. According to Angela King, the Head of the mission:

UNOMSA was one of the UN's first experiences of a preventive diplomacy mission as defined in the *Agenda for Peace*. It became a model rich in lessons in how to develop community involvement and national ownership of a peace process. Although the mandate of the mission was to observe and to be the Security Council's eyes and ears, the teams rapidly developed quiet supportive diplomacy in harmony with the peace accord counterparts, and once they had gained trust and confidence took a much more proactive role in negotiating, persuading, nudging and sometimes shaming South Africans to return to the peace tables at all levels and though often characterized as low-key, has been followed by the UN in other areas.[21]

From the very first day, UNOMSA's teams reached out to all eleven regions of the country. Channels of communication were established across the political spectrum with all 25 political parties and entities. The Head of Mission met and had regular consultations with the leaders of all parties and entities and more importantly, heads of the police and military in the various provinces. This ensured inside information of political developments, likely areas of new unrest where bombs were likely to be placed, early warning on both sides of impending outbreaks, and for the most part ensured the safety of the mission's

South African counterparts as well as of UNOMSA staff, though some received wounds from bullets, strafing and stone throwing.

Those contacts were useful in carrying out the mandate, in particular in explaining the importance of the design of political institutions for a sustainable democratic settlement, getting peace negotiations back on track, and defusing violence and tensions between the security forces and the population, as well as between various political and ethnic factions.

NGOs, religious and tribal leaders played a useful role in the political process. Numerous caucuses and meetings were attended and legal and logistical support was provided to independent watchdog organizations, among them the Goldstone Commission. South Africans everywhere grew accustomed to seeing the UN's face – women and men dressed in blue caps and smocks, carrying the UN flag proudly.

In the view of Angela King, the primary lesson of UNOMSA was what was later called by Lakhdar Brahimi, who had come to watch over the successful elections, a 'light footprint' in national reconciliation when, instead of sending an international mediator or military peacekeepers, the international community chose to encourage local parties and observe their direct negotiations and intervened only at vital junctures. This included assisting the setting up of a Transitional Executive Council, Independent Electoral Commission and furthering of the election process that culminated in the holding of the first democratic non-racial elections in April 1994.

Through all of this, UNOMSA's main ally was the framework and people of the Peace Accord signed by all parties. Its structures at the national, regional and local levels gave entry points to all parts of the country, to different strata of society and access to all disputes and settlements. It gave the mission access to the courts to monitor that judges were being even handed, to hostels where migrant workers had been kept in often dire conditions, to prisons, to the seat of power in Ulundi, Bophutaswana, Ciskei, Western Cape and elsewhere. The Peace Accord drawn up by South Africans before the arrival of the UN saw its implementation under UNOMSA.

Another key lesson learned from UNOMSA, according to Angela King, was the critical role of women in political processes. From the very beginning, a special effort was made to select UNOMSA staff for the teams on the basis of gender balance, ethnic diversity and varied occupational experience. The presence of so many women in leadership positions in UNOMSA, over 50 per cent in the first 14 months, acted as a catalyst to change the views and attitudes of many local women irrespective of their party affiliation. International and local women in partnership with men, proved to be successful negotiators and capable of proposing non-traditional approaches in finding the means to establish dialogue between polarized groups.

With the assistance of UNOMSA, South African women emerged to participate in peace committees, church groups and non-governmental organizations. Through traditional mediation means such as family ties, oral narratives, and prayers and songs, women raised awareness of the need for reconciliation and the restoration of trust between communities. With compassion and understanding, they explained the benefits of peace, and the futility of violence and conflict, thus contributing to a non-threatening environment. During electoral campaigns, women advocated increased integration of a gender perspective into decisions and policies concerning their communities.

A Corps of Humanitarian Observers

In a path-breaking report that he submitted to the Commission on Human Rights on ways and means of tackling the human rights root causes of mass exoduses, the late former UN High Commissioner for Refugees, Prince Sadruddin Aga Khan, made the case for the formation of a corps of humanitarian observers who could be deployed to situations of concern as soon as possible.[22] Prince Sadruddin, based on his experience with many humanitarian situations, thought that such an urgent deployment could have a calming influence and also a protective one. While this idea was not followed up by UN bodies, Prince Sadruddin himself put it into practice when he was called upon to serve as humanitarian coordinator in the situation in Northern Iraq in the aftermath of the first Gulf War. The idea proved very successful on that occasion and Prince Sadruddin pointed to its success and called for the emulation of the method elsewhere.[23]

The Contemporary Human Rights Roles of Peacekeeping Operations

A presentation on the web-site of the UN DPKO which discuss the contemporary principles and doctrines of UN peacekeeping, asserts that the promotion and protection of human rights is central to and cuts across all areas of peacekeeping and has become a standard element of most Security Council mandates. All UN entities have a responsibility to ensure that human rights are promoted and protected through and within their operations in the field.[24] Moreover, all peacekeeping personnel, whether military, police or civilian, are bound by international human rights law and have an individual responsibility to protect, promote and advocate for human rights. OHCHR, as 'lead agency' on human rights issues, has a central role to play through the provision of expertise, guidance and support to the human rights components of UN peacekeeping operations.[25]

The same document notes that Security Council resolution 1325 (2000) on Women, Peace and Security places binding requirements on all UN peacekeeping operations to mainstream gender issues into operational activities. In this regard, it is widely recognized that the international community's objectives in countries emerging from conflict will be better served if women and girls are protected and arrangements are put in place to allow for the full participation of women in the peace process. Missions should ensure that their operations are undertaken with due consideration for the needs of different demographic groups, and in particular their differing impact on women and men. Furthermore, UN peacekeeping operations have a responsibility to ensure a coordinated response to Children and Armed Conflict (CAAC) concerns, and to monitor and report on child protection issues to the Secretary-General.

A UN Handbook on UN Multidimensional Peacekeeping Operations lists the following human rights functions of UN peacekeeping forces, depending on the mandate of each operation:

- Reporting human rights violations and working to prevent future abuse;
- Investigating and verifying past human rights violations;
- Promoting and protecting civil, cultural, economic, political and social rights;
- Conducting capacity-building initiatives with local governmental agencies and NGOs, including national and local human rights institutions;
- Assisting relevant judicial and truth and reconciliation processes to foster a culture of accountability and address impunity;
- Collaborating with UN and international development and emergency relief organizations on human rights issues;
- Designing and conducting human rights training programmes for UN peacekeeping personnel and local and national institutions, such as the military and police forces;
- Providing advice and guidance on human rights to all peacekeeping components;
- Working to address human rights of problems associated with most modern conflicts, including massive movements of refugees and internally displaced persons (IDPs), the increasing conscription of child soldiers and the sexual exploitation and trafficking of women and children; and
- Identifying and integrating a human rights perspective into programmes to disarm, demobilize and reintegrate combatants.[26]

Notwithstanding the foregoing impressive list of human rights challenges, there are formidable protection challenges in the field, as the next sections will show.

Protection Challenges

Protection of Civilians in Armed Conflict: UN Aide Memoire

The UN *Aide Memoire on the Protection of Civilians in Armed Conflict*[27] set out an agenda for protection of civilians placing emphasis on prioritizing and supporting the immediate protection needs of displaced persons and civilians in host communities through measures to enhance security for displaced persons, measures to enhance security for civilians who remain in their communities and for host communities living in or around areas where refugees or internally displaced persons take shelter.

The Aide Memoire called for facilitation of safe and unimpeded access to vulnerable populations as the fundamental prerequisite for humanitarian assistance and protection through appropriate security arrangements, engagement in sustained dialogue with all parties to the armed conflict, facilitation of the delivery of humanitarian assistance, compliance with obligations under relevant international humanitarian, human rights and refugee law, and counter-terrorism measures in full compliance with all obligations under international law.

It urged strengthening of the capacity of local police and judicial systems to physically protect civilians and enforce law and order through deployment of qualified and well-trained international civilian police, technical assistance for local police, judiciary and penitentiaries, reconstruction and rehabilitation of institutional infrastructure, and mechanisms for monitoring and reporting of alleged violations of humanitarian, human rights and criminal law.

The Aide Memoire stressed the importance of addressing the specific needs of women for assistance and protection through special measures to protect women and girls from gender-based discrimination and violence, rape and other forms of sexual violence; implementation of measures for reporting on and prevention of sexual abuse and exploitation by humanitarian workers and peacekeepers; mainstreaming of gender perspective, including the integration of gender advisers in peace operations. It also emphasized the need to address the specific needs of children for assistance and protection through prevention of and putting an end to the recruitment of child soldiers in violation of international law. The Memoire called for specific provisions for the protection of children, including where appropriate, the integration of child protection advisers in peace operations.

Finally, the Aide Memoire called for putting an end to impunity through the establishment and use of effective arrangements for investigating and prosecuting serious violations of humanitarian and criminal law; the exclusion of genocide, crimes against humanity and war crimes from amnesty provisions; and the referral of situations, where possible and appropriate, to international courts and tribunals.

Protection of Children in Armed Conflicts

A Report of the Secretary-General submitted to the General Assembly in 2004 provided a Comprehensive Assessment of the UN System response to children affected by armed conflict.[28] The report grouped recommendations for improving and sustaining efforts on Children and Armed Conflict (CAAC) into four categories, which constitute the medium-term strategic priorities for the UN system to improve its response to children affected by armed conflict: (a) Continued vigorous advocacy for children and armed conflict; (b) An effective and credible monitoring and reporting system on child rights violations; (c) Enhanced mainstreaming of CAAC issues across the UN system; and (d) Improved coordination of CAAC issues across the UN system.[29]

On advocacy, the report concluded that there was continuing need for a Special Representative of the Secretary-General (SRSG)-CAAC as an independent advocate reporting directly to the UN Secretary-General and recommended the introduction of appropriate mechanisms for measurement of progress against benchmarks established each year. The mandated functions of the SRSG-CAAC should focus on the following: integrating children's rights and concerns into the UN' peace and security, humanitarian and development agendas throughout all phases of conflict prevention, peace-building, peacemaking and peacekeeping activities; unblocking political impasses to secure commitments from political actors on child protection at national and regional levels and ensuring adequate follow-up to these commitments; and ensuring the inclusion of children and armed conflict concerns in all relevant reports submitted to the Security Council by the Secretary-General. It called for reporting of child rights violations to relevant bodies, e.g. the Secretary-General, the Security Council, governments and regional mechanisms, and advocating the inclusion of appropriate measures in resolutions, such as sanctions, for actors who are violating CAAC norms and standards. The report called for a collaborative process to produce the annual Secretary-General's report to the Security Council on children in armed conflict, which should focus on progress in the application of CAAC norms and standards, including reporting on child rights violations in situations of conflict; suggestions for measures to ensure compliance with norms and standards; and high-level analysis of CAAC trends with recommendations on improvements to the UN system response, particularly with suggestions on how UN peace and security mechanisms can respond better to CAAC, and progress on the development of a monitoring and reporting system for child rights violations.

The document recommended producing an annual report using input from key UN actors. It also recommended providing proactive advocacy support to the Secretary-General, Heads of Agencies, SRSGs, Resident Coordinators/ Humanitarian Coordinators (RCs/HCs) and other high-level UN officials, primarily through inter-agency committees, and annual meetings of RCs and HCs; co-chairing a coordination mechanism at UN Headquarters on children affected by armed conflict; and maintaining a high-profile public awareness on CAAC issues as required to achieve political advocacy objectives including cooperation with the Department of Public Information.[30] The report urged that the advocacy role of the Resident Coordinator and the High Commissioner for Human Rights be systematically resorted to in support of CAAC concerns and issues.[31]

The report recommended that a robust monitoring and reporting system for child rights violations in conflict situations be developed in three distinct stages: developing an accepted, standardized and practical methodology to identify, document and verify child rights violations; setting up and coordinating networks of actors on the ground to document child rights concerns, and establishing responsibilities and procedures for disseminating and leveraging the information.[32]

Protection of Women

In its resolution 1325(2000), the UN Security Council called upon all parties to armed conflict to respect fully international law applicable to the rights and protection of women and girls, especially as civilians, in particular the obligations applicable to them under the Geneva Conventions of 1949 and the Additional Protocols thereto of 1977, the Refugee Convention of 1951 and the Protocol thereto of 1967, the Convention on Elimination of All Forms of Discrimination against Women of 1979 and the Optional Protocol thereto of 1999 and the Convention on the Rights of the Child of 1989 and its two Optional Protocols from 25 May 2000, and to bear in mind the relevant provisions of the Rome Statute of the ICC.[33] The Council further called on all parties to armed conflict to take special measures to protect women and girls from gender-based violence, particularly rape and other forms of sexual abuse, and all other forms of violence in situations of armed conflict.[34]

Protection of Internally-Displaced Persons

The Guiding Principles on Internal Displacement[35] provide that national authorities have the primary duty and responsibility to provide protection and humanitarian assistance to internally displaced persons within their jurisdiction. Certain internally displaced persons, such as children, especially unaccompanied minors, expectant mothers, mothers with young children, female heads of household, persons with disabilities and elderly persons shall be entitled to protection and assistance required by their condition and to treatment which takes into account their special needs. All authorities and international actors shall respect and ensure respect for their obligations under international law, including human rights and humanitarian law, so as to prevent and avoid conditions that might lead to displacement of persons. The Principles contain, in addition to general principles, guidance on protection from displacement (prevention), protection during displacement, humanitarian assistance, and principles relating to return, resettlement and reintegration.

UN Field Operations and Human Rights: The 'Brahimi Report'[36]

Keeping in mind the foregoing protection challenges, it would be useful to recall the recommendations of the 'Brahimi Report', which advocated, *inter alia*, the essential importance of the UN system adhering to and promoting international human rights instruments and standards, and international humanitarian law in all aspects of its peace and security activities. It also called for improving respect for human rights through monitoring, education and investigation of past and existing abuses, providing technical assistance for democratic development, and promoting conflict resolution and reconciliation techniques.

The Report furthermore stressed the importance of integrating human rights specialists in peace-building missions; upholding the rule of law and respect for human rights through team work on the part of judicial, penal, human rights and policing experts; training military, police and other civilian personnel on human rights issues and on the relevant provisions of international humanitarian law; a doctrinal shift in the use of civilian police, other rule of law elements and human rights experts in complex peace operations to reflect an increased focus on strengthening rule of law institutions and improving respect for human rights in a post-conflict environment.

The Idea for the Establishment of a Rapid Reaction Force

The idea for the establishment of a Rapid Reaction Force has been under discussion in UN circles for some time but has so far seen only partial implementation. It is, however, an important preventive idea that has great relevance to the future of the UN. Ramsbotham, Woodhouse and Miall provide a neat summary of the journey of the idea.

In the 1990s, a group, the 'Friends of Rapid Deployment', worked with the DPKO to secure support for developing a rapidly deployable mission headquarters (RDMHQ). Since 1994, DPKO had organized the UN Stand-by Arrangement System (UNSAS) to expand the quality and quantity of resources that member states might provide. To complement this arrangement, the Danish Government, in cooperation with thirteen regular troop contributors, organized a multinational Stand-by Readiness Brigade (SHIRBRIG). The concept was also advocated in the UN High-level Panel on Threats, Challenges and Change.

In 1995, the Netherlands published 'A UN Rapid Deployment Brigade: A Preliminary Study' which argued that developing crises necessitated a rapidly deployable 'fire brigade'. The report called for a permanent rapidly deployable brigade. In 1995, the Government of Canada also published a study, 'Towards a Rapid Reaction Capability for the UN' which could include an early warning mechanism, an effective decision-making process, reliable transportation and infrastructure, logistical support, adequate finances, and well-trained and equipped personnel.

In the academic writings on the subject, Longville made the case for a UN Emergency Peace Service which Ramsbotham, Woodhouse and Miall supported:

> The development of a UN Emergency Peace Service, or of a mechanism similar to it, is ... a progression of the idea of collective human security agenda to which the UN is committed ... this does indeed require new ways of thinking about the nature and roles of peacekeeping and about the function of peace operations in the emerging global order.[37]

The Case for Flexible, Rapid Deployment of Peacekeepers and Observers

From the perspective of human rights protection, it can no longer be satisfactory that one waits until there has been a crisis before considering the deployment of peace forces or observers, UN or regional. One must in the future seek to head off atrocities before they take place. This means that observers or peace forces must be called into the picture much earlier to help support democracies, head off state failures, and to address transnational threats before they deteriorate. We deal with each of these in turn.

Support for democracy

There are fledgling democracies in many parts of the world and it will take time for them to take roots and become stable. It is crucial that they be encouraged and supported. There are many situations in which problems of underdevelopment or internal strife test fledgling democracies. In some of these situations it would help to have international observers stationed in key areas to help promote confidence and to ward off problems.

With the consent of the government it would be helpful in some of these situations to deploy observers in preventive or confidence building mode. As could be seen in the case of UNPREDEP, they could also act as a channel for defusing ethnic grievances or human rights problems. A more pro-active approach is called for to support democracies, and thereby promote human rights, through the deployment of observers in sensitive situations.

Heading off State Failures

If, as Hume has argued, the international community will need to deal with increasing cases of state failure, then, for the sake of international peace and security, as well as for human rights, it is important to heighten efforts to head off such state failures. For the reasons adduced in the preceding section, the preventive deployment of observers, could, in many situations, help avoid the descent into the abyss. Proactive peace forces can thus help, including with human rights.

Containing and reducing Transnational Threats

Terrorism, narcotics trafficking, intentional criminal activities, trafficking in human beings and similar problems threaten the security of fragile states and international peace and security. They also contribute to gross violations of human rights. One cannot generalise here about the potential role of international observers in containing the problem. A class case would be the build-up of international terrorist activity in an area. International observers could help by monitoring the contours of the situation and reporting on it. That, in turn, could help organs such as the Security Council have a better assessment of the situation and act to contain it. Here also, issues of security are intertwined with issues of human rights.

Protecting population groups at risk

In many countries of the world insecurity and gross violations of human rights are caused by lack of protection of minorities or indigenous populations. The resulting situations can lead to strife, rebellion, or open conflict. One could imagine situations where the causes of security and human rights would be well served by a preventive deployment of peacekeepers or observers.

The UN Peacebuilding Commission

Peacebuilding, at is core, is a preventive idea. It is meant to head off the resurgence of conflict and, in the long term, to remove the root causes that led to conflict in the first place. *Agenda for Peace*, in 1992, first defined the concept of peacebuilding, which was later elaborated upon in the *Supplement to Agenda for Peace*. According to an *Agenda for Peace*, peacebuilding included:

> [C]omprehensive efforts to identify and support structures which will tend to consolidate peace and advance a sense of confidence and well-being among people. Through agreements ending civil strife, these may include disarming the previously warring parties and the restoration of order, the custody and possible destruction of weapons, repatriating refugees, advisory and training support for security personnel, monitoring elections, advancing

efforts to protect human rights, reforming or strengthening governmental institutions and promoting formal and informal processes of political participation.[38]

The High-level Panel on *Threats, Challenges and Change* saw peacebuilding as an inherent part of the efforts of the UN to prevent, contain, and resolve conflicts and it therefore recommended the establishment of a Peacebuilding Commission, which after a further recommendation of the Secretary General in *In Larger Freedom*, was formally established in 2005.[39] It is intended to marshal resources at the disposal of the international community and propose integrated strategies for post-conflict recovery, focus attention on reconstruction, institution-building and sustainable development, in countries emerging from conflict.

The Commission is expected to bring together the UN capacities and experience in conflict prevention, mediation, peacekeeping, respect for human rights, the rule of law, humanitarian assistance, reconstruction and long-term development. Specifically, the Commission will:

(a) Propose integrated strategies for post-conflict peacebuilding and recovery.
(b) Help to ensure predictable financing for early recovery activities and sustainable investment over the medium to longer term.
(c) Extend the period of attention by the international community to post-conflict situations.
(d) Develop best practices on issues that require extensive collaboration among military, humanitarian and development actors.

The deployment of observers in situations of concern must surely be one of the methods of action of the Peacebuilding Commission.

Conclusion

From the foregoing, it will be seen that new challenges require new approaches to the deployment of peacekeepers and observers in the cause of human rights. A world seeking to prevent conflicts and gross violations of human rights must aim for prompt, adequate, and effective protection approaches and methods. It will no longer be satisfactory to consider the human rights role of peacekeeping forces in the aftermath of conflict. The accent must be placed in the future on the preventive role of peacekeepers and observers in protecting human rights.

Peacekeepers and observers can, in the future, serve the cause of human rights through preventive deployments in support of democracy, to ward off state failures, in dealing with transnational threats, in protecting population groups at risk, and the process of peacebuilding generally. The challenge at hand is for prompt, adequate, and effective human rights protection. That means we must have more preventive action on the ground. Peacekeepers and observers can play a crucial role.

Such an approach would not be easy from the point of view of acceptability, financing, logistics and management. We are all well aware of this. But that is not the central issue. The central issue is the kind of world we wish to build and the imperative need to protect human rights before violations take place. We can build a world of universal respect for human rights by striving for it and by having the resolve to take the actions needed. The flexible, rapid deployment of peacekeepers and observers for human rights protection along the lines we have advocated is certainly feasible and affordable. Tomorrow's generation will demand it!

NOTES

1. See on this Linos-Alexander Sicilianos (ed.), *The Prevention of Human Rights Violations*, The Hague: Martinus Nijhoff, 2001.
2. Oliver Ramsbotham, Tom Woodhouse and Hugh Miall, *Contemporary Conflict Resolution* (2nd ed.) Cambridge: Blackwell/Polity Press, 2005, p.xiii.
3. Ibid., p.125.
4. See, generally, Bertrand G. Ramcharan, *Preventive Diplomacy at the UN. The Journey of an Idea*, Indiana University Press, 2007.
5. Cameron Hume, 'The Security Council in the Twenty-First Century.', in David Malone (ed.) The *UN Security Council from the Cold War to the 21st Century*, New York: International Peace Academy, 2004.
6. Ibid., p.615
7. Gregory Fox, 'The Security Council and Democratization', in Malone (n.6 above).
8. See David W. Wainhouse, *International Peace Observations: A History and Forecast*, Baltimore: Johns Hopkins Press, 1966.
9. GAOR, Third Session, Supp. No. 1, UN Doc. A/565, 5 July 1948.
10. Third Annual Report, Collected Papers, 156.
11. Report to the General Assembly, reproduced in Andrew W. Cordier and Wilder Foote (eds.), *Public Papers of the Secretaries-General of the UN, Volume I: Trygve Lie*, New York: Columbia University Press, 1969, p.167.
12. Ibid.
13. Ibid., p.171.
14. Cordier and Foote (n.12 above), pp.187–188.
15. Ramsbotham, Woodhouse and Miall (n.3 above), p.331.
16. Ibid., pp.143–144.
17. *Report of the Secretary-General on the Former Yugoslav Republic of Macedonia*, UN Doc. S/24923, 9 December 1992.
18. Background paper submitted by the FYROM Command to Brainstorming Exercise on the future of UNPROFOR, Zagreb-Mokrice, 15–17 February 1994. Paper in the possession of the author, who participated in the exercise.
19. Henryk J. Sokalski, *An Ounce of Prevention: Macedonia and the UN Experience in Preventive Diplomacy*, Washington, D.C.: United States Institute for Peace, 2003, p.108. See also, Abiodun Williams, *Preventing War: The UN and Macedonia*, Lanham, MD: Rowman & Littlefield, 2000.
20. This account is based on Angela King, 'Internal Conflict Prevention: The UN Observer Mission to South Africa (UNOMSA) 1992,' in Bertrand G. Ramcharan (ed.), *Conflict Prevention in Practice*, Leiden: Martinus Nijhoff, 2005, pp.151–156.
21. Angela King in Ramcharan (n.21 above).
22. See UN Doc. E/CN.4/1503.
23. See his letter, 'UN Guards Can Help Contain Civil Conflict', *New York Times*, 15 January, 1992.
24. See Decision No. 2005/24 of the Secretary-General's Policy Committee on Human Rights in Integrated Missions.
25. See the 'Capstone' presentation, version of 30 June, 2007.
26. *Handbook on United Nations Multidimensional Peacekeeping Operations*, Peacekeeping Best Practices Unit, DPKO, United Nations, December 2003.
27. *Protection of civilians in armed conflict, Aide Memoire, For the coordination of issues pertaining to the protection of civilians during Security Council's deliberations on peacekeeping mandates*, UN Doc. S/PRST/2003/27, 15 December 2003.

28. *Comprehensive assessment of the United Nations system response to children affected by armed conflict*, UN Doc. A/59/331, 3 September 2004.
29. Ibid., para.46.
30. Ibid., para.49.
31. Ibid., para.51
32. Ibid., para.52.
33. UN Doc. S/RES/1325 (2000), 31 October 2000, para.10.
34. Ibid., para.9.
35. See Addendum in *Report of the Representative of the Secretary-General, Mr. Francis Deng, submitted pursuant to Commission resolution 1997/39*, UN Doc. U.N. Doc. E/CN.4/1998/53/Add.2 (1998), 11 February 1998.
36. *Report of the Panel on UN Peace Operations*, UN Doc. A/55/305-S/2000/809, 21 August 2000. See generally William J. Durch, Victoria K. Holt, Caroline R. Earle and Moira K. Shanahan, *The Brahimi Report and the Future of UN Peace Operations*, Washington, D.C.: The Henry L. Stimson Center, 2003.
37. Ramsbotham, Woodhouse and Miall (n.3 above)., pp.157–158
38. *An Agenda for Peace Preventive diplomacy, peacemaking and peace-keeping*, UN Doc. A/47/277-S/24111, 17 June 1992, para.55. On *The Supplement to An Agenda for Peace*, see UN Doc. A/50/60-S/1995/1, 3 January 1995.
39. See *A More Secure World: Our Shared Responsibility, Report of the High-Level Panel on Threats, Challenges and Change*, UN Doc. A/59/565, 2 December 2004, and *In Lager Freedom: towards development, security and human rights for all*, UN Doc. A/59/2005, 21 March 2005.

DIGEST

Editor: Alexander Ramsbotham

The Digest is produced using United Nations sources

PEACEKEEPING MISSION UPDATES: January–March 2006

DARFUR

Security situation and the role of the African Union

There were no major breakthroughs in the resolution of the crisis in Darfur during 2005, with violent clashes carrying on through December between Sudanese government forces, militia and rebel groups. There were also many instances of banditry and inter-tribal fighting. During December, attacks by unidentified armed elements continued on internally displaced persons' (IDP) camps. Elements associated with the Sudanese Armed Forces also continued to harass and intimidate displaced persons. January 2006 saw an escalation in violence, and tensions also increased on both sides of the border with Chad. Attacks were further levelled against humanitarian workers and members of AMIS.

As at 3 March 2006, AMIS had a total of 6,898 personnel in Darfur, comprising 715 military observers, 1,385 civilian police, 27 international civilian staff, 11 Ceasefire Commission personnel and a protection force of 4,760 troops. The efforts of the African Union Mission in Sudan (AMIS) succeeded in enhancing the security situation in many areas of its deployment to some extent, and in offering limited improvements in protection for IDPs. Increased AMIS patrols around IDP camps managed to reduce the number of incidents in some locations.

The seventh round of the AU-led inter-Sudanese peace talks, which had started in Abuja, Nigeria, on 29 November 2005, failed to achieve significant progress by early January. At this time, armed movements appeared more interested in deliberating their internal hierarchies than in achieving progress in the Darfur peace process. However, the decision of the AU Peace and Security Council (PSC) to recommend – in principle – the transition of AMIS to a United Nations mission succeeded in stimulating some progress in Abuja, as on-going advances in the wealth-sharing commission were matched in the commissions on power-sharing and security arrangements.

Transition of AMIS to a UN mission

Despite AMIS' limited success in helping to protect civilians, in late 2005 it remained clear that security was continuing to deteriorate beyond the mission's control. In response, from 10 to 20 December 2005, the AU Commission conducted an assessment mission of AMIS. This mission was supported by a wide range of partners, including representations from Canada, Norway, the Netherlands, the United Kingdom, the United States, the European Union, the North Atlantic Treaty Organization, representatives of several troop-contributing countries and the UN. The mission carried out a comprehensive review of the operations of the military and civilian police components of AMIS. It sought to assess the security and humanitarian situation in Darfur and to make recommendations on how to achieve progress.

Reflecting on the mission's findings, on 12 January 2006 the AU PSC acknowledged progress made in the deployment of AMIS and noted that the mission had contributed significantly to the protection of the civilian population, despite serious financial, logistical and other constraints. As noted above, the PSC also expressed its support – in principle – for the transition of AMIS to a UN operation, within the framework of the AU/UN partnership in the promotion of peace, security and stability in Africa.

In a Presidential Statement issued on 3 February 2006, the UN Security Council requested the Secretary-General to initiate immediately contingency planning for the transition proposed by the PSC. It stated that such planning should be undertaken jointly with the AU, and should look at a range of options for a possible transition. The Council decreed that planning should be undertaken on the basis of: a unified, integrated approach; maximum use of existing resources of AMIS and of the UN Mission in Sudan (UNMIS), subject to the agreement of troop-contributing countries; an assessment of the essential tasks to be carried out in southern Sudan and Darfur with a view to re-allocating existing troops and assets to the most practicable extent; and a readiness to review and adjust the current structure of UNMIS, including command and control and logistics.

Kofi Annan, in a 30 January 2006 report to the UN Security Council, asserted that, given the volatility of the situation, the logistical constraints facing AMIS and the hugely demanding operational environment, any future international presence in Darfur would need to be enhanced, multifaceted, robust and mobile. He further stated that such a deployment would need to be in place for as long as was necessary to see peace take root. The Secretary-General noted that the support requirements for such a presence would be enormous, and pointed out that Security Council members and other Member States with appropriate military capabilities would need to be prepared make major contributions to such an effort.

Annan stated that the UN would work closely with the AU and other key stakeholders to take forward the PSC's suggestion to transfer AMIS to a UN mission, noting that this would be a very difficult and costly exercise, requiring extensive logistical, human and financial resources. He urged widespread support to AMIS in the meantime.

Planning for transition

The Secretary-General reported on his efforts at contingency planning on a range of options for a possible transition from AMIS to a UN operation. On 14 February, Annan's Special Representative met with senior AU officials to discuss transition. Dedicated planning teams were established at UNHQ in New York and in Sudan, within UNMIS. In late March, Annan reported that the initial phase of planning was well advanced, based on strategic guidance which his office had supplied. Focus was at the time concentrating on collecting information in preparation for the deployment of a technical assessment mission. A report on options for transition would be finalized for presentation to the Security Council following the technical assessment mission.

Annan stated that any UN-led operation in Darfur would rely heavily on African contributions and support, as well as those of other capable contributors. However, a UN successor mission would need to be qualitatively different from AMIS, especially regarding force mobility. He highlighted the necessity for cooperation by the Sudanese government to transition, as the 3 February Security Council Presidential statement cited above had stressed that preparation should occur in cooperation and close consultation with the parties to the Abuja peace talks.

Planning would need to take into consideration the ongoing violence and consistent violations of human rights in Darfur, the displacement of more than 3 million people and increasing instability near the border with Chad. Annan asserted that the primary goals of international efforts in Darfur should be to help protect vulnerable civilians, with a view to establishing an environment conducive to national reconciliation. A multidimensional presence, including political, military, police, humanitarian and human rights elements, would be necessary to achieve these objectives.

The Secretary-General asserted that the size, composition and capabilities of the military component of a UN mission would depend on a range of factors. However, the key factor would be the status of ceasefire arrangements in Darfur: the absence of an effective and functioning ceasefire would require any international security presence in Darfur to be mandated and resourced to take robust action to protect vulnerable civilians.

IRAQ

A 3 March 2006 report of the UN Secretary-General to the Security Council acknowledged that the results of the December election in Iraq were certified on 10 February 2006. This represented the completion of the transition timetable, which had been set forth in the Transitional Administrative Law and endorsed by UN Security Council resolution 1546 (2004). However, Kofi Annan stressed that, while all of the key benchmarks of this timetable had been met in Iraq, the country still faced formidable political, security and economic challenges.

Political situation

The 22 February 2006 bombing of the shrine of Imams Al-Hadi and Al-Askari in Samarra and its aftermath demonstrated how sectarian violence had become a primary threat to the security and stability of Iraq. Kofi Annan asserted, therefore, that the establishment of mutual trust and national reconciliation must remain a key priority in steering Iraq towards a peaceful and democratic future.

The Secretary-General stressed that Iraqi political and civil society leaders needed to promote their commitment to the unconditional respect for individual human rights and the establishment of the rule of law throughout the country, and pledged long-term international support for this endeavour. The best prospects for improving the overall security situation in Iraq, consolidating democracy and enhancing Iraqis' welfare remained the promotion of an inclusive, participatory and transparent political process that could respond to the aspirations of all of Iraq's communities.

The current situation emphasized the need for inter-communal dialogue and confidence-building measures to promote national reconciliation, which the UN remained eager to assist. To support this endeavour, Kofi Annan stated that the UN would continue to strive to implement the mandate it had been given through Security Council resolutions 1546 (2004) and 1637 (2005) to maintain its core political, electoral and constitutional activities, as well as its reconstruction, development, humanitarian and human rights activities. In the long term, its overarching political strategy was to institutionalize these processes internally within Iraq, and to promote national dialogue and reconciliation.

Electoral process

The December 2005 election for the new Council of Representatives was the third national electoral event held in Iraq during that year. However, it was particularly significant as the first election in which all Iraqi constituencies participated in large numbers, both as candidates and as voters. The ballot by and large met international standards and had a high turnout, in spite of its ambitious timetable and the highly problematic political and security environment in which it was carried out. During the various electoral processes in 2005, Iraq's Independent Electoral Commission built a significant indigenous capacity, which would provide a solid foundation for electoral processes. The UN would continue to provide electoral support in 2006, in correspondence with a request by the Iraqi government.

Annan stated that he believed the new Council of Representatives to be broadly representative of Iraq's communities, including a substantial percentage of women. The early formation of a fully inclusive government remained a key challenge, representing a mechanism to demonstrate responsible leadership by uniting to develop an agreed national agreement that can fulfil the aspirations of all Iraqi communities. Iraq's Constitution envisaged a constitutional review process, which represented a key step in forging such a national agreement. The early establishment of a Constitutional Review Committee of the Council of Representatives that was also foreseen in the Constitution represented a useful mechanism to achieve national consensus on a strong framework for the Iraqi State.

United Nations Assistance Mission in Iraq

The Secretary-General stressed that the United Nations Assistance Mission for Iraq (UNAMI) would continue to focus on implementing the targets set out in Security Council resolution 1546 (2004). However, the mission also planned to strengthen its activities in key areas of its mandate beyond political facilitation, in particular in relation to reconstruction and development. In support of the new government of Iraq's key priority of establishing tangible improvements of the quality of life for all Iraqis, UNAMI would maintain an important role in donor coordination.

UNAMI's most recent bi-monthly human rights report stressed ongoing concern over the human rights situation in Iraq. It highlighted incidents of mass detention, torture and extrajudicial killings. The Secretary-General stressed that the Multinational Force and the Iraqi security forces maintained a particular responsibility to act in full accordance with international humanitarian and human rights law. Initial steps taken by the government to address the situation needed to be supplemented by additional measures to ensure that both past and present abuses are dealt with on the basis of the rule of law and in accordance with international obligations. Improving the human rights situation was seen as key to the development of mutual trust and national reconciliation.

Security situation

There continued to be large numbers of casualties among Iraqi civilians as a result of terrorist, insurgent, paramilitary and military action. Violence in Iraq was taking on an increasingly sectarian character, especially in ethnically mixed areas, with militias and irregular armed elements of particular concern in this regard. The most effective means to improve security was to ensure a credible and inclusive political process and rapid improvements in basic living conditions. In the shorter term, training of Iraqi security forces represented an essential task, and Multinational Forces were making efforts to achieve progress in this area. Insecurity continued to have a major impact in constraining UNAMI's activities, and Kofi Annan reiterated the need for a dedicated protection force for all UN personnel in Iraq. Operational and logistical constraints, including insufficient air assets, also needed to be urgently addressed.

DOCUMENTATION

TEXT OF THE COMMUNIQUÉ OF THE AFRICAN UNION PEACE AND SECURITY COUNCIL, 46TH MEETING, ADDIS ABABA, ETHIOPIA, 10 MARCH 2006

The Peace and Security Council (PSC) of the African Union (AU), at its 46th meeting, held on 10 March 2006, adopted the following decision on the situation in Darfur,

'*Council*,

1. *Takes note* of the Report of the Chairperson pursuant to paragraph 5 of the PSC Communiqué PSC/PR/Comm. (XLV) of 12 January 2006 on the situation in Darfur [PSC/MIN/2(XLVI)];

2.
   Decides to support in principle the transition from AMIS to a UN Operation, within the framework of the partnership between AU and the United Nations in the promotion of peace, security and stability in Africa;

3. *Decides* to extend the mandate of AMIS until 30 September 2006 to undertake the following:

   - contribute to the improvement of the general security situation, provide a secure environment for the delivery of humanitarian assistance and the return of IDP and refugees, and contribute to the protection of the civilian population in Darfur,
   - monitor and observe the compliance of the parties with the N'djamena Humanitarian Ceasefire Agreement of 8 April 2004 and the Abuja Protocols of 9 November 2004 and all such agreements in the future, and
   - assist in the process of confidence building;

4. *Decides* that, during the period mentioned above, every effort should be made to: ensure the early conclusion of a peace agreement at the ongoing 7th Round of the Inter-Sudanese Peace Talks that opened in Abuja since 29 November 2005; improve the security, humanitarian and human rights situation on the ground; and address the crisis in the relations between Chad and Sudan:

   (a) In order to achieve the conclusion of a peace agreement at the Abuja Peace Talks, Council:

      i) *Demands* that the parties demonstrate their commitment to bring the conflict in Darfur to an end by making rapid progress on the outstanding issues at the Talks, as they relate to power sharing, wealth sharing and security arrangements,

ii) *Urges* the facilitators and the observers at the Abuja Peace Talks to lend a closer cooperation to the AU Mediation Team and to intensify their efforts to persuade the Sudanese parties to make compromise on the outstanding issues,

iii) *Stresses* the need for increased engagement at the highest level by African leaders and other stakeholders, to bring the parties to honour their commitments and negotiate in good faith with a view to ending violence in Darfur and concluding a peace agreement by the end of April 2006.

(b) In order to improve the security, humanitarian and human rights situation, Council:

i) *Requests* the Commission to immediately take all necessary steps for the consistent, flexible, broad and robust interpretation of the mandate provided for in paragraph 3 above and the tasks deriving thereof as spelt out in Communiqué PSC/PR/Comm. (XVII) adopted at its 17th meeting held on 20 October 2004 and in light of the Conclusions [MSC/EXP/Con.(III)] of the 3rd meeting of the Military Staff Committee (MSC) held on 25 April 2005 as endorsed by the 28th meeting of the PSC held on 28 April 2005 [PSC/PR/Comm. (XXVIII)], in order to ensure a more forceful protection of the civilian population,

ii) *Further requests* the Commission to vigorously pursue its efforts towards reaching, as quickly as possible, the authorized strength of AMIS i.e. 6,171 military personnel, with an appropriate civilian component, including up to 1,560 police personnel,

iii) *Also requests* the Commission to take all necessary steps for the full implementation of the recommendations made by the AU-led Assessment Mission that visited Darfur from 10 to 20 December 2005, in order to enhance the capacity of AMIS in the short and medium terms, in particular with respect to operational and tactical planning, command and control, protection of civilians, joint operations management, training, use of personnel and civil military coordination,

iv) *Demands* that the parties cease all acts of violence and atrocities on the ground, particularly those committed against the civilian population, humanitarian workers and agencies and AMIS personnel, and to fully comply with their commitments under the N'djamena Humanitarian Ceasefire Agreement of 8 April 2004 and the Abuja Protocols on Humanitarian and Security Issues of 9 November 2004, as well as with the decisions of the Joint Commission and relevant resolutions and decisions of the United Nations Security Council and the PSC. In particular, Council, once again, *demands* that:

- the Government of the Sudan refrains from conducting hostile military flights in and over the Darfur region, expeditiously implement its stated commitment to neutralize and disarm the Janjaweed/armed militias, and identify and declare those militias over whom it has influence and ensure that these militias refrain from all attacks, harassment and intimidation,
- the Justice and Equality Movement (JEM) and the Sudan Liberation Movement/Army (SLM/A) provide AMIS with the required information to enable it determine clearly the sites occupied by the forces on the ground, ensure the security of commercial activities in the areas occupied by their forces and, regarding specifically the SLM/A, withdraw its forces from contentious areas such as Graida

v) *Urges* the parties to cooperate fully with AMIS and to do all in their power to guarantee the safety of the members of the Mission to enable it to effectively discharge its mandate and guarantee AMIS and the humanitarian agencies unrestricted access,

vi) *Urges* the parties, pending the conclusion of a peace agreement, to contain the ever-deteriorating security situation on the ground by agreeing to the enhanced Humanitarian Ceasefire Agreement proposed to them by the AU-led Mediation Team, which, among others, provides for the strengthening of the mandates of the existing Ceasefire and Joint Commissions,

vii) In the interim, *authorizes* the AU Commission to convene an emergency Joint Commission meeting in Addis Ababa, to be chaired by the Special Representative of the Chairperson of the Commission to the Sudan, to further deliberate on the precarious security situation and take the necessary and appropriate measures against any party that is found responsible for the escalation of violence and tension in Darfur,

viii) *Appeals* to the international community to continue to provide humanitarian assistance to the affected population in Darfur, as well as to the refugees and host communities in Chad,

ix) *Urges* the Government of the Sudan and the rebel movements, to cooperate with the Office of the Prosecutor of the International Criminal Court (ICC) as called for by UN Security Council Resolution 1593 (2005) of 31 March 2005 and to take all necessary steps to combat impunity to ensure lasting peace and reconciliation in Darfur, and *requests* the Commission to cooperate with the ICC,

(c) In order to effectively address the crisis in the relations between Chad and Sudan, Council:

i) *Urges* the Government of Chad and Sudan to fully implement the commitments made and to facilitate the work of the existing mechanisms that have been agreed upon in the Declaration and Agreement signed in Tripoli in February 2006. Council *endorses* the Tripoli Declaration and the Agreement,

ii) *Requests* the Facilitators of the Tripoli Agreement to remain actively engaged in the efforts to defuse the tension on the ground and normalize the relations between Chad and the Sudan and ensure the effective functioning of the existing mechanisms agreed upon in the Tripoli Declaration and Agreement,

iii) *Further requests* the Commission to take all necessary steps and extend all necessary assistance to contribute to the implementation of the Tripoli Declaration and Agreement. Council *also requests* the Commission to prepare and submit proposals on how best AMIS can assist in the implementation of the Tripoli Declaration and Agreement, including the necessary adjustment to its current mandate;

5. *Reiterates* that, given the progress made in the initial stabilization phase of Darfur and the ongoing efforts to conclude a peace agreement, steps should be taken to sustain the peace support operation in Darfur in 2006 and beyond, bearing in mind the requirements for an increased integration of the different aspects of the peace efforts. In this respect, Council *welcomes* the adoption by the Security Council, on 3 February 2006, of Presidential Statement S/PRST/2006/5 commending the efforts of the AU and requesting the Secretary-General to initiate contingency planning without delay, in close and continuing consultation with the Security Council, and in cooperation and close consultation with the parties to the Abuja Peace Talks, including the Government of National Unity, on a range of options for a possible transition from AMIS to a UN operation. Council *takes note* of the announcement by the Sudanese Government that Sudan is prepared to accept the deployment of a UN operation in Darfur after and as part of the conclusion of a peace agreement at the Abuja Talks. Consequently, Council *requests* the Chairperson of the Commission to continue his consultations with the United Nations, the Government of Sudan and other stakeholders on the modalities of the transition. Council *further requests* the Chairperson of the Commission to work closely with the United Nations Secretary-General on joint planning towards that end;

6. *Stresses* that the transition from AMIS to a UN operation in Darfur should be informed by the following:

   • The preparedness of the Government the Sudan to accept the deployment of a UN operation in Darfur,
   • That the decision on the mandate and size of any future UN peacekeeping operation in Darfur is informed by the evolving situation on the ground. In this respect, a successful outcome of the Abuja Peace Talks and a significant improvement in the security and humanitarian situation on the ground will be key factors in any decision by the UN Security Council on the nature of the peacekeeping operation in Darfur,

- That the African character of the mission, including through its composition and leadership, is maintained in order, as much as possible, to secure the cooperation of all the parties, which is necessary to achieve a lasting solution to the conflict in Darfur,
- That the lead role of the African Union in the overall Darfur peace process is maintained, including the conduct of the Abuja Peace Talks and the Darfur-Darfur dialogue and consultation provided for by the Declaration of Principles (DoP) signed in Abuja on 5 July 2005, as well as in the implementation of existing and future agreements between the parties,
- That, during and after the transition, consultations are maintained between the AU and UN, including between the PSC and the UN Security Council, as well as between the Chairperson of the Commission and the Secretary-General of the United Nations, particularly prior to any decision by the UN Security Council regarding the envisaged UN peacekeeping operation in Darfur;

7. *Recommends* the establishment of a Committee of Heads of States and Government, including the Current Chairman of the AU, the immediate past Chairman, the Chairperson of the PSC, and the Chairperson of the Commission, as well as any other Head of State and Government the Current Chairman of the AU may wish to involve, to engage the Sudanese authorities and other stakeholders on how best to expedite the peace process in Darfur and on the transition;

8. *Reiterates* its appeal to the AU partners to provide all the necessary financial and logistical support to sustain AMIS until 30 September 2006, as well as support the ongoing Abuja Talks. In this respect, Council *welcomes* the envisaged convening of a pledging conference in Brussels, with the support of the United Nations and the European Union;

9. *Calls* for an immediate end to all acts aimed at inciting demonstrations against the international community, in particular the United Nations, as well as to the unacceptable and defamatory characterization of AMIS;

10. *Emphasizes* the critical role of the United Nations Security Council in holding accountable those impeding the peace process and committing human rights violations;

11. *Decides* to remain actively seized of the matter.'

Index

For Product Safety Concerns and Information please contact our EU
representative GPSR@taylorandfrancis.com
Taylor & Francis Verlag GmbH, Kaufingerstraße 24, 80331 München, Germany